ABOUT ARCHITECTURE

Hugh Pearman

ABOUT ARCHITECTURE

An Essential Guide in 55 Buildings

YALE UNIVERSITY PRESS, NEW HAVEN AND LONDON

Contents

Introduction 7

Civic 13
- **The Acropolis** Athens, Greece 16
- **Isfahan** Persia (Modern Iran) 20
- **Town Hall** Säynätsalo, Finland 24
- **Seaside** Florida, USA 27
- **Spreebogen Government District** Berlin, Germany 30

Houses 35
- **Fitzwilliam Square** Dublin, Ireland 38
- **Blackwell** Cumbria, UK 41
- **Villa Tugendhat** Brno, Czechia 44
- **Vanna Venturi House** Philadelphia, USA 48
- **Nora House** Sendai, Japan 51

Education 55
- **St John's College** Oxford University, UK 58
- **Munkegaard School** Dyssegård, Denmark 62
- **The Beinecke Library** Yale University, USA 65
- **Gando Primary School** Burkina Faso 68
- **Universidad de Ingeniería y Tecnología** Lima, Peru 71

Offices 75
- **Somerset House** London, UK 78
- **Chilehaus** Hamburg, Germany 82
- **Johnson Wax Headquarters** Racine, Wisconsin, USA 86
- **Centraal Beheer Insurance Offices** Apeldoorn, Netherlands 89
- **CCTV Headquarters** Beijing, China 92

Industry 97
- **Shrewsbury Flaxmill Maltings** Ditherington, UK 100
- **Moulin Saulnier Cocoa Mill** Noisiel, France 103
- **The Van Nelle Factory Complex** Rotterdam, Netherlands 106
- **Salk Institute for Biological Studies** La Jolla, California, USA 109
- **Shenzhen Energy Ring** Shenzhen, China 112

Transport 117
Canal du Midi Southern France 120
Chhatrapati Shivaji Terminus Mumbai, India 123
Fiat Tagliero Service Station Asmara, Eritrea 126
Washington Dulles International Airport Washington, DC, USA 129
Yokohama International Port Terminal Yokohama, Japan 133

Museums 137
The Uffizi Florence, Italy 140
Dulwich Picture Gallery London, UK 144
Pompidou Centre Paris, France 148
Ningbo History Museum Zhejiang Province, China 152
National Museum of African American History and Culture Washington, DC, USA 156

Performance 161
Theatre at Epidauros Greece 164
The Globe Theatre London, UK 167
Bayreuth Festspielhaus Bayreuth, Germany 170
Sydney Opera House Sydney, Australia 173
Walt Disney Concert Hall Los Angeles, USA 176

Religion 181
Angkor Wat Siem Reap, Cambodia 184
Portuguese Synagogue Amsterdam, Netherlands 188
Basílica de la Sagrada Família Barcelona, Spain 191
Notre Dame du Haut Ronchamp, Eastern France 194
The Ismaili Centre Toronto, Canada 198

Retail 203
Grand Bazaar Istanbul, Turkey 206
Galleria Vittorio Emanuele II Milan, Italy 210
Ljubljana Central Market Arcades Ljubljana, Slovenia 214
Langham Place Shopping Mall Mong Kok, Hong Kong 217
Magna Park Milton Keynes, UK 220

Gardens 225
Gardens of the Villa d'Este Tivoli, near Rome, Italy 228
Gardens of the Generalife Palace Granada, Spain 232
Kyoto Temple Gardens Kyoto, Japan 235
Gardens of Stowe House Stowe, Buckinghamshire, UK 240
The High Line Manhattan, New York, USA 244

Further Reading 248 **Index** 249 **Acknowledgements** 254 **Picture Credits** 255

Introduction

Architecture is the art and science of designing buildings and places. While the built environment directly affects us all, the process behind its construction can sometimes seem somewhat baffling. The aim of this book is to demystify that process. Rather than starting from a style or theory, location or period, it presents existing buildings from across the world, built at different points throughout history, and brings out some of the personalities and stories involved in making them.

This is a different way into architecture. The book is organised by building type – that is, by the particular use or mix of uses it was designed for. The way that the various types arise and evolve helps to explain what architecture does, and makes it a perennially fascinating subject. Since there are very many building types, and this must be a concise guide, I have chosen a basic 11 types, in a sequence that broadly follows our life patterns: how our towns and cities are organised, where we live, learn and work, how we get around and interact with others, enjoy ourselves, and feed our minds.

Beyond the function of buildings is of course something else: their expression. This is the art of architecture and relates to what buildings look like, how they sit in the city or open landscape and how we respond to them aesthetically. The requirements of architecture were reduced to just three words by the early seventeenth-century English diplomat and scholar Sir Henry Wotton (1568–1639), paraphrasing a work of the Roman architect/engineer Vitruvius (c.80–15 BCE): 'Firmness, Commodity, and Delight'.[1] That is, a building must be well built, useful and pleasing. Everybody agrees with this, if not always with what constitutes 'delight'.

That formula, however, sidesteps the pressures of human society that lead to this or that building type. So, while taking Wotton/Vitruvius as read, we can overlay today's three main determinants: society, technology and style, in that order. Society decides what it wants (useful and desirable buildings and places) and can afford to build; technology allows it to build as humbly or ambitiously as it wishes and in accordance with, or overcoming, environmental factors; style determines the aesthetic appearance of the finished article. Looking back across architectural history, these three together provide the necessary information to understand why any building looks and works the way it does.

Society concerns the way we live, behave, trade, fight and are governed. Societal habits and pressures, concentrations of power and wealth, government edicts, the influence of religion, wars and persecution, riches amassed from foreign (often colonised) lands and the ugly proceeds of slavery, patterns of agriculture and industrialisation – these have all fed into the way we shape our places and our buildings. Above all, for architecture to flourish, societies need long periods of relative stability.

Portal at the megalithic temple complex of Ħaġar Qim, Malta, as photographed in 1960. The architecture dates from more than 3,000 years BCE and is regarded as one of the most ancient religious structures on Earth.

Technology brings in the complementary skills of the engineer and environmentalist. The disciplines of architecture and engineering did not become formalised and separated until the early nineteenth century. Indeed, all but the smallest buildings have always been collaborations between people with different sets of skills. Most good buildings in modern times have the name of an architect or designer attached to them, sometimes several. The solo 'hero architect' who does everything is a mythical creature.

Technology concerns how the designers and constructors of a building exploit the materials and techniques available to them, whether sourced locally (stone, timber, clay for bricks and ceramics, concrete, steel, glass, recycled materials) or from further afield. It allows them to produce zero-carbon buildings, for example, and even those that can generate more power than they use. From ancient temples to today's skyscrapers, people have always tried to build what was not previously possible, using new technologies and revisiting old ones. The quest for lightness, transparency and reflectivity, for instance – usually associated with modernism in the twentieth century – goes right back to the medieval cathedrals, solid walls dissolving into delicate frameworks of light and colour.

Style – the appearance of the building outside and in – is more complex and no less intriguing. As much an intellectual as an artistic pursuit, it can reflect national or international aesthetics and can be personal or impersonal. Style is infinite: nobody has yet exhausted all of the ways you can make even a small house look, let alone any more complex building type such as a theatre, law court or transport interchange. As to whether one style is superior to another, there you fall into the realms of subjective judgements. Tastes differ and change over time. One person's timeless beauty is another's eyesore. Part of the great appeal of architecture is that the same set of requirements, the same budget and the same site will always yield different responses from different architects, even if they are of the same stylistic persuasion. There is, and can never be, any single 'correct' way to design a building so long as it fulfils its function.

To over simplify what is not as binary a situation as this suggests, today we think of architectural styles in two, very broad, overlapping and sometimes opposing camps: modernism, which is usually regarded as beginning in the early twentieth century; and traditionalism, which is the continuation or revival of earlier styles. The two co-exist, if at times spikily, often interbreeding. There are endless variations, but wherever a particular example of architecture finds itself on this stylistic spectrum, one thing always holds true: everything in architecture depends on and refers to what has gone before.

While style varies for each building type, in the case of some types the 'essence' – that is, the way in which the building serves its users – remains surprisingly constant. Types such as the stadium and theatre hark back to

Ancient Rome and Greece. Granaries and tithe barns are the ancestors of distribution warehouses. Home layouts are recognisably domestic from Neolithic times to today. The 'community hub' has existed as long as the village hall or meeting place beneath a tree. The first office buildings date back to the sixteenth century[2], while public museums and art galleries as we recognise them today originated in the seventeenth century. Industrialisation gave us factories, mills and worker housing, the railway station, the airport and the multi-storey car park: transport architecture is one of the most fluid of the types. Moreover, there have been monuments and 'icon' buildings ever since the Seven Wonders of the Ancient World. What does change are the technologies we use in everyday life. From transport to online shopping, new building types emerge to serve them.

Architecture does not have to be built to exist. As an art, architecture is as real in drawings or in writing as in bricks and mortar. But if and when that drawing is finally built, it engages nearly all of our senses. It is unusual, though not unknown, to taste buildings, but we see, hear, smell and feel them as we interact with them. We can also 'read' them. Buildings contain narratives about what they do, about their designers and builders, and the society and conditions in which they were made. They contain the design intention, made full-size and fully functional. Built architecture is the point at which the organism emerges from its larval stage and begins its adult life.

That life can be eventful. All buildings change over time as part of the ageing process. Existing buildings can act as raw material for successive generations with new patterns of social behaviour and new technologies. If they are accommodating enough, their use can change. This book records such changes of use where they have taken place. Too many buildings, though, are just needlessly thrown away – demolished when they could be adapted. The construction industry is a huge emitter of carbon: existing buildings lock up carbon. To reduce carbon emissions and help combat climate change requires a considerable rethink in many areas, especially materials. More sustainable timber and stone buildings are now appearing, replacing concrete or steel. It is important to build to last, and the most sustainable building is the one that already exists. The mantra of 'long life, loose fit, low energy' – meaning adaptable and sustainable – was first coined in the 1970s and guides many architects today.[3] Happily, all of the buildings in this book survive at the time of writing, with some several centuries old and two well over a millennium.

Buildings sometimes exist in splendid or forgotten isolation: the large country house, the barn or the power station, say. Architecture is, however, nearly always about more than a solitary design. Buildings are as sociable as the humans who make them. Obviously enough, they slot into villages, towns, cities and megalopolises. They have to respond to their neighbours in one way or another, even if that response – as has been the case throughout history – is to haughtily ignore them. The resulting urban variety, a mishmash of styles and materials, heights and (less commonly) widths, is what you find in all old towns, and it is this that gives the town its character. Planned large urban complexes in consistent style and proportions – such as the Plaza Mayor in Madrid (first begun in 1580 and rebuilt several times subsequently) or the kilometre-long housing estate of Karl-Marx-Hof (1927–30) in Vienna – are marvellous set pieces, which even the best all-new towns and cities struggle to emulate. But one of the most appealing aspects of architecture is the chaotic opposite, the cheek-by-jowl jostling of buildings by different hands and from different times, all co-existing in the present.

A city will contain landmarks – a castle or city hall, main place of worship, cultural buildings, railway terminus, ultra-tall skyscraper – but these are not the basic urban material. That consists not only of the steady accumulation of more 'humdrum' buildings but also of the parts that are not buildings, but which are just as designed. On the grandest end of the scale, you get nation-defining civic gestures such as the boulevards of Washington Mall or the Champs-Élysées in Paris. At the other end, public parks and gardens define a city just as much as any building.

The way old cities have evolved teaches us vital lessons for what we build today, the most prominent of which might not seem like architecture at all. This lesson is that the most important factor in designing any new settlement or suburb is the balance between the road layout and the buildings. Related to this, the second most important is density. If the buildings are too small and scattered, the roads too dominating, no sense of place emerges. In the 1937 phrase of Gertrude Stein (1874–1946), lamenting the loss of her childhood home to the urban expansion of Oakland in California, 'there is no "there" there'.[4]

Some building types can die. There is understandably little call for toll houses or stable blocks any more, familiar parts of any eighteenth or early nineteenth-century journey. But overall, the variety is proliferating. The 'visitor centre' scarcely existed before the 1980s. The architecture of power production now includes wind and solar farms, onshore transformer buildings and large energy storage banks. The world is peppered with data centres powering the internet: again, often in buildings converted from other uses.

The stories of the buildings, architects and clients in this book help to explain our world. Different as these places are, whatever their age or style or function, all can aspire to the purely aesthetic definition written by the Swiss-French modernist architect pioneer Le Corbusier (1887–1965) in 1923: 'Architecture is the masterly, correct and magnificent play of masses brought together in light.'[5]

Author's note

This guide aims for simplicity. There are short introductory essays to each of the 11 building types, followed by a quintet of individual case studies per type, ordered chronologically. Each of the five examples per type is from a different country. The examples are chosen to demonstrate diversity of approach and location, and evolution of a type across time. Overall, the book is structured to be easy to dip in and out of, section by section and project by project.

Naturally, the built environment often resists easy categorisation and some of my examples straddle types either through multi-functionality or changes of use. If, occasionally, my choice of type for a building seems odd, that is why.

I assign each a style category, and this gets even more subjective. Such labels are always debatable, especially with recent buildings where stylistic consensus can be rare. They are there to help place a given piece of architecture on the style spectrum for those who find that useful. Feel free to devise your own.

The buildings and places I cite have to be a personal selection, so these inevitably reflect my background, tastes and interests, though they include some examples that I do not necessarily like. I have considered, and in some cases written, many others which I later rejected. With the whole of history and all the world to choose from, many more types and vastly more examples are available, but such a book has to stop before it becomes unwieldy. Architecture is so rich and diverse that one could produce several alternative versions of this book with entirely different examples.

The 'we' frequently invoked in this book is generally us, the users and beholders, rather than 'they', the clients and designers and makers of buildings and places. Then again, everyone is a consumer of architecture, whether involved in the process or not. Whatever the audience, I hope this way of presenting different types of architecture will intrigue the reader enough to want to know more.

1 Sir Henry Wotton, *The Elements of Architecture*, 1624, based on *De architectura* by Marcus Vitruvius Pollio, 30–20 BCE.
2 Antwerp Town Hall, 1561–65, was essentially office buildings; see Nikolaus Pevsner, *A History of Building Types*, 1976, trans. 1987, p. 213.
3 Coined by Alex Gordon, President of the Royal Institute of British Architects, 1972.
4 Gertrude Stein, *Everybody's Autobiography*, 1937.
5 Le Corbusier and Amédée Ozenfant, *Towards a New Architecture*, 1923, trans. Frederick Etchells, 1927.

KAY'S PLAN
OF
EDINBURGH
Containing all the
Improvements
TO THE PRESENT TIME
1836.
Drawn & Engraved by Kirkwood & Son
Being a reduction of their larger Plan laid down from
Actual Survey on a Scale of 1½ Inches to the Mile.
COMELY BANK
Distillery
Edinburgh Academy
HENDERSON ROW
Canon Mill Haugh
ROYAL CIRCUS
CUMBERLAND
NORTHUMBERLAND
ABERCROMBIE PLA.
HERIOT ROW
MORAY
DARNAWAY ST.
QUEENS STREET
GEORGE STREET
PRINCES STREET
CHARLOTTE SQUARE
YOUNG STREET
HILL STREET
THISTLE
St. Andrews Ch.
Assembly Rooms
ROSE
ALBYN PLA.
St. Bernards Well
St. Georges Well
WATER OF LEITH
Road from Queensferry
Quarry
MELVILLE PLACE
WILLIAM
ATHOL CRESCENT
Wester Coates
MAITLAND
TORPHICHAN ST.
CANNING STREET
MORRISON STREET
Hay Market
Glasgow Road
ST CUTHBERT STREET
LOTHIAN
CASTLE TERRACE
Charity Work House
ORINDLAY STREET
Burying Ground
St. Cuthberts
NEW WEST APPROACH
CASTLE HILL
LAWN
GRASS MARKET
Royal Institution
Bank of Scotland
MOUND
Kings Stables
Meal Mar.
Heriots Hospital
LAURISTON PLACE
PORTLAND PLACE
Watsons Hospital
Merchants Maiden Hos.
MORTON CRESCENT
BREAD STREET
CASTLE BARNS
Chapel
GROVE SQUARE
FOUNTAIN
Lochrin Distillery
Basin
UNION CANAL
Lanark Road
Bainfield
From Glasgow
Dalry
GILMOUR PLACE
MEADOW ST.
Wright's H.
Gilmore House

Civic

Civic buildings are those at the heart of every town and city. Narrowly defined, they are the local seat of government: the town or city hall, parliamentary buildings and some cultural buildings often associated with the civic authorities such as libraries and museums (covered elsewhere in this book). The broader 'civic realm' concerns the urban nature of our town and city centres as used by us, the citizens. The two intertwine: the buildings and the spaces together make up the grain, the character of the place. The job of the architect is to read this and react to what is there already, designing in response to the existing context. If planning a new settlement from scratch, the architect should look to the precedents.

Venice is not Venice without its hierarchy of canals. But Venice is equally Venice because of its parallel hierarchy of alleys, streets and squares, from the small and quirky to the grand set piece of the Piazza San Marco with its adjoining Byzantine cathedral, towering campanile and ducal palace. Although it is futile to attempt to replicate a topographically unique city such as Venice, which has evolved over a millennium and a half, its urban grain holds lessons for today's architects and planners.

We citizens own the civic realm, or think we do: the awkward fact is that increasing numbers of seemingly public spaces are in fact privately built, owned and policed. With seats of government it is a constant battle to balance democratic accessibility with the necessary security. Subject to these provisos, it is mostly still the case that these are *our* streets, *our* squares, *our* places of congregation, celebration and sometimes protest. Government, commerce, entertainment and workplace have always combined to make good places to be in and to meet up.

An important point was reached in the early twenty-first century – 2008, to be precise – when for the first time in history as many of us lived in cities or large towns as in rural communities.[1] The urban population is predicted to rise to two thirds of the population by 2050, some seven billion people. How we urbanise – how we design our towns and cities – is crucially important. Architects and planners must mend damaged cities, densifying and extending them judiciously, as well as plan new ones to meet rising demand.

In selecting examples of civic design for this section, I have chosen places that have either evolved over time (even if sometimes convulsively, such as Central Berlin) or are relatively small-scale. A study of modern built-from-scratch capital cities such as Brasília, Canberra or Nur-Sultan (previously Astana) in Kazakhstan would fill a book itself. Here, Isfahan, effectively rebuilt in a short period centuries ago to be a capital, provides historical perspective.

Architects have always designed on the larger scale of urban planning, even if – as with Sir Christopher Wren's (1632–1723) plans to rebuild London after the Great Fire of 1666, or Le Corbusier's equally speculative 'Plan Voisin'

James Kay's 1836 *Plan of Edinburgh* shows the shift from the tight medieval city south of the castle to the spacious 'modern' grid plan of the late Georgian New Town north of Princes Street.

for Paris in 1925, involving the wholesale clearance of a Parisian district for a grid of skyscrapers set in parkland – they think too big for what the city wants. But the imposition of a grid of streets over the previously spidery medieval road pattern became relatively commonplace from the seventeenth century, Glasgow in Scotland and Mannheim in Germany being examples. Meanwhile, in Edinburgh, the medieval Old Town faces the more rational New Town across a valley, the New Town being based on the eighteenth-century grid plan, first laid out by James Craig (1739–1795). The grid-plan approach was widely adopted for the building of new cities in the United States. In Manhattan, only meandering Broadway, originally a Native American track, recalls its pre-grid and pre-colonial origins.

Architects also design new rural settlements, whether actual or imagined. An example of the former would be the original British 'garden cities', proposed first by social reformer Ebenezer Howard (1850–1928). Some of these, including Letchworth Garden City (started in 1903), were successfully built and went on to inspire many others in the United States as well as continuing to influence new town planning today.

Suburbia, often derided, has its champions too. Consider the American architect Frank Lloyd Wright's (1867–1959) 41-square-kilometre 'Broadacre City' proposal, which evolved from 1924 onwards with many revisions. This was to be an ultra-low-density settlement (America had the space), in which every citizen would be given an acre of land to farm and a place to live on it. Although some public transport was indicated, Wright was in love with the motor car and fast motor roads, and his design leaned heavily on car usage (he also imagined his residents using fanciful personal flying machines). Broadacre City, never built, was a curious mix of top-down planning and libertarianism. As things turned out, the sprawling car-dependent suburbs never became self-sufficient in the way Wright imagined they would.

For working populations worldwide the standard of living tends to be higher in cities than in farm villages, though the rapid growth of planned cities is usually accompanied by the growth of unplanned shanty towns or slums. This was as true of the First World Industrial Revolution from the late eighteenth century as it is of the continuing rapid urbanisation of China, India, the Middle East and Africa. The twenty-first-century equivalents of the hell-for-leather nineteenth-century manufacturing and trading cities of Manchester and Chicago, say, are China's Guangzhou, India's Bangalore or Angola's Luanda. Despite this, the number of slum-dwellers globally has been steadily declining for many years.

Mistakes of the past are inevitably repeated. With urbanisation and rising personal and business wealth comes a proliferation of motor vehicles, the roads to carry them and the associated pollution. Older First World cities suffered the onslaught of the motor car from the 1930s and in some cases lost much of their pre-existing urban character in consequence. The free-market United States became the home of the 'doughnut effect', where the middle-class car-owning populace decamped to the suburbs, shops moved to out-of-town malls and the old centres decayed into ghettoes, endless surface car parks and highway intersections.

European cities – usually more centrally planned and with more restrictions on land and development – faced a period of reconstruction following the Second World War when many cities were left in ruins. During this time adaptations were made to central urban areas with the ease of motor-car movement in mind. This push towards car usage, whether in Europe or the United States, had the result of loosening the weave of the city fabric, allowing holes to emerge. Some convincing attempts have been made to correct this. Boston in the United States has removed an elevated urban freeway (which had proved to be a catastrophically divisive barrier within the city), put it in a tunnel and made a linear park on top, all at huge expense. But the effects of sprawl on older centres continues. Beijing, notorious for its smog, might still have 13 million bicycles but also no fewer than seven roaring ring roads or beltways, with all the traffic that implies.

Today, modern architecture that acknowledges and references history is on the rise, along with people-based, rather than machine-based, urban planning. However, this is mostly happening in the older centres. Most of the world's new and fast-expanding cities, especially in the Middle East and Asia, still seem more than prepared to make the old twentieth-century mistake of domination by vehicle movement. One hopes this will be put right eventually, along with urban designs that can accommodate and ameliorate extreme climate conditions rather than worsen them. Meanwhile, destruction by warfare continues.

From civic and national governance to the interconnected streetscape of the places where we live and work, the question facing architects and urbanists is nothing less than the expression of civilisation itself. Civilised centres privilege the human scale, the face-to-face meeting, a fair balance between the movement of people on foot and by machine. The best town and city centres of the world achieve this.

---

1 United Nations Population Division report, *An Overview of Urbanization, Internal Migration, Population Distribution and Development in the World*, January 2008.

The Acropolis Athens, Greece, 460–407 BCE

ARCHITECTS: ICTINUS, KALLIKRATES, PHIDIAS AND MNESIKLES (ACTIVE MID-FIFTH CENTURY BCE)

STYLE: HELLENIC (ANCIENT GREEK CLASSICAL)

Pericles' city of temples on the hill served an administrative as well as religious purpose and concluded a civic processional route.

An acropolis is the high part of a city (or a citadel occupying a high place), where civic seats of power – such as fortresses, palaces or main places of worship – are typically located. While the term is generic, derived from the Greek meaning 'high city' or 'city in the air', the most famous acropolis can be found on the main plateau in Athens, as built up over a long period from the Bronze Age. The golden age of the Acropolis of Athens – for architecture, democracy and culture – came in the time of Pericles (c.495–425 BCE). Pericles was a general and an effective leader of Athens and its empire from 461 to 429 BCE, responsible for ushering in a period of relative peace among the warring city-states of the region. Enough of the buildings and public spaces of the Acropolis of Athens have survived the vicissitudes of time, earthquake, war, religious dogmatism and cultural plunder to give us the preserved ruins of classical Greece we see today. The influence of the immensely sophisticated buildings of the Athenian Acropolis is all-pervasive in architecture, overtly or covertly.

Its principal building, the great temple of Athena Parthenos, commonly known as the Parthenon (448–432 BCE), is an endless source of inspiration for architects, even though much of its sculpture has been removed. The majority of the sculpture went to the British Museum, due to the work of Thomas Bruce, Seventh Earl of Elgin (1766–1841), at the start of the nineteenth century, when Greece was ruled by the Ottoman Empire. His actions were controversial then and even more so now. The ransacking of this flowering of Ancient Greek

Dedicated to Pallas Athene, the Parthenon and its sculptures continue to influence architecture to this day.

art, stimulated by fascination on the part of wealthy European patrons of the seventeenth and eighteenth centuries on their 'Grand Tour', made Greek classicism the first widely imitated international architectural style of the Western world from Renaissance times onwards. Although it was never intended that way, this removal of sculptures from the Parthenon to museums also happened to preserve them from two centuries of atmospheric erosion.

The other key buildings within the Acropolis are the never fully completed monumental gateway building to the site, the Propylaia (437–431 BCE), by architect Mnesikles; the little temple of Athena Nike (426–421 BCE) by Kallikrates (a Nike is a winged goddess of victory and the commemoration of military victories was an important part of the Acropolis); and the Erechtheion (421–407 BCE), also by Mnesikles, consolidating a number of shrines and cults. The latter is notable for its south porch, where instead of columns the roof is supported on six caryatids – clothed standing female figures, mourning the losses of the Persian War, which had destroyed the preceding Parthenon. As with all the surviving buildings and fragments of the Acropolis, this porch became a widely imitated motif in the Western Greek Revival of the eighteenth century.

But the mothership here is the Parthenon. In this great temple to Athena, the protective goddess of Athens, stood a 12-metre, gilded statue of the deity, dominating the interior, within the large enclosed space known as the *cella*, the actual seat of the god. At the Parthenon, Kallikrates, Ictinus and the sculptor/architect Phidias (whose high-level relief sculptures around the exterior of the *cella* were an unusual feature) made a building that is as near perfect as any building could be, from its overall plan and proportions through to its intrinsic sculpture. We have yet to come to terms with the fact that these buildings and their sculptures would originally have been very colourful, more Las Vegas than British Museum.

The Parthenon did not spring from nowhere. Earlier timber-built temples of a similar form, dating back over 200 years, had been replicated in stone, which as a material behaves differently to timber. Previously functional pegged wooden joints, exposed beam ends, roof gables and spreader plates at the top of the columns became purely decorative and increasingly refined to the point of fetish. It's a form of skeuomorph, replicating the form of one material in another. And perhaps here also there was the sense that these buildings were recognisable as the houses of the gods (and also, usually, the local treasury, presumably guarded by the god in question), so best not to tinker about with the form.

The Parthenon was, therefore, a culmination of a particular line of architectural development. This was to be the ultimate template, capable of changes of size and detail, but always true to its origins. The strong, simple fluted Doric columns and circular column heads (capitals) of the Parthenon, in contrast to the more delicately slender Ionic columns with 'ram's horn' capitals of other buildings on the Acropolis, signified power, authority and continuity.

Here we have a celestial city, a ceremonial place which – accessed by the winding Panathenaic Way, up from the main city square on the plain below – was carefully laid out over a relatively short period to be a visually dramatic conclusion of what had become the dominant city-state of the region. Down below, commerce and everyday life rubbed shoulders with the affairs of state – quite literally, given the governance structure of Athens. High above on the plateau, the gods looked down.

But all of this was, in historic terms, quite late. The Athens that Pericles took over and transformed was itself part of a city-building tradition derived from the earlier civilisations of the eastern Mediterranean, from Mesopotamia to Ancient Egypt and the Minoans of Crete. Both the palace of Knossos in Crete and the Mycenaean civilisation of the Greek Peloponnese flourished a thousand years before Pericles made his mark on Athens. But he re-established an order and

The temple of the Erechtheion, with its caryatid columns, is possibly a fragment of a once-larger building. The use of caryatids in this way has been much copied.

hierarchy, an intertwining of the life of the citizen with the arts and architecture of the time, which we recognise as urban planning of the highest calibre. It contains architecture which, insofar as any architecture can be, is timeless. The much larger and longer-lasting Roman Empire adopted and adapted it in turn.

Today we do not build pyramids very much, but the Greek temple at the heart of civic and cultural life is entirely familiar to us. The British Museum itself is a case in point. Meanwhile, in Athens, since 2009, the Acropolis Museum, an impressive building by French-Swiss architect Bernard Tschumi (b.1944), has displayed its fragments among the white plaster casts of the works they hope and believe one day will return.

The urban planning of power: Abbas the Great's rebuilding of the Persian city included the immense Naqsh-e Jahan Square.

Isfahan Persia (Modern Iran), 1598–1722

ARCHITECTS: SHAH ABBAS I (1571–1629), ALLAHVERDI KHAN (C.1560–1613) AND OTHERS

STYLE: SAFAVID ISLAMIC

Shah Abbas I, Abbas the Great of Persia, was a highly astute ruler who revived the fortunes of his Safavid Empire, bridging Central Asia from east to west. Abbas was a great builder and made Isfahan his capital. Centrally and strategically placed in a fertile basin on the Iranian plateau, the settlement dates back to the Bronze Age and had an earlier cultural flowering in the pre-Islamic Achaemenid Empire under Cyrus the Great (c.600–539 BCE). However, it was the high-status city planning of Abbas that made Isfahan into one of the most celebrated cities in the world.

To set this in a global context, the golden age of Isfahan began a century before Peter the Great (1672–1725) of Russia established St Petersburg in 1703, and two centuries after the construction of the Ming Dynasty 'Forbidden City' (completed in 1420), in what is now Beijing. In Mexico, Tenochtitlan, capital of the Aztec Empire had flourished from 1325 to its conquest by the Spanish in 1521. The mysterious Inca mountain citadel of Machu Picchu in Peru – a royal estate rather than a large city – had been built around 1450 and abandoned only 80 years later, despite not having been discovered by the invading Spanish. There the spread of virulent European diseases did the work of many armies. In southern Africa, the city of Great Zimbabwe, thought to have been the royal city of the Shona people, rose and fell between the eleventh and fifteenth centuries, probably falling victim to changing trade patterns rather than war.

Isfahan was an ancient oasis city defined by commerce, but its importance waxed and waned over the centuries and rulers did not always make it their base. With a recurring reputation for cultural and religious tolerance, it stood at the crossroads of two great trade routes, running north–south and east–west. To this, Abbas brought a panoply of palaces and squares as well as that cooling and calming speciality of Islamic architecture: the 'paradise garden' (see Granada, p. 232). He also established a considerable financial centre powered by forcibly resettled Armenians, the human booty of his wars with the neighbouring Ottoman Empire.

The historic set pieces of Isfahan include one of the largest city squares in the world – the enormous Naqsh-e Jahan Square, approximately 560 metres by 160 metres – around which Abbas brought together mosques, his palace of Aali Qapu and commerce. The square links northwards to the city's ancient covered bazaar, which runs two kilometres and a half long. Other great gardens with subsidiary palaces extend west to the grand boulevard – itself a linear park – that Abbas ran south to the Zayanderud river. Beyond is the new town of the Armenian quarter where Vank Cathedral (officially the 'Holy Saviour Cathedral'), built from 1606 to 1664, is more than somewhat in the style of a mosque, although it has always been Christian. Joining the two is an extraordinary meeting place taking the form of the double-deck Allahverdi Khan Bridge.

Usually referred to locally as the *Si-o-se-pol* ('Bridge of 33'), it was completed in 1602. The official name of the bridge is that of the military engineer and senior politician who oversaw its construction, while its popular one refers to its 33-arch construction across the wide, flat (and now usually dry) bed of the Zayanderud river. When the river flows, the bridge acts also as an impounding weir. When dry, this forms a low-level stone-paved walkway and you can wander in and out of the arches. Rather than having mere balustrades on top, it is given a stately presence by twin rows of tall arched alcoves, their rhythm being double that of the arches below. Unlike its close contemporary, the Rialto Bridge over the Grand Canal in Venice, these side-rooms were not for shops, although one once functioned as a tea house. Rather, they are places to meet, pause-points to either side of the broad street running along the centre of the bridge. It is therefore a destination in itself.

Although the city created by Shah Abbas I later declined, as control of this vast area shifted once again, his legacy remains, most notably in the planning of the city's civic infrastructure. To an extent, the waxing and waning of Isfahan's importance over the centuries has helped preserve its character. Recent rapid expansion and industrialisation is, however, destroying what, until the mid-twentieth century, was the finely balanced ecosystem of the city region – an enclosed basin with no outlet to the sea, which had a carefully designed irrigation network as part of the overall civic works of its golden period.

The now rare appearance of the river water (extraction upstream means that it is generally allowed to flow through the city only at Persian New Year) has made the surrounding urban area a less appealing spot. It speaks too of the environmentally damaging Soviet-style industrialisation in the region, introduced by the Pahlavi dynasty, last of the Persian/Iranian monarchies to date, prior to the declaration of the Islamic Republic in 1979. This over extraction of water has not been corrected since.

Safavid Isfahan was one of the great cities of the world. Famed while at its peak, it later became a tourist destination (though it is never as overrun as, say, the great historic European centres). It survives, gloriously, at the heart of a considerably less well-planned modern city, with Naqsh-e Jahan Square now inscribed as a UNESCO World Heritage Site.

The two-storey, 33-arch Allahverdi Khan Bridge – named after the engineer and politician who built it – is as much a place to meet as a river crossing.

Town Hall Säynätsalo, Finland, 1949–52

ARCHITECT: ALVAR AALTO (1898–1976)

STYLE: MODERN VERNACULAR

The little factory township of Säynätsalo sits on its small island near the top end of Lake Päijänne, the second largest body of water in southern Finland. Linked to the mainland and two other islands by bridges, it consists of not much more than a sawmill and plywood works and the things you need to keep a working community of some 3,000 people going: houses dotted about, a few shops, a church, community centre, sports field, little harbour and so on. After the Second World War the Finnish authorities decided that this ad hoc place, which had been uninhabited until the sawmill arrived in 1897, needed some municipal organisation. The result is one of the most celebrated and influential civic buildings in the world.

The tiny town hall's simplicity is matched by its subtlety, for this is a multi-functional building. Such small island settlements did not need a large bureaucracy. There is, of course, a small council chamber, signalled by a little square tower with uptilted roof, which inside is treated in blonde wood

Alvar Aalto's civic complex for the little industrial island town of Säynätsalo adopts a domestic style in rough brick.

supported from beams with radiating trusses in the same material. There are some offices, a meeting room and a public library. There were originally useful shops at ground level such as a pharmacy, bank and hairdresser. These spaces were later taken over by the library. Finally, there were some apartments for municipal employees to live in.

The civic status of this building is signalled not only by its small tower. Its wings, each different in design to reflect their different uses, are set around a raised, grassed courtyard. A set of conventional steps leads up to this on the south-eastern corner, marked by the council chamber. On the south-western corner an informal, irregular set of steps spills down, sprouting grasses, as if the green courtyard was flowing out into the surrounding countryside, in what has become a much-imitated feature.

The courtyard form had been proven since ancient times as a natural gathering place. From a practical perspective, a building around a courtyard has shorter corridors than a solid rectangular building, for example. Those corridors at Säynätsalo do not feel like corridors in any case, since they run around an inner window wall overlooking the courtyard.

There are echoes of groups of traditional farm buildings or houses, and the largely traditional external materials are relatively low-maintenance and can weather, get grimy and erode without spoiling the overall visual effect. This little building showed a new way forward: not slavishly aping the past but learning important lessons from it. It is not a grand civic centre, but it is, nonetheless, an urban acropolis.

The library within the town hall is a light and informal space.

Beginning his career in Finland in the early 1920s as a neoclassicist, Aalto quickly adopted the tenets of the white, modernist International Style of architecture. This is reflected in his design for the famous tuberculosis hospital (1929–33) at Paimio in the south-west of the country, where modernism suited the need for light, air and openness demanded by the treatment regime in those pre-antibiotic days. Indeed, modernism as an approach was largely driven by such early sanatoria, its health benefits extolled for other buildings, especially houses.

By the late 1930s, however, Aalto and his architect-designer wife Aino (1894–1949), were starting to turn away from that kind of modernism and, post-war, they took a new direction. Aino died much too young in 1949, the year that Aalto won the competition for the town hall in Säynätsalo. For this project he wanted a return to a more familiar way of building, adopting a very personal and organic style in which timber, brick and rough textures came to the fore. This and others of his post-war buildings marked a divergence from the earlier thinking of the International Congresses of Modern Architecture (CIAM), which, driven by Le Corbusier, had become the progressive architectural think-tank of

The internal corridor with its large windows runs round a raised green courtyard.

the day. The Säynätsalo town hall is clearly 'modern' to our twenty-first-century eyes some 75 years later, but in a far more nuanced and contextual way than much of what was happening elsewhere at the time it was built. This later Aalto approach has been described as part of an 'alternative tradition' of modernism, which never declared a clean break with the past.[1]

One of the reasons the town hall looks so familiar, inside and out, is that it has been so comprehensively imitated by other architects in buildings ranging from universities and libraries to individual houses. The timber ceilings, brick floors and stairs, minimal paintwork, simple red-brick exteriors with the merest hint of decoration, the raised courtyard design, the way it is both standing in woodland while also elevated above it, as well as the fact that it is on a human scale and seems approachable, are all features that have been replicated. Similarly, the furniture, glassware and other domestic objects designed by the Aaltos defined a kind of 'Scandi-modern' aesthetic that people could readily relate to, and which has proved enduringly popular. It is thoroughly appropriate, given the nature of this timber-products factory town, that much of the Aaltos' furniture was and is made in plywood. Aalto himself subsequently built a modest holiday home on the nearby island of Muuratsalo and sailed his boat around the Lake Päijänne archipelago.

Municipal mergers mean that the structure has not functioned as a town hall since 1991. While this is sad, the building has become a museum of itself – much like Le Corbusier's much showier 1954 chapel at Ronchamp in France (see p. 194) – a place for pilgrims seeking out the key moments of architectural change.

1 See Colin St John Wilson, *The Other Tradition of Modern Architecture: The Uncompleted Project*, 1995.

Seaside Florida, USA, 1980–present

ARCHITECTS: ANDRÉS DUANY (B.1949)
AND ELIZABETH PLATER-ZYBERK (B.1950) WITH LÉON KRIER (B.1946)

STYLE: NEW URBANIST

A new town or village that looks to historic precedents is always an intriguing proposition. It is one with a long lineage, going back at least to the planned picturesque villages of early nineteenth-century England, which reflected the Romantic preoccupation with landscape and rural life, and was later seen in the notion of the 'garden city'.[1] The idea is generally to find a reset for deteriorating urban or rural life by starting again from first principles. Seaside in Florida, revolutionary for its date, takes its place in this tradition. An entirely private development, a civic realm invented from scratch to conjure up how towns and cities used to be and could be again, it marks the start of the movement known as 'New Urbanism'.

As a reaction against the sprawling, car-dominated suburbs of much of North America, New Urbanism emerged in the late 1970s as a campaign in favour of tighter-planned, more traditional, walkable places. Seaside, on Florida's Emerald Coast on the Gulf of Mexico, was the first built example. Its architecture, when it was first conceived back in 1980, mixed the then-fashionable postmodernism (which took traditional motifs and used them in novel ways) with outright traditionalism and added a sprinkling of modernism. However, its main visual reference is to the modest pre-war timber tin-roofed, picket-fenced beach and plotland houses of this part of the Florida Panhandle and other southern states, known locally as 'cracker cottages'. Never an 'official' town, it was built on 32 hectares of private land that had been in the ownership of the Davis family since 1946.

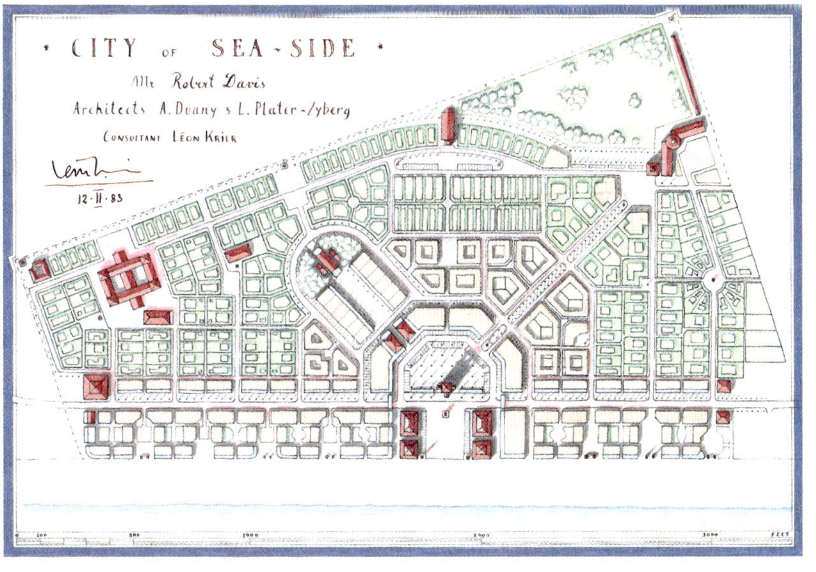

Architect Léon Krier's amended 1983 'New Urbanism' plan for Seaside.

Seaside's architecture is inspired by local vernacular 'cracker cottages' interpreted in a variety of ways.

Robert S. Davis inherited the estate in 1978 and he, his wife Daryl and the architects proceeded to imagine what rediscovered urban principles and building techniques might look like there. It was to be in sharp contrast to the car-dominated, zoned-uses norm of post-war American town planning where the various types of building – residential, commercial, industrial, public – became widely separated rather than all mixed up together.

Seaside is anything but ad hoc, being wholly and intensely planned. Its focus is on the beach, with streets and squares radiating back from there in a deliberately asymmetrical manner. Civic buildings originally ranged from a little post office down by the beach, focal point of the street layout, to a slightly Scandinavian-looking white-painted chapel inland (by 2019 the post office had vanished). There are various eye-catcher follies in the form of a row of pavilions by different hands, marking the points where the streets become paths through the dunes to the beach. Shops and offices are dotted among other larger buildings arranged around a crescent near the beach. To either side of the relatively grand avenues, houses are grouped conventionally enough on plots arranged on a grid pattern of little streets, the blocks also cut through by footpaths. A town council oversees the various street associations but there is no symbolic town hall.

All of this feels almost, but not quite, normal – as is the way of showpiece developments. It is a holiday resort, and as such is seasonal, but with enough of a permanent population to sustain a small school. You will recognise it if you have seen the 1998 movie *The Truman Show*, starring Jim Carrey as Truman Burbank, the only person in a huge film-set town beneath a dome who believes this is real life, not the ultimate reality show with himself as the subject. The fictional town of the movie – 'Seahaven Island' – is the real Seaside, enhanced in places by the movie's designers. Truman's house at 31 Natchez Street (36 in the film) is one of many buildings in the town designed by architect Don Cooper in a kind of turbocharged neoclassicism. Many different architects of all stylistic persuasions were involved in the design of the various buildings and it is this high-design aspect that sets it apart from older, less self-conscious, vernacular towns, which have evolved mostly in the hands of builders rather than architects.

The appearance of individual buildings here is only part of the story, which is mostly to do with the tight and walkable layout: neighbourliness. Florida had suffered greatly from the atomising effects of road-dominated redevelopment of settlements. Enough remained, however, to act as a guide. For Steven Semes, native Floridian and professor of architecture at the University of Notre Dame, Seaside is 'the radical alternative to almost all post-war models and an attempt to reconnect with the formal knowledge and planning techniques that produced the more successful historic towns in the state ... an urban culture that many people want but almost no post-war places provide.'[2]

Seaside's plan, with its recognisable hierarchy of streets, buildings and urban spaces, proved very successful. With it came design codes: regulations governing what buildings must look like within flexible parameters. So there are front porches, gazebos and open loggias everywhere, and largely painted timber construction. Within the rules, design variety is encouraged. There are even a few modernist buildings. The design codes keep Seaside's character more or less intact, though more recent houses are distinctly less quirky and tend to be larger than the early ones. There are lots of vacation rental properties now, and some big houses that sell for eye-watering prices. These are the inevitable result of success in a free market. Young though it is as a place, Seaside is being gentrified.

Today's 'alternative' communities, shaped by individuals rather than official organisations, can take other forms. Some twentieth-century ones such as Arcosanti in Arizona, begun in 1970 by architect Paulo Soleri (1919–2013), are eco-futuristic in feel. Others, in rural corners and coastal plotlands, have something of a junkyard or farmyard quality. Sir Bertram Clough Williams-Ellis's (1883–1978) brilliantly fanciful 'Italian' village of Portmeirion in North Wales (built 1925–75) is an exercise in picturesque bricolage, reusing salvaged parts of demolished buildings. But if that was an outbreak of inspired whimsy, the New Urbanism principles first explored at Seaside are entirely serious and have been applied to many other settlements along the Emerald Coast, elsewhere in America, in Europe and Scandinavia. The village of Poundbury in Dorset, England, masterplanned by Léon Krier from 1987 with the involved patronage of then-heir to the British throne, Prince Charles (b.1948), is planned on the same principles.

Today, the traditionalists meet broadly modernist architects coming the other way. Many more architects now agree on the need for density, walkability and narrow intersecting streets, discouraging fast-moving vehicles in towns. There is similar agreement on the pressing environmental need for more natural, longer-lasting and less carbon-intensive materials. Style is all that separates the two sides. Seaside was at first interesting because of its experimental quality and variety of styles, and is now encouraging because of the way many of its principles have become so widely accepted.

---

1 The idea of the picturesque village started in 1810 with Blaise Hamlet near Bristol by John Nash and George Repton. See also Gillian Darley, *Villages of Vision*, 1975.

2 Correspondence with the author, May 2022.

Spreebogen Government District Berlin, Germany, 1894–2010

ARCHITECTS: PAUL WALLOT (1841–1912), NORMAN FOSTER (B.1935), AXEL SCHULTES (B.1943), CHARLOTTE FRANK (B.1959) AND STEPHAN BRAUNFELS (B.1950)

STYLE: LATE MODERN MONUMENTALIST / NEO-BAROQUE

The Spreebogen area, showing the restored Reichstag building (top right) with the axis of the three new buildings to the left.

Political upheavals have far-reaching architectural consequences. In living memory none is more fascinating and as broadly successful in civic terms as the careful remaking of Berlin since the collapse of the Soviet Bloc symbolised by the breaching of the Berlin Wall in 1989.

The continuing reconstruction is extraordinary in its ambition. It is one thing to build a capital city from scratch, another to rebuild a city after destructive wars. But in recent times only Berlin has undergone three fundamental changes in the space of little more than half a century: first the Third Reich and destruction of the Second World War, secondly brutal division into two parallel cities ruled by two political systems, communist and capitalist; and finally, starting all over again with the decision in 1991 to create the revived capital of a reunited Germany in Berlin. This required a complete new government district to be built in the Spreebogen area, which includes the restored historic seat of government, the Reichstag, and three other new buildings arranged on an east–west axis close by.

The Reichstag was originally an ornate neo-baroque 1894 building by Paul Wallot for the Bundestag or lower chamber of the German parliament. It was wrecked first by the momentous arson attack just after Hitler came to power in 1933 – which he seized on as an excuse for savage repression of political opponents – and again in the battle for Berlin at the end of the Second World War, when it was targeted by Soviet troops. After the war it fell into the western sector, the damaged glazed iron-frame dome was removed and in the 1960s it was modernised but little used. After German reunification it became highly symbolic, not least for the 1916 inscription on its portico: *Dem Deutschen Volke* ('to the German People'). Reunification was formally agreed there in October 1990 and, following the 1991 vote to return government to Berlin, an international competition to redesign it for the Bundestag launched in 1992.

Inside, the Reichstag's new dome has a walkway and light reflector to illuminate the Bundestag chamber below.

The eventual winner was the UK's Norman Foster, who was asked to include a dome to replace Wallot's missing one. In this most politically sensitive of locations, the choice of non-German architect had symbolic value: there was to be no nationalism here. The message was that this was for Europe and the world. Meanwhile, the simultaneous competition to masterplan the adjacent Spreebogen government buildings was won by two Berlin architects, Axel Schultes and Charlotte Frank.

Foster conceived his dome as a glass-clad observation gallery with a spiral ramp rising up through it. The dome was floored in glass, looking straight down into the Bundestag chamber below: democracy on view. It also contained a glittering 'Sword of Damocles' suspended above the chamber, an inverted-cone daylight reflector to illuminate proceedings below.

Foster left many of the surviving Reichstag interiors in a partially raw state, complete with carefully preserved Soviet-troop graffiti, and the new elements in glass, steel and timber are placed in contrast with those. Such niceties were not required in the adjacent Spreebogen, however, where the Schultes/Frank masterplan was for a sequence of all-new buildings running on a straight east–west axis across the meanders of the River Spree immediately north of the Reichstag. The symbolism there was the literal stitching together of the former East and West, for the Berlin Wall had passed through here: and also to connect the government centre with the western commercial heart of the city.

As built, the architectural ensemble of the *Band des Bundes* (or 'Federal Belt') is not quite so ambitious as envisaged, but by any standards grand enough. The proposed line of buildings was shortened, so severing the western end of the great sequence apart from a park. Within this reduced masterplan, Schultes and Frank nonetheless got to build what is thought to be the largest government building in the world, eight times bigger than Washington's White House: the new German Chancellery, base of the German leader elected by members of the Bundestag. The power of the Chancellor is great and, as the leader of the most influential member of the European Union, carries international weight. H-shaped in plan, with a tall central section and lower wings stretching out to either side, lightweight in appearance with pale stone juxtaposed with large areas of glazing, the Chancellery is a curious building. It is an example of modernism aspiring to monumentalism, but in this highly charged political context not too monumental. Its axial composition and restrained neoclassical references suggest a nod to the great Prussian architect Karl-Friedrich Schinkel (1781–1841), but it also refers to the later monumental work of American architect Louis Kahn (1901–1974). The overall effect is of the Late Modern architectural style, with more than a touch of postmodernism. Its structure is cut away in places, its western wings dissolving into open riverside pavilions and an elegant bridge hopping across to the western park.

The German Chancellery, opened in 2001, is the power base of the German leader. It treads a fine line between the merely imposing and the outright monumental.

At its eastern end, across a central square (where a 'citizen's forum' building was originally planned), the baton is passed to another architect, Stephan Braunfels, for two government back-office buildings including library, committee rooms and archives. True to the masterplan, Braunfels designs his two buildings effectively as one, separated by the river and another footbridge. His architectural language is less delicate than Schultes and Frank's, but he deploys some of the same anti-bulk tactics where the two buildings face each other and open up to the river's edge.

This is by no means the end of it: Berlin has plenty more administrative buildings of one kind or another, new and old. But with these four showpiece buildings and their associated parks and riverside walkways, the new government quarter of Berlin fulfils its remit of visual openness and accessibility. Like much of rebuilt Berlin, the scars have not quite been erased: this district does not yet feel properly woven into the fabric of the city. The hierarchy is, however, clear. The star of the show and seat of democracy is the Reichstag. This historic centre looks across to the power base of the Chancellery, while the large back-of-house buildings complete the civic sequence. The spaces between and around are public domain. All of this is just a fragment of the overall replanning and rebuilding of Berlin as a city commercially, culturally and infrastructurally, but without the government's restored civic presence, that would have happened at a much slower pace.

Houses

Design a good house and you can design a good anything. For the Italian Renaissance architect and theorist Leon Battista Alberti (1404–1472) this was a given. 'For if a City, according to the opinion of philosophers, be no more than a great House, and on the other hand a House be a little City; why, may it not be said that the parts of that House are so many little houses; such as the courtyard, the hall, the parlour, the portico and the like?'[1]

This organic relationship between the parts of a house and city is apparent in some of the very earliest recorded settlements. Skara Brae in the Scottish Orkneys is a Neolithic village, which flourished between the years 3200 and 2200 BCE. It later became engulfed by sand dunes until it was revealed by a mighty storm in 1850. Today, visitors can see how the individual sunken houses – with their stone walls, clearly defined common layout and built-in fittings (beds, central fireplace, shelved storage units) – were linked via covered alleys to form a larger whole, complete with drainage system. Built before Stonehenge or the Great Pyramids of Egypt, Skara Brae is immediately comprehensible to us, some five thousand years later.

The Ancient Romans perfected a form of domestic architecture with their *domus* or atrium house. These were often single-storey, sometimes two-floor, rectangular in form, arranged with rooms around an open courtyard and with a small walled garden or *hortus conclusus* at the rear. They did not necessarily have much street presence at first. For the merchant classes, shops were often inserted at the front, while for the more lavish individual country villas of officials across the empire, the emphasis was rather more on the interior than the exterior. These were 'live-work' spaces, and the simplicity and practicality of the Roman courtyard house layout continues to be an inspiration to architects today, especially for landlocked sites where it helps to have daylight from above.

Whereas the *domus* can be argued to have survived around the Mediterranean, evolving for instance into the Moorish courtyard-house, much of Europe began again after the collapse of the Roman Empire. Thus, in the medieval agrarian communities of northern Europe and Scandinavia the prosperous landowner, acting as the local civic or military leader, would build his hall. From the Viking longhouses of Scandinavia, their curving roofs like upturned boats, via the farmhouses of Saxonian northern Germany and the Low Countries to the first iterations of the English country house, the heart of these multi-functional houses was the communal great hall.

There were numerous variations on the hall-house theme depending on various factors, including the status of the individuals doing the building, the materials available locally, the climate and thus the nature of the agriculture. Stalls for animals, haylofts and granaries were incorporated into usually timber-framed buildings, which also functioned as dwellings for the 'yeoman farmers' – landowning mid-status individuals. It was not so very different when it came

The Brümmerhof hall house, Hösseringen in Lower Saxony, Germany, 1644. Now part of a museum village of salvaged farm buildings from Lüneberg Heath, it is a late flowering of a type common across northern Germany and the eastern Netherlands from medieval times. A single large timber-framed hall combines family living with haylofts, granaries and byres.

to the *Minka* farmhouses of Japan across broadly the same period: this was a logical and natural way to build for a hierarchical agricultural-based community.

Typical of the European genre is the *Fachhallenhaus* ('Low German House'), a type common in northern Germany and the Netherlands. The main characteristic, apart from the timber framing, is the huge roof, thatched or tiled, sweeping down low and offering some shelter at the sides. Tall enough for large storage areas and rooms within the roof, it is a type not so different from the earlier Viking longhouses, which in turn had much in common with some Neolithic examples. Within were different areas for different functions but, as time went on, this type settled down to a fairly standard model of human habitation at one end and animals at the other. There would appear to have been little privacy, but certain areas were curtained or partitioned off, placed up on galleries or set at one or both ends of the large central space, always with its central hearth with (before the gradual arrival of the chimney from the twelfth century) smoke rising to filter through the roof thatch or rudimentary vents. Unsurprisingly, fires were commonplace, with evidence of repeated rebuilding following fires on the same sites.

Alberti described a good house as being a machine for the dispersal of water, instructing architects to pay attention to proper roofs and gutters to keep its inhabitants dry.[2] His mention of 'machine' recalls Le Corbusier's 1923 description of a house as 'a machine for living in', a place that functioned efficiently to help us in our daily lives.[3]

Luxury houses across the centuries – and until around a century ago, plenty of the more modest ones too – presupposed the existence of live-in servants and were designed accordingly. In the late twentieth century, small family homes were designed with stay-at-home housewives in mind. Space- and labour-saving fitted kitchens were first invented in Germany in 1926 with the 'Frankfurt kitchen' designed for a social apartment project by the pioneering Austrian-born architect Margarete Schütte-Lihotzky (1897–2000). She called her kitchen 'the housewife's laboratory'. Post-Second World War small prefabricated houses across Europe, many of them timber flatpack types exported from Finland, extended this ultra-functionalist apartment thinking to standalone homes. The two greatest changes in wealthier countries in recent times have been the reinvention of the kitchen as a more general living space, rather than as a place of solitary toil, and the proliferation of bath and shower rooms.

Houses for the comfortably-off are one thing, houses for those affected by natural disasters or conflicts another entirely. In Pakistan Yasmeen Lari (b.1941) – the first woman architect to practise in that country – has devoted her time, since she retired from mainstream practice in 2000, to designing and building simple, dignified homes from readily available local materials, such as mud, lime and straw. Built after emergencies such as earthquakes and floods, and designed to resist recurrences of these events, these homes require little or no money to build. By 2021 she had succeeded in producing 50,000 of them in various places and configurations, along with larger community buildings using the same techniques. By the nature of their materials and techniques, they are virtually carbon-neutral. So what some might regard as 'primitive' houses are in fact quite sophisticated and very fit for purpose. She calls the process of making them 'barefoot social architecture'.[4]

A one-off house is not the same as an apartment in a block or tower, villages of emergency-response dwellings, or a home in a cookie-cutter suburb: mass housing is a fascinating and noble subject in itself. Once inside the house, of whatever kind and however small, though, the Alberti principle applies: in your home, you are in your own miniature city.

1 Leon Battista Alberti, *On the Art of Building*, 1486.
2 Ibid.
3 'Une maison est une machine-à-habiter', Le Corbusier and Amédée Ozenfant, *Towards a New Architecture*, 1923, trans. Frederick Etchells, 1927.
4 Yasmeen Lari in her speech on accepting the Jane Drew Prize for architecture, 2020.

Fitzwilliam Square Dublin, Ireland, 1790–1830

ARCHITECTS: JOHN AND PATRICK ROE (ACTIVE FROM 1790) AND VARIOUS BUILDERS

STYLE: GEORGIAN DOMESTIC CLASSICAL

The terraced or row house first emerged in medieval times and began to be a feature of European urban planning from the seventeenth century. Buildings had always leaned against each other in hugger-mugger fashion in towns and cities, but these generally remained individually styled houses. The essence of the row house is uniformity with its neighbours and this made them the natural preserve of speculative developers, providing a standardised product, the mass housing of their day.

The type reached what many regard as a peak of perfection in the late eighteenth and early nineteenth centuries in Europe and North America. 'Georgian' is a broad term describing the classically derived architecture of the Hanoverian dynasty from 1714 to 1830, usually also including the short reign of William IV (r.1830–1837) until the year his niece Victoria (r.1837–1901) succeeded him. Such identical, joined-together houses – often built by landowners in pattern-book fashion regulated by the authorities – achieved civic status when organised into squares, circuses and crescents, with private or sometimes public gardens at their centres. In Georgian Dublin, the layout of new streets and squares from the mid-eighteenth century onwards transformed what had hitherto been a largely medieval city into a modern one.

Fitzwilliam Square is named after Richard, Seventh Viscount Fitzwilliam (1745–1816), Anglo-Irish landowner, developer and (funded partly by his property holdings) collector of art, antiquities and books. This square was the last to be built of Dublin's famous five, starting with two in the north of the city – Mountjoy and Rutland (now Parnell) squares – then a further three spurring the expansion of the city south of the River Liffey, at St Stephen's Green, Merrion Square (another Fitzwilliam Estate project) and finally this one bearing the family name. By that time the formula was thoroughly tried and tested, with minor variations depending on the date and the builder and the wealth of the target market. The square was laid out by surveyors, and the builders buying the leases for the plots for the 69 houses built according to strict guidelines regarding form, layout and materials – what these days are called 'design codes'. Regulated both by the landowners and Dublin City Council and slotted between the new wide boulevards laid out at this time, these simple well-proportioned flat-fronted houses represent an urban residential ideal.

The square has a large garden at its centre for use by the surrounding householders.

The carefully regulated Georgian houses of Dublin's Fitzwilliam Square. Such uniformity made these upmarket town houses a good prospect for speculative developers.

The Industrial Revolution was under way and cities were rapidly growing, but this was not yet the hell-for-leather expansion of the later nineteenth century. The times were not propitious, economically or politically. Great Britain and Ireland (previously colonially governed and from 1801 part of the new United Kingdom) were in a steadily intensifying war with Revolutionary France. This was only a decade after Great Britain under George III (r.1760–1820) had lost its 13 American colonies. In this uncertain climate the building of Fitzwilliam Square proceeded in fits and starts, or what we would now call 'phases'. The south side was the last to be completed, though this was done against the wishes of the residents of the other sides who rightly pointed out that they would lose their view of the distant mountains.

The appeal of this square, apart from its intactness, is precisely that it is not as grand as some of the others, either here or in British cities from London to Edinburgh. There was no named architect for it: the Roes, father and son surveyors, operated at a less exalted level than John Nash (1752–1835) or Robert Adam (1728–1792) in London, say. So the square is not, for instance, designed so that each side looks like one large mansion, as was happening in places at this time in England and Scotland. Nor does it have grander set-piece insertions of larger town houses, as happened in the earlier Dublin squares.

The individual houses in Fitzwilliam Square, mostly wholly brick-built though some with stone-faced ground floors, just proceed calmly and rationally round all four sides of the square and continue off into the adjacent streets. On north and south sides of the square their halls and stairs adjoin, so the doorways are arranged in pairs: for no obvious reason this rhythm breaks down on the east and west sides. All the houses are tall – five storeys including a semi-basement, often the domain of servants where kitchens and sculleries were to be found. There were two main rooms per floor, plus outbuildings at rear ground level.

Georgian Dublin is noted for its splendid doorways, reflecting the wide halls behind. The doors are all the more imposing for being at the top of short flights of steps. They are set in neoclassical porticos, flanked by columns and surmounted by semicircular 'fanlights', so named because their delicate glazing bars radiated outwards from the base like a fan. Such sparing neoclassical details continue in the doorways and cornices inside but, as was the way at this time, the houses are relatively plain otherwise, despite the wealth of their residents. The windows are tall up-and-down-sliding sashes in proportion with the rest of the frontages, the facades rise to a simple parapet behind which the shallow pitched roofs are concealed. The heights vary minutely according to the phase of building, with some houses being ever so slightly grander than others, not something noticeable at a glance.

The fine rooms of the houses, used for entertaining as much as family life, are on the first floors, with taller ceilings and windows to match – what the Italians call a *piano nobile* or 'noble floor', as you find in the palazzi of Venice. These houses are by no means palaces, but the idea of gracious living in this way persisted for the professional classes. Fitzwilliam Square quickly became a focus for the medical profession, which remains there today, though now more institutional than residential.

The terraced or row house is a very efficient, high-density way to build, in which – unlike apartment blocks housing the same number of people per square metre – everyone gets their own front door and a bit of land at the back, whether that is a small yard or, as here, a sizeable town garden. Here, the high status of the houses is shown by the way the gardens run back quite a distance to (originally) coach houses and stables on the mews streets behind, some of which survive.

For all the lack of individuality, these simple, well-planned and well-proportioned houses represent an ideal. It is relatively rare for a complete Fitzwilliam Square house to come onto the market and, when one does, it is costly.

Blackwell Cumbria, UK, 1898–9

ARCHITECT: MACKAY HUGH BAILLIE SCOTT (1865–1945)

STYLE: ARTS AND CRAFTS

A wealthy country retreat, Blackwell reflects an Arts and Crafts-inspired aesthetic for living.

The period of Arts and Crafts architecture from the late nineteenth to the early twentieth centuries is, by some reckoning, the summit of Western domestic design thus far. This movement was partly a reaction against the modern world – especially the world of mass-production – and partly about planning new ways of living. It was a call to arms for traditional craft skills combined with an upper-middle-class notion of good taste.

Wealthy private clients with servants were essential: this was the last great era of the country house. In America, Frank Lloyd Wright (1867–1959) was a keen Arts and Crafts exponent, taking things to extremes in his sprawling, low-roofed 'Prairie' houses. His contemporaries moved in different directions – Charles Rennie Mackintosh (1868–1928) in Scotland and England towards art nouveau (even latterly jazz-age), Edwin Lutyens (1869–1944) in England towards inventive classicism, Adolf Loos (1870–1933) in the Czech lands towards ultra-plain exteriors and rich, interlocking interiors. Baillie Scott, of the same generation as all of these, was a less stylistically restless type. His best work was at the more traditionalist, externally plain end of the Arts and Crafts Movement, often called 'vernacular' because it draws most obviously on a familiar rural domestic visual language.

Blackwell demonstrates that he was as fluent and inventive in his handling of spaces as his better-known contemporaries. His brief was to build a holiday home for a well-to-do family, the Holts. Sir Edward Holt (1849–1928) was a brewer and politician who did much to improve conditions in his native Manchester. This was a time when such families habitually moved base with children and servants in the summer months.

Set high on a hillside overlooking Lake Windermere, with the Coniston Fells in the distance, Blackwell has a glorious location. Outside, its white-rendered gabled wings and stone bay windows are topped with slender conical chimneys and the house is surrounded by terraced gardens. Inside, the main rooms – hall with gallery and inglenook fireplace (an inglenook being an intimate part-enclosed space by the fire), dining room and drawing room – flow into each other in a way reminiscent of early Wright in the Midwest or Mackintosh's slightly later Hill House outside Glasgow. Upstairs, there are eight bedrooms, two with dressing rooms, and (normal for the time) just two bathrooms for the whole house.

Blackwell contains richly decorated interiors with some exaggerated details.

The contrast between the very masculine main hall, with its medieval-revival feel, and the very feminine White Drawing Room with delicate, almost art nouveau columns around its own inglenook, shows Baillie Scott at his best. As was an article of faith with Arts and Crafts architects, he designed the house in every detail, outside and in, down to the door handles.

The Arts and Crafts Movement looked both backwards and forwards. On the one hand was traditionalism, which fed into the doctrine of 'honesty' in building: an approach that came to be widely known as 'truth to materials'. This often expressed itself in a pared-down style, with fewer and better fripperies (furniture, wall hangings, coloured glass). After all, traditional buildings, especially rural ones as built by their revered crafts folk, were nothing if not functional. So Arts and Crafts, being the antidote to Victorian 'over-richness', was taken by some historians to be a forerunner of modernism, and thus a transitional style. Arts and Crafts houses were far from being copies of historic buildings. They were often heavily stylised, with exaggerated details – oversized roofs and turrets were a speciality. However, the fact that some of these houses were relatively plain and increasingly fluidly planned did not mean that they were necessarily anticipating the modernist sea-change in architecture that was coming. This was a time of much international cross-talk in architecture, fed by magazines, books and exhibitions. America, Britain and mainland Europe, even Japan, were all in on the conversation. This was an evolution of traditional forms rather than the clean-slate modernist revolution. Nonetheless, a visit to this house makes you realise why – along with Lutyens – Baillie Scott's work was admired by some of the new generation of more overtly modernist architects. Architects always have more in common than matters of style might suggest, and that commonality shows itself most clearly in interiors.

Having originally trained as a farm manager before switching to architecture, Baillie Scott somewhat eccentrically based himself at first on the Isle of Man. This does not seem to have hampered his business or his style. He was unfortunate to lose his archive of drawings and correspondence twice – once in a fire in 1911 and again in the London Blitz of 1941. Consequently, his work is much less well documented than it should be.

Blackwell is the indulgence of the arts-conscious, *fin-de-siècle*, self-made business magnate. It now seems a lost world of wealth, craftsmanship, optimism: a stratum of society that was to be devastated by the First World War. The Holts were no exception. Their eldest son died in the trenches and this grand holiday home, containing painful memories, lost its appeal for the family. Remarkably, it survived various changes of use thereafter, including a long spell as a girls' school, with its interior details intact. Finally, it was restored and opened to the public in 2001.

The delicate White Drawing Room at Blackwell has an art nouveau feel.

Villa Tugendhat Brno, Czechia, 1928–30

ARCHITECT: LUDWIG MIES VAN DER ROHE (1886–1969)
WITH DESIGNER LILLY REICH (1885–1947)

STYLE: INTERNATIONAL MODERNIST

This house, a modernist villa for an affluent young family, has a floor-to-ceiling glass wall overlooking its hillside gardens. Its largest sheets of glass each measure approximately 5 metres wide by 3 metres high. These are big even by today's standards. In 1930, in a family home, they were astonishing. The technology used to make such large glass panes was relatively new in the 1930s, and more often used for shop windows. Even more remarkable is the fact that these sections can slide electrically downwards, dropping into slots in the floor to open the house up fully to the gardens and the city beyond. It is a conjuring trick: what on earth is supporting the floor above?

The answer is a row of very slender cruciform steel columns, set well back from the facade. Unusually at a time of concrete and brick in domestic architecture, its architect constructed a delicate steel frame for the top two floors of the house. Cladding the columns in chromed brass plating allowed

Villa Tugendhat, viewed from the garden below. The huge window panels are shown sliding downwards to open.

him to visually dematerialise them. Walls are there where necessary for privacy and to define spaces, but as partitions carrying no weight. Doors in richly grained dark timber rise right up to the ceilings. It is a place designed to impress and delight.

Ludwig Mies van der Rohe (usually known just as 'Mies') was a German architect who had begun his career as a conventional neoclassicist but following the First World War, along with many of his colleagues across Europe, he became convinced that a new style was needed to reflect modern times. A consensus of the avant-garde emerged. This style would be minimalist, reflect the technology of the times and would maximise daylight and fresh air. Nor did it need to be austere: Mies, a bon viveur fond of his cigars and Martinis, was never a hair-shirt architect.

It helped that his newly married young clients here, Grete (1903–1970) and Fritz Tugendhat (1895–1958), were both wealthy scions of separate industrialist families. Grete's father had given her the family's large neoclassical villa as a wedding present. But she and Fritz wanted something new and modern. Towards the end of her life Grete recalled: 'I truly longed for a modern spacious house with clear and simple shapes. My husband was horrified by the idea of having rooms full of objects and cloths as he had known from childhood.'[1] They built it in part of the gardens of the old villa. Money really was no object; they wanted the best.

These, then, were ideal clients for an ambitious architect. Mies had already produced a handful of houses in the modernist manner in Berlin and it was there that he met the Tugendhats. They had been considering an architect from Brno, but rapidly decided that Mies – already with a considerable reputation as a leader of the avant-garde who got things done – was the one for them.

Mies was introduced to the Tugendhats by the designer and teacher Lilly Reich, his contemporary and partner at the time, in life as well as art. Reich's specialisms were textiles, furniture and materials generally. The classic 'Mies' furniture designs of this period, including his 'Brno chair' (originally designed for this house), began and ended with his 12-year involvement with Reich. Experienced in exhibition design – the pair came fresh from their triumphantly successful German pavilion at the Barcelona International Exposition of 1928–9 – Reich may also have collaborated more than previously thought on the overall layout of Mies's buildings. Between them, in Brno they designed a house that is a masterpiece.

The Villa Tugendhat is designed to address the south-western view across the gardens and it steps down the slope on three levels. From the street side it does not look especially remarkable. From this angle all that can be seen is the single-storey top floor pavilion and entrance terrace, with a delicate pergola at the rear looking out across the city. There are bedrooms for parents, children

and a governess on this level, a main entrance hall, a garage and housekeeper's room. The lowest level – the concrete plinth on which the house sits – is a basement utility area, originally full of the coal-fired equipment to heat the house, along with a complex filtered ventilation system. The main event, therefore, is the tall middle floor, the living/dining/kitchen area.

Mies and Reich wanted spaces to flow freely into each other with minimal divisions. The dining area, for instance, is contained within a freestanding semi-circular timber enclosure rather than being a separate room. Only a curtain otherwise separates the spaces. Cream rubber flooring runs right through. At one end, an internal glass wall, matching the exterior one, encloses a built-in conservatory. There is a separate inner living room towards the back of the house, behind a divider wall of golden onyx – translucent stone cut so thin that the low winter sun makes it glow gently when viewed from behind. A private cinema room opens off at the back.

If the rear of the house contains the winter living quarters, then the main space at the front is for summer. Facing south-west, it can heat up on summer days, hence the drop-away glazing, augmented by fold-out awnings. An outside terrace here leads to a broad staircase descending to the gardens below.

The weight of the house is carried on slim, chromed, cruciform steel columns.

The family spared no expense to achieve the rich interiors, including a built-in conservatory, shown here to the left.

Mies and Reich designed everything in the main rooms down to the last detail, with only the sanitaryware in bathrooms and kitchens being off-the-peg. The Tugendhats had achieved a house that expressed their progressive sensibilities, with Grete in particular rushing to defend it when it was criticised by jealous Czech architects.

The idyll did not last. The Tugendhat family lived in the house for just over seven years. They were Jewish and thus forced to flee their homeland as war approached in 1938. They went first to Switzerland, then to Venezuela. Mies himself, the last director of the famous Bauhaus school of design, found his kind of architecture branded 'decadent' by the Nazi regime. He had emigrated to America in 1937 to continue his career there. Reich stayed behind. The house was looted and badly damaged during the war but survived in various uses until finally being faithfully restored, along with its gardens, furniture and materials, in 2010–12. Today, you can visit it as a museum of itself and as a brilliant record of an all too short inter-war period of tremendous optimism and affluence in architecture and life.

1 From a speech given by Grete Tugendhat in Brno in 1969, Villa Tugendhat Research Centre.

Vanna Venturi House Philadelphia, USA, 1961–5

ARCHITECTS: ROBERT VENTURI (1925–2018)
WITH DENISE SCOTT BROWN (B.1931)

STYLE: MODERN MANNERIST

When it was designed in the early 1960s, Vanna Venturi's house, though conventionally built, was revolutionary in style.

A recently widowed mother decides to downsize from the family home. To encourage her bookish, architect son in his career she asks him to design her a small new house. Designing for one's parents is a common enough scenario, but in this case the end result is out of all proportion to the scale of the job. This little home becomes a celebrated moment of radical change in architecture.

That moment was later seen as a harbinger of postmodernism. Often associated with the late 1970s and 1980s, its roots go back much earlier. The reaction against 'International Style' inter-war modernism, such as the Villa Tugendhat (see p. 44) had set in surprisingly soon, and the 1950s was a time of sceptical architects exploring alternatives. One of these was the style commonly referred to as 'brutalism' (usually in moulded raw concrete) but, as the fifties went on, other options were investigated by architects wanting to re-establish a dialogue with the past after the clean break of (mostly European) ideological modernism. Robert Venturi Jr was one such architect.

The Vanna Venturi House therefore stands out at a time – the start of the 1960s – when modern house design was in a state of flux. Everything was available, from exhibitionist glass boxes to ultra-traditionalist eighteenth-century replicas, and the always popular Scandinavian-modern aesthetic occupying a broad swathe of the centre ground, as it does to this day.

Venturi was in his mid-thirties when he began to design his mother's new home in the affluent, wooded Philadelphia suburb of Chestnut Hill. He was the only son of a fiercely independent, liberal and well-read woman, herself the daughter of Italian immigrants. He had previously worked for two other highly original architects searching for more expressive forms of architecture – Eero Saarinen (1910–1961; see Dulles Airport, p. 129) and Louis Kahn (see Salk Institute, p. 109). Like Kahn, Venturi was both a practising architect and an Ivy League teacher and theorist, later collaborating on equal terms with his wife and co-architect Denise Scott Brown.

This house is as much of a manifesto statement as anything the modernists came up with. Venturi, like them, was adept at sloganising. His response to Mies van der Rohe's famous 'Less is More'[1] dictum was 'Less is a Bore'.[2] He later wrote that 'Where the Modern masters' strength lay in consistency, ours should lie in diversity.'[3] Note that he nonetheless regarded them as 'masters'. Much of Venturi and Scott Brown's philosophy was contained in the book *Complexity and Contradiction in Architecture*. Symbolism and ornament, mostly ignored by mainstream modernists, were important to them.

As many generations of architects can attest, having an indulgent client such as your mother to work for makes it a lot easier to get your ideas built. Vanna wanted this house to advance her son's career. Her husband, Robert's father, had died in 1959. For her new life she insisted on a simple house, and no doubt with advancing age in mind, wanted to be able to live at ground level. She had given up driving, so needed no garage. That was about it, but she stuck firmly to her requirements.

The original interior, showing the staircase squeezing past the chimney with its oversized fireplace.

Mother and son found a large plot of land on a quiet lane, Millman Street, and set the house well back behind a long garden approach. Venturi's design was a simplified version of an unbuilt project of his from 1959 for a weekend beach house which played around with complex sloping roofs and a slightly offset tall chimney. Vanna's house is a great deal calmer as a composition – once Robert met Scott Brown, she helped pull the design together but does not claim co-authorship.[4] The sloping roofs are there, however, arranged at the front in a classical manner. The whole front facade is one giant 'broken pediment' (the pediment being the shallow-pitched triangular gable end of a classical temple atop its columns, the break being a central gap which allowed concealed windows behind it).

The back of the house is entirely different and more complicated, with a rearward-facing upper roof slope and a classically inspired Diocletian window/door (semicircular, divided into three sections) with balcony. As Scott Brown later described this front-back divergence: 'You get the Queen Anne front and the Mary Anne behind.'[5] She, as Venturi himself did, rejects the term 'postmodern'.[6]

The 'Mary Anne behind' with its upstairs Diocletian glazing.

Within the front facade is a large rectangular inset porch, marked by a horizontal lintel overlaid with a delicate appliqué arch. This is pure decoration, as is an equivalent, slightly projecting banded frieze visually linking the differently sized windows across the facade. The lack of window symmetry and the just slightly offset chimney gleefully subvert the classical language.

The house contains only a living/dining area, kitchen, tiny bathroom, one bedroom, small upstairs guest room, side porch and a basement. Touches of luxury come with certain materials (the marble floor to the dining area, for example) and some good joinery, as well as in the positioning of the oversized fireplace at the heart of the house with the staircase sidestepping behind it, and in the handling of space and light, with daylight reflected into the interior via a tall curving ceiling.

Modest though it is, the Vanna Venturi House has the scale and ambition of a much grander building. This was Venturi's take on sixteenth-century Mannerism – the style where architects and artists played fast and loose with the classical language. As Scott Brown later remarked: 'It has all the aspirations of a Michelangelo.'[7] It did not launch a wave of imitators at first, but it showed what a built intellectual riposte to modernism, drawing on classical precedents, might look like. In that sense it set the scene for the aesthetic upheaval of the years to come.

1 Cited in Philip Johnson, *Mies van der Rohe*, exh. cat., Museum of Modern Art, New York, 1947.
2 See Robert Venturi, *Complexity and Contradiction in Architecture*, 1966.
3 Robert Venturi and Denise Scott Brown, *A View from the Campidoglio: Selected Essays 1953–1984*, 1984.
4 Conversation with the author, August 2022.
5 Denise Scott Brown, quoted by Amy Frearson, 'Postmodern Architecture: Vanna Venturi House, Philadelphia, by Robert Venturi', *Dezeen*, August 2015.
6 Conversation with the author, August 2022.
7 Denise Scott Brown, quoted by Amy Frearson, 'Postmodern Architecture', op. cit.

Nora House Sendai, Japan, 2008

ARCHITECTS: ATELIER BOW-WOW (YOSHIHARU TSUKAMOTO (B.1965) AND MOMOYO KAJIMA (B.1969))

STYLE: MODERN VERNACULAR

This small house with large ambitions draws on traditional Japanese forms.

Atelier Bow-Wow (known in Tokyo as Atelier Wan-Wan, because that is how the sound of a barking dog is pronounced in Japan) began fruitfully experimenting with domestic architecture when they set up business in 1992. Like many other Japanese architects, they find great appeal in making ingenious use in urban houses of what, to Western eyes, are impossibly tiny spaces. Tsukamoto and Kajima take this further, finding inspiration in the junk structures that spring up on leftover scraps of land in the city, jammed between other buildings, under highway overpasses and so on, making use of whatever materials come to hand. For this home, however, they looked to something very different: the traditional *minka* farmhouse.

Minka is a very broad term encompassing any number of styles and historical periods in rural Japan, but timber construction and tall roofs are frequently recurring features. To anyone familiar with the lushly animated films of Hayao Miyazaki (b.1941), which lovingly track the contrast of urban and rural Japan, the image of the idyllic old house, set amid intensively cultivated market gardens within reach of the city, is a compelling one. Nature is inclined to burst through in often unexpected and mystical ways.

The clients – a young family of three – were returning to the suburbs, to what was originally an ad hoc settlement in a farming area where the mother had grown up. The site was a vegetable patch the family owned. The space available was small, but the architects were able to arrange the house

horizontally rather than vertically, as is more usually the case in dense Japanese cities. The result is a kind of architectural yearning for a pre-urban way of life as much as an intellectual exercise, but it remains true to the material – timber – and to traditional ways of shaping a building.

In the West, this approach had a brief flourishing in the 1970s as the 'New Vernacular', a response to disenchantment with mainstream modernism. It was short-lived as a movement but elements of it periodically recur, usually in the form of abstracted barn-like shapes. Modernists and traditionalists alike generally love traditional agricultural buildings because they are entirely functional and responsive to climate and materials. They hold many lessons in an ecologically aware age.

This is a real house for real clients, but it is also, to an extent, a pedagogical exercise. The architects worked with students from their alma mater, the Tokyo Institute of Technology. They were clearly keenly aware of the city/rural interface as explored by Miyazaki, not because of those films, but because it is the lived experience of so many Japanese people. The original settlement seems to have been something of a 1960s bohemian drop-out community, set amid fields growing vegetables. It is a similar story with plotland developments at one time or another the world over. The place, a few kilometres outside the medium-

This is a modern hall house with very few dividing walls in the multi-level interior.

sized city of Sendai, about 320 miles north of Tokyo, had grown somewhat since its bohemian origins, but that character remains. Nora House is not a response to the immediate context, which is distinctly varied, rather to an idea of rural 'house-ness' more generally.

Roughly rhomboidal in plan – a slightly skewed rectangle – it is built of a complex, undulating timber frame providing a roof rising to two offset peaks, which bring daylight from above: a glorification of the rooflight which also recalls chimneys and the steeply angled peaked roofs of many *minka* houses. The design plays with our perceptions in that it has a scale befitting a rather larger building: in fact, this is a very compact little house, opening out at the front where the roof flares out to provide a canopy over a glazed porch. This porch can be closed off from the rest of the house, which is particularly necessary here as inside it is mostly just one large space with little by way of partitions. Instead, the various areas are defined by changes of level. It is an interior landscape, stepping up and down, reflecting the architects' observation that it is the circulation areas in many conventional homes which are the most interesting: a landing on the turn of a stair, say.

The traditional *minka* farmhouses that inspired this modern house (much like European medieval hall houses) took varying forms depending on location and wealth, but are generally also based around a large communal open space and hearth. This, of course, raises questions about privacy, but these are modern Western questions: there is more of a tradition in Japan of families living in a very disciplined way, the landscape of loose furnishings changing between day and night. Single-room dwellings, or dwellings where the various spaces open up into each other, are very common. The traditional sliding *shoji* (latticed rice-paper screens) are visual, not acoustic, dividers and even those are dispensed with here.

There is some vertical stacking at the rear of this house. A home office and living space both sit above a sunken bedroom, which is the only fully enclosable space in the house, other than a bathroom situated in one corner. One living area is set low, the other up high, which was the domain of the daughter when the house was first completed.

Planting in the porch and a little front garden provides a visual filter to the street, while on the other side of the street – at least at the time of completion – was an open space, a remnant of the local field system. The Nora House is an example of minimal living that is both ancient and modern in the Japanese context, set beneath a roofscape that works, both inside and out, as a recollection of an older, if not so very different, way of building.

Education

Nobody forgets their early experience of schooling, wherever it takes place. At its most basic, you are in some kind of intimate space and somebody is telling you a story, or explaining something. You ask questions – 'Why?' – and you like repetition, familiar phrases. You learn. The physical and social experience changes as you grow older and the numbers of people involved increase. You find yourself in a classroom of fellow-pupils, or in a lecture theatre or among others in a library. You move between places in a large school, educational campus or district. Or it might be just you and a tutor, in person or online, and the question–answer routine of early childhood reasserts itself on a different level.

Teachers are said to be *in loco parentis* – taking the place of your parents – and this means, among other things, that the place of schooling has elements of domesticity about it. This applies especially to schools for the youngest, from kindergarten onwards. If your course is structured for meetings in your tutor's study, the relationship is no different from that of the earliest European universities, where the masters brought students into their own homes to teach them. That's the micro level, but the architect, when designing for education, must work at all scales, span the gulf between the domestic and the institutional, with more than a touch of the performance building as well. A school classroom might accommodate anything from a dozen to 50 pupils. A typical university lecture theatre might seat from 100 to 1,000, by which point acoustics and sightlines are as important as in a dramatic theatre or music venue.

As we age, we move from one stage of education to another. The architecture of education works on a similarly graduated level. As we have seen, a school (elementary or high) or university has to provide a variety of very different-sized spaces and buildings depending on the numbers and functions involved. There is always the juxtaposition of the small and the large. For younger children physical play in the open is involved as well as book-learning. For older cohorts, provisions for more organised sport may be required. Large halls are needed for gyms, dining and assembly, and these are often multi-purpose. Some schools, like most universities, are places where you can live as well as learn and teach.

Schools must be secure: younger pupils cannot just come and go individually in the way that university students can. That other self-contained institution, the monastery, became the template for the college, the monkish cloister became the residential quad or court. The college then coalesced with other nearby colleges to form the prototypical university, the earliest claimant being that of Bologna in Italy which can (with caveats) date itself back to 1088. Bologna in fact began as a *studium*, a network of foreign students in the city, acting as tutors, usually operating from their own homes. It was not until such places and people organised themselves into officially recognised

Where earlier universities would have had a chapel, Thomas Jefferson's 'academical village' of the University of Virginia had its library (1822–6) in a building modelled on the Pantheon in Rome.

degree-awarding institutions that the university as we understand it – the word essentially meaning 'all in one' – came to be.

In collegiate universities, such as Oxford and Cambridge in England, each college remains independent. There are later variations on the collegiate theme, usually with all or most of the (usually residential) colleges being directly owned by the university. There are also federal universities, urban or rural, which come into being as a result of administrative get-togethers by previously separate places of learning. In the enormous University of London, for instance, the constituent parts can be universities in their own right.

The oldest universities in the United States are the eight-strong Ivy League contingent in the north-east, dating from the time of British rule. Of these, Harvard (originally New College) was founded in 1636, Yale 1701, Princeton 1746. Broadly, they continued the tradition of the court or quad and in time spawned their own sub-colleges or houses. As private universities they have built up colossal endowment funds, which means that they can build extensively and even lavishly, latterly employing some of the world's best architects.

The typology broadened out after American Independence when, in 1817, the third President of the United States, Thomas Jefferson (1743–1826), an excellent self-taught architect and polymath, founded and designed the University of Virginia in his home town of Charlottesville. This was fresh thinking from an old man who, in his prime as American ambassador in Paris, had studied the neoclassical architecture and landscapes of France and England.

Jefferson, main author of the Declaration of Independence, saw a wide-ranging educational system as being essential to democracy. His university was a clean break from the pre-existing university tradition in three ways. Firstly, his university was (like the American Constitution) secular – earlier universities nearly always had a clerical connection. Secondly, it offered courses in several subjects rather than specialising in only one or two, such as law or divinity. This was the start of the 'liberal arts' approach to universities. Finally, it adopted a different form. Jefferson envisaged and built what he called an 'academical village' for his university, organised on a symmetrical U-shaped layout with four rows of linked neoclassical pavilions, halls and dormitories flanking lawns leading up to a large rotunda, based on the temple of the Pantheon in Rome and containing the university library. This more open configuration, with the university designed as a small, self-contained town (he even incorporated walled vegetable gardens and farm fields in the design), marked the birth of the purpose-built campus university.

This being plantation-owner Jefferson and Virginia in the early nineteenth century, the university depended on a slave economy to build and run it. Those were the times and the practices and they cannot be ignored or condoned. Jefferson's contribution as an intellectual and architect to the evolution of both modern democracy and the modern university is, however, indisputable.

The choice between urban and semi-rural universities has continued ever since: as a student, do you want to be part of city life, or of more self-contained campus life? In the latter, the design of landscape is as important as the buildings, and the overall masterplan is key. In the former – especially the ancient universities – today's architects find themselves having to densify existing tightly landlocked sites, frequently digging down to make space, responding much more directly to the urban grain and the work of their predecessors. Overall, the buildings we learn in are central to our human existence. For good or ill, we remember them.

St John's College Oxford University, UK, 1555–present

ARCHITECTS: FROM THE MID-TWENTIETH CENTURY ONWARDS: ARCHITECTS CO-PARTNERSHIP, ARUP ASSOCIATES, RICHARD MACCORMAC AND WRIGHT & WRIGHT

STYLE: GOTHIC, RENAISSANCE CLASSICAL, MODERNIST

If you are lucky enough to be invited to descend the flight of steps into St John's well-stocked wine cellar you find yourself in a stone-vaulted Cistercian undercroft from the early fifteenth century: the vaults are undecorated, plainly functional. This space pre-dates the foundation of St John's in 1555 by clothier Sir Thomas White (1492–1567), a leading member of the powerful Merchant Taylors' Guild, who had served as Lord Mayor of London. White bought and altered the buildings of an unfinished monastic college, St Bernard's, dating back to 1437. The college had been established by Henry Chichele (c.1364–1443) when Archbishop of Canterbury, but it was going spare after Henry VIII's (r.1509–1547) great asset seizure, the Dissolution of the Monasteries in 1539.

White and his successors started building out from the original college in a process that has continued in bursts ever since. The most recent new building to be added, a library and study centre by architects Wright & Wright, was completed in 2019 and follows the line of a fifteenth-century garden wall. The money is there to build well: St John's is Oxford's richest college in terms of endowment income. Its wealth largely derives from the land where much of north Oxford was built in the nineteenth century. For all this, it is a relatively

The Canterbury Quad, where late Gothic meets Renaissance classical of the William Laud kind.

modest college. Far from being Oxford's grandest, its street frontage with its stumpy gatehouse tower, screened by large trees, is easily overlooked. Despite this reticence it has all the right ingredients: a sophisticated balance of buildings with open space, demonstrating the careful evolution of this building type from medieval to modern times.

The University of Oxford was one of the first wave to form across Europe in the early centuries of the second millennium. As with its slightly later rival, Cambridge, its monastic origins came to define the familiar form of its colleges, arranged around a quadrangle or court of buildings where tutors and students lived, taught and learned, their rooms laid out around staircases. There was always a prominent chapel, library and refectory or dining hall. In Oxford, St John's takes its place among dozens of such quad-based colleges, ancient or modern. It is a model that has proved to have lasting international appeal as an alternative to the freer-form campus university.

St John's began to flourish under the leadership of another Archbishop of Canterbury, William Laud (1573–1645), who built the Canterbury Quad along with its library between 1633 and 1635. Laud employed a variety of master

Modernism arrived in Oxford in the quirky form of the 'Beehive' set of student rooms.

masons, surveyors and sculptors and it is a delightful piece of Jacobean architecture, from the period when English medieval architecture first dipped its toes into classical, Renaissance waters.

In the seventeenth century, sited on what was then the northern edge of a small market town playing host to 20 quadrangular colleges, Laud's St John's resembled a nobleman's country house: seen from the east across its Great Lawn today it still does. There are two grandly decorative classical centrepieces in the centre of the east and west sides of Canterbury Quad: to the west, a statue of Charles I (r.1625–1649) and to the east one of his queen, Henrietta Maria (1609–1669). Both were invited to the grand opening by Laud along with their court: the banquet and entertainment cost half as much as the building itself. Laud's Royalist sympathies were to cost him his life: he was beheaded in the English Civil War. During the Restoration in 1660, the college exhumed his body, reattached his head, and quietly brought it back to be buried in the chapel.

Things stayed relatively quiet from an architectural perspective until the late nineteenth century, when building resumed in earnest north and south, continuing in a traditionalist style until the 1940s. By then it consisted of several quads and gardens spreading out from the original entrance quad with its battlemented Gothic gatehouse, chapel (much altered inside over time) and dining hall.

Then came a shift in mood. The student population was getting more numerous and was increasingly coming via scholarships from state schools and poorer backgrounds rather than the elite fee-paying 'public' schools. Society was getting more go-ahead: St John's was seen as old-fashioned. The last traditionalist architect to be employed, Sir Edward Maufe (1882–1974), had contributed neo-Georgian buildings to the college, including the small Dolphin Quad in 1947–8. Henceforth, the college's architects for new buildings were to be different shades of modernist.

First came Michael Powers (1915–1994) of Architects Co-Partnership, with a cluster-block of hexagonal student rooms (the 'Beehive', 1958–60). This filled an awkward gap to complete the North Quad and was one of the first modernist buildings in Oxford University. Next was Philip Dowson (1924–2014) of Arup Associates who, in 1975, completed the open-sided Thomas White Quad: an L-shaped sequence of 11 dourly muscular pavilion-like buildings with concrete exoskeletons and stone panels, at one point stepping delicately across a retained boundary wall. 1993 saw the most openly ambitious expansion to date. Architect Richard MacCormac (1938–2014), in full historic-postmodern mode, designed the Garden Quad as a stepped series of buildings with a semi-open undercroft, inspired by buildings from Elizabethan to Georgian times. It is picturesque, romantic and more than a little overwrought.

The new library, indirectly daylit, presents a seemingly windowless facade to the semi-private garden behind. It is ornamented with a stone-relief frieze by Susanna Heron (b.1949).

In 2010 MacCormac returned for the much calmer Kendrew Quad, situated at the very north end of the St John's site, arranged around a large existing beech tree. All these new student blocks included teaching/learning facilities but more were needed. Then, in 2019, Wright & Wright's new library and study centre was completed. Bridging the garden gap between the Canterbury and Thomas White Quads, it created another place of enclosure in which the carefully tended garden landscapes and the buildings continue their monastic dialogue. St John's is an unfolding sequence of spaces and places as much as buildings; a self-contained world.

Munkegaard School Dyssegård, Denmark, 1949–57; extended 2009

ARCHITECTS: ARNE JACOBSEN (1902–1971) AND DORTE MANDRUP (B.1961)

STYLE: MODERNIST

Not so much a giant grid, more a composition of domestic-scale courtyards, most shared by two classrooms.

Arne Jacobsen was a Danish architect who has become better known for his furniture and product design – mid-century modern classics, from bent-plywood chairs to lighting and doorhandles, most of which are still in production to this day – than he is for his buildings, which are perhaps more for the cognoscenti. Jacobsen, a noted perfectionist, had this much in common with the late nineteenth-century Arts and Crafts Movement and the inter-war cross-discipline German design school, the Bauhaus. He routinely designed every element of his buildings down to the tiniest detail: in the case of his St Catherine's College, Oxford of 1964, he even designed the very distinctive cutlery used in the dining hall.

His austerely modernist architectural style – the kind which holds tenaciously to the function of the building, with no ornamental distractions – was therefore enriched by his facility and talent as a designer, along with the sheer refinement of his design. His children's desks and chairs at Munkegaard, offered in three sizes according to age from six to 16, are a delight. Even so, the Munkegaard school at first glance seems somewhat over-rigorous, arranged as it is in an intersecting grid of single-storey classrooms. But if you see it not as a grid, rather as a companionable courtyard cluster, it starts to make sense.

The school was built to serve an area of suburban post-war expansion just north of Copenhagen. Although there is a loose arrangement of long four-storey brick housing blocks set in an open green landscape to the north of the school, it turns its back on those, instead being oriented south towards a different kind of grid, of agreeable residential streets where little houses are set in patches of garden: the suburban dream. The school had to be big – for 850 pupils – but Jacobsen wanted each part of it to feel small. He had noted the move towards well-ventilated and well daylit single-storey post-war schools in England, and took that idea to a new level. You can regard the Munkegaard school plan as a tighter assemblage of those suburban homes. Instead of designing the school as a monolithic block, he broke the whole thing down to child scale, each part being almost domestic in feel.

The four rows of classrooms, arranged in pairs with single rooms on the ends, are brick-built with shallow-pitched aluminium roofs and big picture

Arne Jacobsen also designed the classroom furniture, which was produced in different sizes according to age range.

windows overlooking the courtyards. Each classroom also has a clerestory (high level glazing) set into the roof to ensure that daylight and ventilation gets to the back of the rooms. The rows are linked by short glass-walled corridors and also by the bigger entrance building, which houses the main hall and school offices. Jacobsen used the larger blocks all schools need, such as the gym, to define the edges and corners of the site, including a two-storey range with science labs forming a wall across the back. At the western edge of the built area, flights of open-tread steps take you down to the school playing field. In all there are 17 courtyards, 11 of them serving pairs of classrooms and six on the flanks serving the single rooms. Some of the courtyards are mostly paved, some mostly planted, with all the variations in between. A few now have sizeable mature trees growing in them.

When the committee tasked with finding the architect for the first all-new, post-war Oxford college – St Catherine's – came to Denmark to visit a number of Danish architects' buildings, this was the building that most impressed them. They loved its geometric rigour, variety of functions and precise detailing, all of which could be scaled up to offer something intriguingly different in the Oxford context, which is exactly what happened. For all of that, the school faded from prominence somewhat over the years, just quietly getting on with its job. It later came back into focus as a new generation recognised it as a notable achievement and since 1995 it has been officially protected by the Danish government as being historically and architecturally important.

We show the original configuration on p. 62, but pedagogy has changed over the intervening years in Denmark as elsewhere, with more emphasis given to larger and more informal groups for teaching, sometimes across age groups. So when another fine Danish architect, Dorte Mandrup, won the commission to upgrade and extend the school for the twenty-first century, it was clear that this new flexibility and adaptability should be incorporated – but without spoiling the clarity of Jacobsen's classic design.

Mandrup is a much more expressive, less hard-line functionalist architect than Jacobsen. However, she is especially alert to the context of her buildings and as a Dane she reveres the modernist master. Her solution was to extend the school underground and to pick up on Jacobsen's courtyard theme by daylighting it via sunken glazed courtyards set in a row across the entrance plaza. She reconfigured other areas of the school, such as inserting a freestanding library into the original entrance hall, and restored the original buildings. That project was completed in 2009: the two eras of the school, one tightly organised and one much more loosely, are clearly distinguishable and complementary.

The Beinecke Rare Book and Manuscript Library

Yale University, USA, 1960–63

ARCHITECT: GORDON BUNSHAFT (1909–1990)

STYLE: MODERNIST

The tower of books, rising from the lower levels, is a building within a building.

The centre of any good university should be a library, the physical embodiment of human knowledge. One of the masterpieces of American mid-century architecture, the Beinecke Library at Yale demonstrates how sophisticated and subtle the steel-framed building could be in the post-war years. In its abstract richness it shares ambitions with the highly decorative commercial buildings of late nineteenth-century Chicago and New York. This was a real test for post-war modernist architects: were they up to the task of building an enduring, even monumental, centrepiece to an august and architecturally conservative institution?

Bunshaft was. He devised three conceptual masterstrokes. The first was the way he made the building visually float, setting it above a recessed ground level of darkened glass, its bulk not meeting the ground with columns but perching lightly on just four pyramidal granite staddle stones – like a traditional farm granary – in a way that appears barely to touch them. This looks effortless but required the kind of structural frame engineering normally associated with bridges.

The second big move was the way the architect dealt with the challenge of the low daylight levels needed in a building that houses delicate materials. Bunshaft clad the building in square panels of thin translucent veined Vermont marble, three centimetres thick. He organised these panels on a grid of five levels expressed in a subtly sculpted granite-clad frame, visually held within top and bottom bands of identical proportions. By day the light glows gently inwards, by night the building becomes a lantern. Externally the projecting frame generates a rippling play of light and shadow across the facade.

Thirdly, Bunshaft expressed the collection – mostly stored in two levels of underground stacks – in the form of a metal-framed glass tower of books in the middle of the interior, rising calmly from the depths. This book tower is a classic modernist bronze-framed building in itself, a miniature skyscraper of the kind Bunshaft's firm, pioneering modernist practice Skidmore, Owings and Merrill, was well versed in. Here, it retains the proportions of the whole building, but scaled down slightly so that it sits in the space without quite touching the ceiling. This powerful idea swiftly became a point of reference for the architectural profession, openly borrowed for the King's Library of George III in the British Library, London by Colin St John Wilson (1922–2007) and M.J. Long (1939–2018), which opened in 1998. At the Beinecke, the six-storey tower contains 180,000 volumes, the basement levels more than a million, making this one of the largest such repositories and research centres of its kind in the world. Its reading room sits in a basement level, opening up to a sunken courtyard in the plaza in front of the main building.

Seen across the plaza, the Beinecke Library is a cool, mysterious building, perhaps deliberately given that what you see above ground is a kind of marker iceberg for the large expanse of stacks running beneath the plaza. Inside, its tones are warm. The view from the entrance is nothing if not dramatic, as your eyes adjust to the reduced light and you gaze up through clear space right to the roof. You take broad stairs down to the basement levels, or up around the glass tower to a mezzanine floor, home to changing exhibitions and events. It is a stately space, an internal public piazza in itself. The materials – dark wood, bronze, light floors, the glowing marble – are good, restrained and long-lasting.

A rare books library might seem a rarefied environment where few would normally enter, but the Beinecke attracts some 175,000 visitors a year and stages exhibitions, concerts and conferences. A café spills out of the building into the plaza on

Mid-century modernism in all its richness lands on Yale's 'collegiate Gothic' campus.

The thin sheets of veined Vermont marble glow gently in the daytime while also keeping the collection out of direct daylight.

one side. All this activity led on occasion to some difficulties maintaining the right climatic conditions in the lofty space. This was finally resolved with a full replacement of the building's (by then) antiquated heating and ventilation systems during a thorough and faithful refurbishment of the building in 2015–16.

The grid rhythm of the coffered ceiling exactly matches that of the walls, while the bronze-framed glass book tower, like the whole building, carries its weight with magical lightness. However, this is no graph-paper exercise. Bunshaft modelled his facade with the eye of a sculptor. The gentle zig-zag undulation of the projecting stone grid softens each square of the facade into an octagon, and doubles up where the grids meet on the corners to make strong vertical elements worthy of the sculptor Brâncuşi (1876–1957).

The Beinecke Library sits in the 1902 'collegiate Gothic'[1] and neoclassical context of what is officially Yale's Hewitt Quadrangle though – such is the power of the newer building – it is generally known as Beinecke Plaza, perpetuating the name of the philanthropic family who financed it. While obviously very different in style from its neighbours, its proportions, materials and craftsmanship are such that it works successfully with them as a focus of attention. Opulently cool but far from retiring, it is an expressive building, and what it expresses is that it is the brain of the university, a powerhouse of learning.

1 A variant of Gothic Revival architecture common in North American universities in the late nineteenth and early twentieth centuries and periodically revived since.

Gando Primary School Burkina Faso, 2001

ARCHITECT: DIÉBÉDO FRANCIS KÉRÉ (B.1965)

STYLE: MODERN VERNACULAR

This modest little school, originally just three classrooms in a row beneath a single sheltering, overhanging roof, was the opening shot in what has swiftly become an illustrious career for Diébédo Francis Kéré. Kéré was born in the rural village of Gando in the West African nation of Burkina Faso, previously Upper Volta and until 1960 a French colony. Since qualifying as an architect in Berlin, where he remains based, he has returned to his home country and village periodically to contribute buildings that have become exemplars in how to combine traditional methods and materials with fresh architecture and engineering.

It is a very personal building for Kéré who, as the son of the village chief, was the first child there to be sent away to school in order to learn how to read and write. At the age of seven he went to live with his uncle in the country's capital, Ouagadougou. From there he went on to learn carpentry, won an apprenticeship in Germany in development aid supervision, then studied architecture and eventually graduated in 2004. But as early as 1998 he had set up a foundation with the aim of building a school back in his home village.

Keeping cool in equatorial Africa: low-cost materials and techniques are used alongside passive cooling via a vented double roof.

Kéré brought education to his home village and with it hope for a brighter future.

The tropical savannah climate is harsh and hot, while the wet-season rains are torrential. There are traditional ways of dealing with this for houses, but school-building had not typically been a high priority in the area. Kéré's training allowed him to develop a low-cost, low-technology school building to work year-round. The people of farming communities such as Gando are used to depending on each other, and Kéré collaborates fruitfully with them to plan and build his projects: this was the first.

Buildings made of clay with sheet-metal roofs are common throughout the region. Kéré has simply adapted these materials to work more efficiently, particularly by making them cool the spaces. He achieves this at the primary school by having a heat-absorbing perforated arched roof made of local bricks (in a clay-cement mix to be stronger than pure clay), with the metal roof spaced some distance above it, springing from a concrete ring beam, which holds the tops of the walls together. This separation of roof from walls allows air to move freely underneath it via a 'chimney effect', drawing in cooler air through the various apertures in the walls. The building is set on a plinth built of local stones with large run-off channels – very necessary in a region where areas of land can simply wash away in floods.

Those are the practicalities, but it is in the simple details that it shines. For instance, the roof is supported by a painted filigree of slender steel rods, the cheap kind normally used invisibly to reinforce concrete. The concrete ring beam extends out beyond the walls at both ends of the buildings to conclude in brick columns, suggesting outdoor spaces, which could be shaded by an awning, or a more permanent extension. The brick walls are given a regular rhythm by strengthening buttresses and by the air gaps left between the three classrooms. This elevates the sloping roof into something like a crown.

The school opened in 2001, and was later extended along with ancillary buildings, including a library and teachers' accommodation. Both the school and Kéré became famous when it won the international Aga Khan Award for Islamic-

Classrooms (here in the first phase) are basic and adaptable.

society architecture in 2004. Encouraged by this, he set up his own practice in 2005. Kéré calls his style 'Afro-futurism', suggesting that it lies 'at the intersection of utopia and pragmatism'.[1]

Kéré has now built and taught internationally, but Africa remains key to his thinking and with variations he has essentially repeated and enlarged the design of the original Gando school for his Centre for Earth Architecture in Mopti, Mali. In contrast, he shifted to a different form – a series of arches – for his teachers' homes back in Gando.

The project continues. As the newly literate children grew up, the need emerged for a secondary school, which was duly built on the same collaborative method involving all the villagers in various tasks. At the secondary school Kéré experimented with other 'passive' (non-mechanical) cooling techniques, including surrounding the school with a tree-planted earth bank threaded through with perforated clay pipes, which emerge beneath the classroom floors. Such earth-pipe air cooling is an increasingly well-used technique in the West, so here Kéré is adapting such knowledge to the very different conditions of sub-Saharan Africa.

For him architecture is not just about making buildings. Rather, it concerns itself with a whole improved environment, which goes beyond literacy and learning into living and subsistence. In another example, he has introduced an extensive programme of mango tree planting using techniques he has developed in natural fertiliser and simple root-watering systems. Mango trees are a traditional source of both food and shelter in the region. Starting with his simple village school and returning at frequent intervals, he has become a practical utopian, a hands-on social planner. Kéré's work is proof that architecture has the power to change things very much for the better, both on a local and national scale.

1 Taken from the Kéré Architecture mission statement at www.kerearchitecture.com.

Universidad de Ingeniería y Tecnología (UTEC) Campus

Lima, Peru, 2015

ARCHITECTS: GRAFTON ARCHITECTS (YVONNE FARRELL (B.1951) AND SHELLEY McNAMARA (B.1952))

STYLE: BRUTALIST

There are buildings that are assembled from components and there are buildings that seem carved as if from a single piece of rock. The UTEC campus in Lima is a visually carved building, a tectonic, geological affair, a woman-made cliff-face. Its Dublin-based architects, led by Yvonne Farrell and Shelley McNamara, had been steadily growing in reputation over the decades, since the founding of the firm in 1978. Their projects moved outside of Ireland onto the international stage and they developed a particular specialism in sculptural university buildings, balancing great mass with space and light. With this building however, something finally clicked: they became fêted. Top awards streamed in. In 2020 they won the world's two highest architectural honours for lifetime achievement: the UK's RIBA Royal Gold Medal and the USA's Pritzker Architecture Prize. Female recipients of these awards are scandalously rare.

There is something about the Lima campus that has always been present in their work, indeed is a hallmark of good architecture more generally. It does a great deal more than the requirements of the brief: it provides public spaces

Building as geological outcrop: UTEC, with its multiple outdoor terraces and walkways, rises above the highway, which skirts its base.

with no particular function other than to be such places. Fully reflecting the steep topography of the city, it is a mysterious landmark that draws on historic forms without ever directly copying them. There is something of the ancient world about it, and there is also a great deal of the more recent past – the 1960s world of brutalist institutional buildings, reimagined for the early twenty-first century.

It is an unusual example of a building where the back is the dominant facade. It is built at the intersection of two busy multi-lane highways. One of these, heading down a valley to the nearby Pacific coast, runs along the foot of its northern flank, while a slip road curves up past its western end to join the other main road heading south through the city. As this was not the most promising of sites, the architects chose to make its northern flank a visually defensive wall, rising from a blank, curving and slightly undulating plinth at its base, behind which are the big inward-looking spaces of the faculty: auditorium, conference rooms, theatre. From the base it rises and opens up to its full height in a beautifully detailed and modelled way.

Its southern side, on a much quieter, mostly residential street, is a different matter – not that the craggy aesthetic of the building diminishes. But it does step down in a series of planted terraces, nodding to Peruvian architectural history such as the Inca royal city of Machu Picchu. From the point of view of students and staff, it steps up rather than down, the various rooms generally becoming smaller towards the top. The whole vertical-campus sequence concludes in a rooftop library set in a loggia (covered gallery) looking out across the city.

There was a 1960s architectural notion of 'streets in the sky',[1] usually applied to social housing, not always happily if the 'streets' were too narrow or unmanaged. Here, that concept is refined for the academic world. It is not so much a building as a generous climbing-frame of circulation space – broad walkways, ramps and steps – into which all the usual functions of a university faculty are slotted. Aptly enough the faculty housed here is engineering and technology.

All this circulation space is not just useless beauty: it is the whole point of the design. Students and staff are mixed up together, laboratories are treated as display objects rather than hidden away, chance encounters between people are built into the fabric of the place, and at all levels the space provides release from the hermetic nature of academic life into a world visually connected with the city and beyond to the sea.

The building is also a hymn to concrete and was completed just as the use of this material was starting to become controversial for reasons other than the aesthetic: construction is a very significant source of carbon emissions, with the making of concrete one of the chief offenders. Progress is now being

Inside, seminar rooms and laboratories are inserted into the giant climbing-frame-like structure.

made worldwide on reducing the material's carbon footprint and finding alternatives such as renewable timber: meanwhile, UTEC is designed for a long life and is low-energy in use. You could regard this raw-concrete monolith as one conclusion of a particular line of architectural inquiry that arguably began with the moulded concrete dome of the Pantheon in Rome (c.126). While it was the nineteenth-century invention of steel-reinforced concrete that really opened up new possibilities for architecture and engineering, the problem is that, over time, exposed to the weather, reinforced concrete can degrade and flake as the steel inside it starts to corrode. The chemistry is now better understood and there are well-proven techniques for restoring older buildings. UTEC is more than honest about how it is made: concrete is not just the underlying frame material, as is more usually the case, rather it is celebrated as both structure and surface finish.

UTEC is a tough building on a tough site, built in an economy particularly accustomed to the material, but it opens up into something much more fascinating. This is a high-density teaching building conceived primarily as a place of encounter and social interaction, but it also addresses the civic duty of such a building to mark its importance, acting as a landmark from a distance, enhancing the city.

1 'Streets in the sky' is a term originally coined in 1952 by British architects Alison and Peter Smithson (respectively 1928–1993 and 1923–2003).

183

Offices

My father worked in the Post Office Headquarters in London. Although his work was the modern business of telecommunications, his office building in the 1940s and early 1950s, as he described it, had scarcely changed since it had been built in the late Victorian period. It was a large building full of small rooms. He had a desk with a phone, a filing cabinet and a small working fireplace, the only form of heating. Every morning a man would arrive to fill up the coal bucket. The trick was to ensure that the bucket was always empty when the coalman came round. If my father had any coal left at the end of the day, he would tip it into the bottom drawer of his filing cabinet, kept empty for this purpose, and so he built up a handy reserve for really cold days. Everyone else did the same.

Imagine a large city full of hundreds of thousands of such office workers, each with a coal fire. Architects had designed such cellularised office blocks much as they did apartment buildings. No wonder my father also described the thick, lethally choking smog that London used to be famous for. The result, in 1956, was London's Clean Air Act. Even at the time, the Post Office Headquarters was a throwback building. Since the late nineteenth century, architects and social scientists had been rethinking the office building as a type.

A famous early example was Frank Lloyd Wright's fortress-like Larkin Soap Company Headquarters of 1904–6, located in Buffalo, New York State. Here, everyone was arranged in efficient rows, out in the open, with the soap coupon clerks working at long tables the length of the floor of a five-storey atrium. The bespoke filing cabinets were arranged between the ranks of clerks. This was a mail-order concern, with efficiency of turnaround vital. It was a well-lit and ventilated place, with an early form of air conditioning and even lush planting at each end, but it was almost wholly internalised as a workspace. The windows were placed so high that you could not see out. Your Wright-designed chair was fixed to your Wright designed desk so you could not move it except to swing it in and out. Productivity and dedication to the company were everything.

This was a highly influential model, and much copied. Decades later Wright was to return to this theme with his headquarters for the Johnson Wax Company in Racine, Wisconsin (1936–50, see p. 86). Eventually, office planning started to loosen up with the German idea of *Bürolandschaft* or 'office landscape', devised by brothers Wolfgang (1930–2005) and Eberhard Schnelle (1921–1997) in the late 1950s. This thinking was all about informal groupings of furniture, with curving screens and potted plants – less hierarchical perhaps, but still everyone in the same big room together. This idea also swept the world.

The origins of the office building are numerous. Large organisations, public or private, have always needed their administrators and workers, along with places to house them. The administrators of Ancient Egypt, the scribes or *sesh*, were anything but lowly, quite the reverse: they were a superior caste of highly literate and numerate civil servants. The scribes worked in teams in royal palaces

A 10th-century day in the office. Monks set to work in the scriptorium of the Spanish monastery of San Salvador de Tábara, which was founded in the 9th century. This is a copy from 1220 of the original 970 version.

and from their own substantial homes, which were also places of business. They were expected to enrich themselves in the process by taking a cut of any transaction.

Ancient Greek administrative buildings included *bouleuterion*, which were secular, local government buildings, and *stoa* – buildings with open colonnades usually flanking town squares – which were public meeting places and market halls, often with shops and offices included. As ever, the Romans developed these models. Throughout the empire, wherever the Romans built their towns with their amphitheatres and temples and baths and barracks, they would also build a lesser-known building type, the *basilica*. These had evolved from the Greek *stoas*. They often incorporated the administrative functions of the *bouleuterion* and usually formed one side of the forum or main square. They were regional administrative centres. The one in London, largest in the northern empire, was over 152 metres long and three storeys high. By this time (70–120 CE), *basilicas* were enclosed buildings. They were still multi-functional – they would include courtrooms and the city treasury – and archaeological investigations show them to have been heavily cellularised, with many small rooms for bureaucrats.

Basilicas were the forerunners of what became town halls and, at the more commercial end of things, market halls. The Roman-era shape of the *basilicas* – nearly always a tall central 'nave' flanked by lower wings or aisles – came to be adopted by the early Christian Church for its buildings and so the word 'basilica' changed its meaning.

Medieval monasteries can also stake a claim to this building type. If the libraries of the monasteries were places of learning, then their spin-off, the *scriptoria* – where manuscripts were copied and illustrated – were places of production. This was desk-based clerical work (appropriately, the word 'clerical' has its other religious meaning), so the *scriptoria* – which could be single-person cells or larger spaces – can be regarded as offices, existing from around the sixth century onwards in various monastic denominations.

In the early Renaissance period, sites of administration and general clerical work became a single building type rather than part of a multi-function building. The Latin-derived word 'office' is one with many meanings relating to service (especially public or state service), but its most common modern meaning as a place of white-collar work probably originates from the sixteenth-century building in Florence known as the 'Uffizi'. Built at first to house the civil servants of the Medici family, relatively soon after its completion it became an art gallery (see p. 140).

Office buildings for state and imperial administrators began to multiply in the eighteenth century (see Somerset House, p. 78) and, in the nineteenth century, office work was revolutionised. The Pitman shorthand system appeared in 1837, the typewriter began to become commonplace from the 1870s and, by the late nineteenth century, a new cohort of workers had arrived to join the clerks: women learning secretarial skills through exams devised for just this purpose. The aim was to provide a new form of employment at a time when jobs for female servants (being 'in service' as maids, cooks and so on) were in decline.

By then, with the emphasis increasingly on efficiency and new iron- and steel-framed buildings allowing large open floors, clerical staff began to resemble factory workers: assigned to specific tasks on identically laid-out floors. The workbench for the blue-collar worker became the office desk for the white-collar.

Today, office design is changing again. More people are working from home, if not quite in the manner of the Egyptian scribes. Many organisations do not allocate specific desks to their staff at all on the basis that not everyone will be present at the same time. Other buildings provide desk space on a pay-as-you-go basis; whatever city you are in, you can find a desk, office or meeting room as required.

In all cases, access to fresh air and daylight via courtyards, landscaped roof terraces and natural ventilation is on the rise where the climate allows. This is increasingly important as a matter of worker wellbeing, and stands opposed to the energy-hungry sealed air-conditioned building that arrived in the 1950s and is still all too common. To understand this change, look up: rooftops that used to be crammed with nothing more than water tanks and air-handling equipment are now an inhabited world of workers looking out across the city.

Somerset House London, UK, 1775–1856; restored and adapted 1998–2022

ARCHITECTS: SIR WILLIAM CHAMBERS (1723–1796) AND SUCCESSORS

STYLE: NEO-PALLADIAN

Looking towards the south-east corner of the Somerset House complex, originally a palace for civil servants and Navy officials.

George III desired to have a palace built: not for himself or his family, but for his government officials, who were scattered in an assortment of rooms all over Westminster. Thus, one of the first and greatest office buildings of the modern age came about – just as the headquarters of today's large organisations do – in a drive for efficiency and centralisation. The king did not at first expect splendour as well, but his Parliament had other ideas. In a debate about the cost of it all, the politicians abandoned penny-pinching in favour of not just a building but 'an ornament to the Metropolis and a monument to the taste and elegance of His Majesty's Reign'.[1]

William Chambers, born in Sweden to Scottish parents, had travelled the world in his first career as a 'merchant adventurer' with the Swedish East India Company. This had allowed him to study Chinese architecture as well as the more usual Roman and Greek – he later designed the famous Pagoda in London's Kew Gardens (completed in 1762). He went on to study in Paris and with this unusually broad experience became tutor in architecture to the young Prince George, who soon succeeded his grandfather, becoming George III in 1760.

Chambers, successful on his own account, also became senior architect in the King's Board of Works. Opportunities to design a public building on the scale of Somerset House, he wrote, 'do not occur above once in five centuries'.[2] When the architect first appointed by Parliament to design Somerset House conveniently died in 1775, Chambers was more than ready. He had already started sketching out his own ideas. He was 52, at his creative peak, and the job was to last him the rest of his life.

There had always been taxes and there had always been administration, but Somerset House was the first concerted attempt in England to separate out these functions from Crown and government, who had their own centres further west. The brief was to replace the decrepit former subsidiary royal palace of the same name, which was situated downriver from Westminster on the street called the Strand. The new Somerset House would contain offices for several Navy and tax-collecting departments: eventually, the tax office would grow to take over the whole place. There was also to be a large cultural element, the so-called 'Learned Societies', led by the Royal Academy of Arts which was already in the old building and needed rehousing. Bringing these ingredients together in a unified classical composition would have been tricky enough, but

Thomas Rowlandson (1757–1827) and Augustus Charles Pugin (1762–1832), *The Stamp Office at Somerset House*, 1809. This coloured aquatint shows the clerks at long tables stamping legal documents with desktop presses.

Chambers also had to contend with a narrow entrance on the Strand hemmed in by other buildings, opening onto a broad site that descended over 12 metres to the edge of the Thames. The site included two lanes from the Strand to the river, which he somehow had to include.

The building he designed is a stately composition around a courtyard, each wing with its own central portico topped with turret or dome. He set the courtyard high like a tabletop to remove the slope. The southern riverside wing, itself on a palatial scale, absorbs the final drop down to the river, and includes a raised 137-metre-long riverside terrace, beneath which was originally a water gate for the Navy's barges (now largely hidden behind the late nineteenth-century Thames Embankment).

By setting his courtyard high, Chambers was able to design his surrounding buildings with deep basement areas, traversed by bridges. The two inherited lanes could then run at low level out of sight behind the backs of the east and west wings. Meanwhile, up on the northern edge, the Strand entrance side, Chambers housed the Learned Societies on either side of a triple-arched entrance, layering them across the backs of the pre-existing buildings on the Strand to give the illusion of a north wing to the courtyard as substantial as the other three. The whole composition is extraordinarily ingenious. Its multi-level structure is at first scarcely apparent to the casual visitor, its variety of rooms, from clerks' offices to grand boardrooms, organised behind regular facades and served inside by some spectacular, elegant staircases. As so often in the top echelon of architecture, it took great skill and effort to make something so complex seem somehow inevitable. It is, of course, not just a building: it is a complete urban square with side streets.

Somerset House perfectly exemplifies the unifying power of classicism over time, for in it Chambers directly echoed the earlier work of Inigo Jones (1573–1652), England's first Renaissance architect who had remodelled parts of the old Somerset House. Jones had based his own work on that of the progressive Italian Renaissance master Andrea Palladio (1508–1580) who, in his turn, had studied the buildings of Ancient Rome and Greece as Jones and Chambers also did. This is, thus, a mature work of Palladian architecture as understood and adapted by successive generations of architects for different uses. The classical line of descent from the ancient world to the world of Georgian London was unbroken. This, the architecture of Somerset House asserts, is the *correct* way to design a grand public building. Modernism and other 'isms' might disagree, but they too learn from the classical tradition, which continues as a vigorous architectural strand to the present day.

From first to last, Somerset House took more than 80 years to build, though such complexes always continue to evolve. Key to its success is that,

Somerset House, as seen from the Strand. A palazzo for the 'Learned Societies' acts as gateway to the grand courtyard behind.

just as Chambers took the baton from Inigo Jones, so, following his retirement, his successor architects James Wyatt (1746–1813) and James Pennethorne (1801–1871) took it on and stayed true to the Chambers design. Despite many changes over time, its primary function remained: the tax offices that eventually became Her Majesty's Revenue and Customs continued to occupy parts of the building until 2011.

Today, after several phases of refurbishment, it is a public arts venue, run by a cultural trust which, among much else, houses the Courtauld Gallery, recently refurbished and expanded by architectural practice Witherford Watson Mann, alongside the Courtauld Institute and many 'creative industry' businesses. The tax collectors may have gone, but this is still a place of work for many.

1 William Chambers, cited in John Harris and Michael Snodin, eds, *Sir William Chambers: Architect to George III*, 1996.
2 Ibid.

Chilehaus Hamburg, Germany, 1923–4

ARCHITECT: JOHANN FRIEDRICH 'FRITZ' HOGER (1877–1949)

STYLE: EXPRESSIONIST

Building design does not necessarily evolve in a straight line: there are always separate strands. Just because iron- and steel-framed buildings in the early twentieth century were leading to proto-skyscrapers in America and parts of Europe, and early attempts at fully glazed 'curtain walls'[1] were happening, this did not exclude other ways of building. In the 1920s in Hamburg, architect Johann Friedrich 'Fritz' Hoger devised another kind of office block entirely. Enormous, irregular and dramatically composed, it was arranged around courtyards and made of solid dark textured brick, with 2,800 windows.

Hoger's architecture falls into the category of northern European expressionism, a style lasting from around 1905 to 1925 (though any building aspiring to sculpture rather than mere function can be described as 'expressionist', including many a recent 'icon' building). By the time Hoger got to work (his career opportunities were delayed by the First World War), the style was in its mature phase: this building can be seen as its triumphant conclusion.

His brief, following the ignominious end of the First World War for Germany, was to house the expanding businesses of the thriving port of Hamburg: shops lining the streets at ground level, offices above. The project could easily have come unstuck. This was the economically disastrous period when Weimar Germany, the republic that lasted from 1919 until the coming to power of Hitler's Third Reich in 1933, was suffering from hyperinflation,

OPPOSITE
The prow of the Chilehaus became one of the great images of Weimar-era Hamburg.

BELOW
The Chilehaus, as seen when new in 1925; the composition of the long undulating flanks is masterly.

Hoger worked with sculptor Richard Kuöhl on the decorative details of the building, such as this window-bay crown.

a consequence of printing money in an attempt to pay its crippling war debts. The value of the currency dropped to practically zero.

In most circumstances this would halt any building project, especially one as ambitious as this. Nonetheless, Hoger's immensely wealthy client, the Anglo-German industrialist and financier Henry Brarens Sloman (1848–1931), had personal, gold-backed reserves. He had made his fortune mining and processing potassium nitrate in Chile and shipping it worldwide. His family was involved in shipbuilding in Hamburg also. His site was close to the docks in an area where clearance of tightly packed medieval buildings regarded as disease-ridden slums led to what became Europe's first planned new merchant city: there is a group of buildings here on the same scale by Hoger and others. Sloman named his building the Chilehaus in honour of the source of his wealth and mounted a sculpted Andean condor on its prow.

Hoger designed the complex, using the happy coincidence of the irregular shape of the site, to resemble the sharp prow of a ship. Physically, this was an immense structure for its time, the biggest office block in Europe, and it is still mightily impressive today. At ten floors high, it was verging on high-rise for Hamburg but is nonetheless a 'groundscraper'. The building occupies two urban blocks to make a plot 200 metres long, with the facade, as measured around the building, totalling 480 metres in length. It forms what is a large perimeter block surrounding three courtyards, the central one public. Fischertwiete Street runs right through it, from side to side, via grand arches. Its reinforced concrete frame, a technique first used for warehouses before being adopted for office buildings, was set on foundations driven 16 metres into the uncertain marshy ground, with a watertight basement for its heating plant.

For all its ambition and dramatic appearance, it was based on two particular traditions of the region: the dark, roasted 'clinker brick' architecture of many of the North German Hanseatic ports and the earlier merchant *Kontorhaus*, a building type where the merchants lived in the same building as their offices and goods warehouses. Hoger, who specialised in commercial and industrial buildings, elevated these practical brick structures to the scale of a cathedral. It was not to be for living in or for storage of goods: it would be a 'landship' full of the workers of the international trading companies.

Hoger, a portly man with round spectacles given to wearing a fedora, used millions of the familiar dark bricks arranged in a highly textured manner, in places working them into twisting columns, picking out details in glazed coloured terracotta and ornamental doorways. Money not being a problem, he was able to work with the sculptor Richard Kuöhl (1880–1961) on these details, both inside and out. The art is not an add-on, rather, it is intrinsic to the whole composition. Interiors are relatively plain and hard-wearing, again with the odd ornamental flourish.

It is impossible not admire the urban effect of the way the building zig-zags to its ship-like prow with its sharply projecting cornice high above, but the whole building is an object lesson in how to compose a very large block for an everyday use without resorting to large areas of dull facades. It helps that the site is irregular – this provides interest as the facades curve this way and that – while Hoger packs his composition with just the right level of detail to sustain interest all the way round, from his little street-level pavilions to the penthouses on top.

Courtyards are enlivened by semicircular towers. The pattern of windows is a rhythm of square and round-topped types. The top three floors step gently back to reduce the apparent mass. At one corner it happily absorbs a pre-existing building. It is a composition that works at all scales, from a distance or close-up, stitched into the grain of the city. That is by no means easy to achieve. Some architects are good at planning but less good at facade detailing, or vice versa, but Hoger was exceptionally good at both.

His career continued on into the Nazi era – he seems to have been entirely at ease with the regime – but his best work was undoubtedly in the tumultuous preceding Weimar era. At the Chilehaus he suggested a different, more urbanistic and richly modelled, future for the large office building. It came to symbolise the whole city, and today, long-lasting and adaptable, serves exactly the same function he originally designed it for.

1 In this context, a curtain wall is one that carries none of the structural load of the building, which is typically carried instead by columns set inboard of the edges of the floors.

Johnson Wax Headquarters

Racine, Wisconsin, USA, 1936–50

ARCHITECT: FRANK LLOYD WRIGHT (1867–1959)

STYLE: ORGANIC MODERNIST

The Johnson Wax Headquarters is the apotheosis of the open-plan office. Its main space is a science-fantasy temple to the drudgery of administration, all in the service of a company making household cleaning products and floor polishes. But the Midwestern company S.C. Johnson is a family-owned firm to this day, and such firms tend to build with a greater sense of corporate pride than some.

It is a curious building to approach. From the street outside it appears at first to be nothing more than a high, windowless redbrick wall, set on a square plinth, curving gently round its corners. Towards its rear it rises higher, with penthouse offices in symmetrical, splayed, round-ended wings. Behind that is another low, windowless courtyard block. Rising from the centre of the courtyard is a mysterious shimmering tower. It is all somewhat alien, but inside the front block it is revelatory: an enormous lofty workroom like a forest floor, the 'trees' being columns widening from their slender bases to broad discs at the top. Diffused light filters down through this canopy. This is Frank Lloyd Wright, who often claimed his architecture was 'organic', at his audacious best.[1]

On the face of it, Wright was an unlikely architect for the company to have chosen. The dandy shaman of twentieth-century American architecture, he cultivated the persona of a seer and had had something of a scandalous private life. Yet by the mid-1930s, in his late sixties, he had hit a fallow period and was in danger of being forgotten, but that was about to change.

Born in 1867, Wright was of the same unorthodox generation as the art nouveau Scottish architect Charles Rennie Mackintosh, the Austro-Moravian proto-modernist Adolf Loos, the Slovenian progressive classicist Jože Plečnik (1872–1957; see p. 214) and Britain's inventive traditionalist Sir Edwin Lutyens. Yet despite his ups and downs, Wright outlived them all and reinvented himself and his architecture several times, always at a tangent to the mainstream. Fond of decoration, pattern, experimental materials and all-round risk-taking, Wright was a maximalist.

Wright was perhaps known best for a sequence of remarkable houses from the turn of the century onwards, in particular his ground-hugging, low-roofed 'Prairie' houses. However, he had produced an earlier temple to work, the tall, severe-looking

The streamlined exterior of Johnson Wax Headquarters, with its mysterious totem of a laboratory tower, gives little away.

Larkin Building of 1904–6 in Buffalo, New York, for a paternalistic, mail-order soap company (see p. 75). In Racine, company boss Herbert F. 'Hib' Johnson (1899–1978) was already planning to start building a design by another architect when his company officials suggested he try Wright instead. Johnson had never heard of Wright and it is said that all the two men had in common was the fact that they both drove the same kind of car at the time, the ultra-modern streamlined Lincoln Zephyr.[2] Nonetheless, Johnson signed Wright up.

Typically of Wright, he immediately tried to expand the commission into something much larger, a complete company town. To achieve this, he wanted Johnson to move his factories out of Racine – a small town on Lake Michigan 35 kilometres south of Milwaukee that had nothing much to recommend it to Wright. Johnson did not buy the idea. Eventually, Wright was dissuaded by his wife Olgivanna (1898–1985) with words that architects the world over will ruefully recognise: 'Give them what they want, Frank, or you will lose the job.'[3]

Wright, subconsciously or otherwise influenced by the streamlining aesthetic popular at the time, as reflected in cars of the period, designed a very fluid, low-slung complex, all soft curves and sleek lines. For a later phase he added a campanile with research laboratories in it, again with curving corners, alternating square and circular floors inside. Throughout the complex he used glass Pyrex tubing, stacked together with the joints sealed, to filter daylight and glow mysteriously at night. This was a problem at first: the joints tended to leak. Nonetheless, Hib Johnson invited Wright back to do the second phase with the tower in the late 1940s.

Inside, the 'great workroom' is intended as an architectural forest floor, with light filtering down through the interstices in the canopy.

For Wright, work was an almost sacred activity that should have no distractions. Even in his own studios, there were no windows to look out of. Instead, he designed office buildings where daylight came from above, or from windows placed too high to serve any other function. In a way this was like many of the schoolrooms of the period and, like them, if you worked there you were in no doubt as to who was the boss and where you sat in the hierarchy. Wright also designed bespoke oval tubular-steel desks for the clerks with (originally) three-legged chairs, on the grounds that you could not slouch in them without falling over. People did indeed fall over – Wright himself did when he tried one – and so he produced a conventional four-legged version.

Wright was frequently over-optimistic in this way, and at first Wisconsin state officials had grave doubts as to whether his 'dendriform' (tree-like) columns with their flat hollow circular canopy-capitals would be strong enough. So he built a test column, overloaded it with weights, and found it could take five times its design load. Wright scampered up and kicked it, just to be sure. Thus, the 'great workroom' was built – the main floor overlooked by two gallery levels – and Wright achieved his woodland-for-office-workers aim: 'being among the pine trees, breathing fresh air and sunlight'.[4]

By the time the first phase was finished, Wright was 70 and famous again. He had recently built a bravura rural house over a waterfall ('Fallingwater') and was soon to design the circular spiral of the Guggenheim Museum in New York, a project which would occupy him until his death in 1959.

S.C. Johnson continues to use its building as intended, with the exception of the research tower which is now open for architecture pilgrims only. Meanwhile, the Johnson Wax complex bears more widely a resemblance to a university faculty or civic centre than a humble office block. Perhaps Wright never stopped thinking of that new town he had wanted to build, out on the prairie.

---

1 See Frank Lloyd Wright, *An Organic Architecture: The Architecture of Democracy*, 1939.
2 See Brendan Gill, *Many Masks: A Life of Frank Lloyd Wright*, 1987.
3 Ibid.
4 Ibid.

Centraal Beheer Insurance Offices

Apeldoorn, Netherlands, 1968–72

ARCHITECT: HERMAN HERTZBERGER (B.1932)

STYLE: STRUCTURALIST

The Centraal Beheer Offices are the very opposite of the generic office block. In fact, this building is an attempt to subvert that formula. The 1960s brought a desire for greater democracy in the workplace which, in Dutch architect Herman Hertzberger's view, included personal space customised by the individual workers. It is certainly significant that this building was designed in 1968, a year when anti-authoritarian protests swept the world.

This thinking was expressed quite literally in the shape of the building. What would normally be a conventional large rectilinear block was broken down into an interlinked collection of 60 small cubes, more like houses, within which were domestic-sized workspaces with corner balconies serving as what we would now call 'break-out spaces' – places of escapes from formal working. From these you are aware of the other people around you – you can wave and call out and throw paper darts – but back at your desk your space is your space, and you make it so. In this sense, Centraal Beheer is a human hive. Here there are certainly bosses, but also a sense of mutual dependency.

Outside, the materials are concrete set off by red-painted steel window frames. Inside, materials are functional, tough: concrete and glass blocks and dark-painted timber and steel. There is ample daylight. All this was just the blank canvas. The office workers – Hertzberger's brief was to house 1,000 – then personalised their parts of it, as they would their own homes, bringing in not just the usual family photos but their own plants, even fish tanks and bird cages.

Herman Hertzberger's creation: an interlinked collection of house-sized cells with roof terraces: the very antithesis of a conventional office block.

This way of organising a building was the architectural interpretation of the philosophical approach known as 'structuralism'. It consisted of paring architecture back to the basic elements that derive from the way people interrelate. It was a social – in Europe often socialist – approach rather than a style, but inevitably the repetition of the component parts led to a recognisable geometric look. Given that Hertzberger's basic element was the cube repeated over and over, Centraal Beheer became somewhat like a crystalline rock formation. Outside, the roofs of these cubes provide linked open terraces. Inside, the interlocking cubes are carved away at key points to open up the space with floor-to-roof atria.

This anti-office-block building is a complex device that in diagrams starts to resemble one of the impossible drawings of fellow Dutchman M.C. Escher (1898–1972), who was still alive and starting to receive belated recognition at the time Centraal Beheer was being built. The way the steps descend to the many roof terraces from the sides of adjacent cubes reinforces this feel. But a stronger reference is that of the North African medina quarter, or European medieval towns, where houses lean out close to each other across narrow streets. Although arranged here on a formal grid rather than by happenstance, this proximity, and the overall human scale, is intended to be much the same. 'The idea was to make it a Mediterranean city, to make the inside like the outside', Hertzberger said in 2011.[1]

So successfully social did the place become, in fact, that it came to resemble what in Britain is called a 'pick-up joint'. With eye contact easy from perch to perch and an excellent in-house restaurant, relationships blossomed, sometimes to the detriment of people's marriages. However, this made the sense of community all the stronger among the workforce who became ever more tightly knit. This was no doubt of benefit to the company.

Other architects experimented with such democratic workplaces, so to some extent Centraal Beheer was influential when it came to office layouts. Other socially minded architects such as the Anglo-Swedish Ralph Erskine (1914–2005) experimented fruitfully with 'townscape' interiors and informal nooks and crannies. However, Centraal Beheer remains the extreme example of how this approach was built into the very shape and structure of the building.

Office buildings tend to have a shorter lifespan than other building types and are vulnerable to company restructuring. Centraal Beheer had something of a charmed life for 45 years, but in 2013 this audacious insurance company, by then part of a larger conglomerate, moved out. For some years the building languished empty: at the time of writing a new owner is planning to transform it into a mixed-use development of homes with associated workspace. The elderly, but active, Hertzberger helped to draw up the plans to revive his building and, although when built this was by no means a 'signature' building in the modern sense of an architect striving for visual recognition, the new owners put his name on it: henceforth it is to be known as Hertzberger Park. In 2022 plans for the conversion project were revealed by Dutch architects MVRDV, working with Hertzberger's office.[2] Such proposed reuse is evidence of the success of Hertzberger's original idea of bringing domestic-sized spaces to the workplace, in that it has proved adaptable enough to bring actual homes into the mix in what seems to be a logical way.

Inside, it is a kind of covered casbah, with personalised workstations suspended over the circulation areas.

Looking back, Centraal Beheer is very much a product of its time. It did not immediately usher in the workplace revolution that it was meant to – the already established open-plan office landscape survived and flourished. But well into the twenty-first century the thinking it embodies finally started to appear in modern offices, which have steadily taken on a more domestic or clubbish feel, where more and more of the floorspace is given over to cafés and restaurants and there are roof terraces aplenty. The irony is that this has been a capitalist rather than socialist change, to do with attracting tenants at good rents who in turn want to attract and retain a good workforce, many of whom are likely to work at least part of the time from home. Nevertheless, Hertzberger can feel satisfaction at seeing some of his ideas from 50 years ago become widely adopted, even if today's speculative office buildings do not take the form of a Mediterranean casbah.

1 From Hertzberger interview with Tom Dyckhoff on Channel 4 / Open University series, *The Secret Life of Buildings*, August 2011.
2 MVRDV Press Release, 16 June 2022.

CCTV Headquarters Beijing, China, 2002–12

ARCHITECTS: OMA (REM KOOLHAAS (B.1944), OLE SCHEEREN (B.1971), ELLEN VAN LOON (B.1963) AND OTHERS

STYLE: DECONSTRUCTIVIST

Sometimes what seems to be an utterly perverse gesture in architecture gets built. The CCTV building, the enormous HQ of China's state television broadcaster, is the shape it is because of what it is not: a skyscraper. Or if you prefer, for what it is: a skyscraper tied into a knot. As a place to work – it contains 10,000 people – it has all the facilities, from studios to office suites, that you would expect of a TV behemoth. Its public areas are spectacular and on its south side it includes an urban park. As a symbol of modern China, however, it can be seen as baleful. It certainly does its best to sidestep conventional notions of beauty. And yet, there it is and, in a world full of jostling, largely indistinguishable towers, it is unique.

Rem Koolhaas, the *éminence grise* of the Rotterdam-based architecture firm OMA that designed it, put it like this: 'It aims at an alternative to the exhausted typology of the skyscraper. Instead of competing in the race for ultimate height and style within a traditional two-dimensional tower "soaring" skyward, CCTV's loop poses a truly three-dimensional experience, culminating in a 75-metre cantilever. The building is visible from most of Beijing; it sometimes comes across as big and sometimes small, from some angles strong and from others soft.'[1]

Its facade reflects the lines of force of its asymmetrical steel frame, culminating in the structural audacity of the 'overhang'.

A cantilever in architecture is a visually unsupported part of a building: a part that sticks out. Of course it *is* supported, the gravitational pull on it being transferred into the rest of the structure for balance. For the CCTV building OMA conceptually took a tower, broke it into four pieces and reassembled them: two sections rise at angles from the ground, their bases joined by a right-angled plinth building. This is then echoed by a mirror-image piece at the top, cranking in the other direction, which connects the tops of the angled towers, its elbow hanging in the air. That is the big cantilever, which turns the whole building from a tower complex into a loop. And finally, this top piece is not a uniform size: it tapers from one side to the other, so it is not flat on top but rises gently to a peak of 234 metres, 51 storeys in all. For a building that sets out not to look like a skyscraper it is still impressively high.

Easy enough to sketch, rather harder to construct. I saw it being built in 2007, when its latticework leaning steel towers had reached maximum height and were starting to sprout the stumps of what Koolhaas called

The CCTV Headquarters both is and is not a skyscraper. Either way, it commands the skyline of eastern Beijing.

the 'overhang', groping for each other like blindfolded party guests.[2] This was formidable work: structural engineer Cecil Balmond (b.1943) of design company Arup (see Sydney Opera House, p. 173, and Pompidou Centre, p. 148) devised a structure that does all of this while also being earthquake-resistant and able to flex with changing temperatures, its lines of compression and tension forces delineated in the facade design. The arms of the overhang were finally and rapidly linked at the optimum moment: eight o'clock on a cold, still winter's morning, when both sides were exactly the same temperature, so avoiding differential expansion.

With a park at its base and a smaller companion building on its left (seen here after a construction fire) this is as much an urban district as a building.

The 'overhang' is not a small thing: this right-angled section is itself a big office block where most of the administration work of the company takes place. The main lobby at the base is itself 10,000 square metres in area, set in a six-floor atrium – three levels upwards, three down into the ground – where it is directly connected to Beijing's subway network. This colossal scale was a large part of the attraction for Koolhaas, who observed:

> Beyond a certain scale, architecture acquires the properties of Bigness. The best reason to broach Bigness is the one given by climbers of Mount Everest: 'because it is there.' Bigness is ultimate architecture ... through size alone, such buildings enter an amoral domain, beyond good or bad.
>
> Bigness is no longer part of any urban tissue. It exists: at most, it coexists. Its subtext is fuck context.[3]

Such 'hyper-architecture',[4] as he also called it, raises questions such as: how big does any single building really need to be? At what point should it conceptually disintegrate into a township of smaller, linked buildings? How important is it for a corporate building to be a landmark-sized logo for a company?

Koolhaas is a highly intellectual architect and theorist who began his career as a film scriptwriter and journalist before training as an architect in London and the United States during the late 1960s and early 1970s. His mission was to revolutionise architecture, especially cultural buildings such as museums, concert halls and libraries, but also to complete ideal-city plans in the Middle East. He succeeded in gathering like-minded people around him and by the early twenty-first century the Office for Metropolitan Architecture (OMA) had become one of the most radical and successful design studios in the world. Fascinated by China's explosive urban growth, he saw the chance to do what few architects get a chance to do: reinvent a building type.

Much odder and much worse architecture than this sprouted in the Chinese property boom as other architects started to design large, strangely shaped buildings with none of the rigour, elan or structural knowhow of Koolhaas and his team. As landmark buildings do, it acquired a nickname in the city, however: 'Big Pants'.[5] In 2014 President Xi Jinping (b.1953), who became leader two years after the CCTV building was completed, made a speech at a cultural symposium calling for a rethink. 'No more weird architecture' was the gist of it, along with a call for a return to more traditional art forms.[6] China was starting to disassociate itself from certain Western values again. Relations cooled somewhat, but architecture continued to be an international affair, and at the time of writing the workers of the state broadcaster still occupy the ultimate architecture that it chose back towards the start of the century.

---

1 Koolhaas's account of the CCTV building, OMA website, www.oma.com.
2 Ibid.
3 Rem Koolhaas, 'Bigness, or the Problem of Large', in *S,M,L,XL*, 1995.
4 Ibid.
5 Megan Willett-Wei, 'Chinese President Xi Jinping: "No More Weird Architecture"', *Business Insider Magazine*, 21 October 2014.
6 President Xi Jinping speaking at a literary symposium in Beijing, October 2014, reported by Xinhua News Agency.

Industry

An industrial building, far from being an unsightly thing to hide away, can be an architectural showpiece. This was especially true of the Industrial Revolution of the late eighteenth and early nineteenth centuries. But buildings for manufacturing existed long before then. Things have always been made and places set aside to make them in, even when economies were predominantly agrarian.

The premises of blacksmiths, wheelwrights, ceramicists, coopers, brewers, brick and tile makers, carpenters, weavers, dyers and all the other medieval fabrication activities – some organised into guilds, some not – were industrial, if relatively small-scale at a time of small populations. Nor is there any functional difference between an enormous monastic tithe barn for the collection, processing, storage and distribution of grain, with doors large enough for loaded wagons to pass in and out, and today's motorway-intersection goods distribution warehouses.

If you take as your definition that people should operate machines in order for such places to be regarded as proper factories, again you do not have to wait until the eighteenth century to find examples. The years either side of the second millennium, specifically 900 to 1300, were a period of great industrial advance across the world. No more was this the case than in China, with its paper-making, printing, gunpowder and weapons manufacture, and its infrastructure to transport goods such as the 1,770-kilometre Grand Canal waterways system dating back to the Sui Dynasty (581–618).

In Europe, the moveable-type printing press was invented around 1440 in Mainz, Germany, by Johannes Gutenburg (d.1468). Printworks were factories, even though the word had yet to be coined. Their products formed the first mass communications network and were a stimulus both for education (you had to be able to read to take advantage) and for the growth of cities as industrial centres formed.

Gradually these places crystallised into recognisable building types. Water or wind mills are good examples, highly recognisable buildings full of ingenious machinery dependent upon an external power source to keep everything moving. Water came to be the preferred, more reliable motive force for most industries, especially with associated engineering works to impound water for use precisely when needed. Building technology lagged behind to some extent, though post-and-beam timber buildings allowed for the large window openings necessary for those activities (like printing), which required good light levels.

What is described as the Industrial Revolution was a matter not only of new processes and machines being invented, but also of an unprecedented scaling-up and centralising of production, which had previously been dispersed. Crucially, it also required the mobilisation of the population, since large numbers of millworkers were needed. As water was vital for power and often also for the

Philippe Jacques de Loutherbourg (1740–1812), *Coalbrookdale by Night*, 1801. This oil painting portrays the iron-smelting Bedlam Furnaces (1756) in Madeley Wood, Shropshire, a county at the heart of the acceleration of Britain's industrial economy from the mid-eighteenth century.

transport of goods, it made sense for the first large textile factories to grow pretty much where the old water mills had been. Among the very first was the Caraglio Silk Mill in Piedmont, Italy (1676–8), a three-storey water-powered mill designed by the Duke of Savoy's architect Amedeo di Castellamonte (1613–1683) to resemble a simplified turreted castle. The whole production process for luxurious silk organzine thread took place there using the latest spinning machinery. It included housing for the millworkers, a century before the conventionally accepted start of the Industrial Revolution. The Caraglio Mill, which still exists as a museum, was the template for the modern 'manufactory' or factory.

The secrets of the Caraglio Mill were stolen by an English entrepreneur, John Lombe (1693–1722). Lombe also recruited Italian millworkers to work in his Silk Mill in Derby (1717–21), which the English naughtily like to claim as the first modern factory. It too, much rebuilt and changed over the years, is now a museum. Lombe died suddenly in 1722 – poisoned by a female Italian assassin sent by the Duke of Savoy, or so the story goes. What Lombe's engineer George Sorocold (c.1668–c.1738) did, however, was to build what became a very familiar building type: the plain multi-storey factory building with its grid of windows. It was a rectangular brick and stone box of five storeys, 34 metres long and housing 300 workers, on an island in the River Derwent.

If the large brick, stone or, later, iron-framed box became the universal factory template, other arrangements were tried, such as the industrial village. The most evocative example is the Royal Saltworks (1775–8) at Arc-et-Senans near Besançon in eastern France, designed by Claude-Nicolas Ledoux (1736–1806), 'architect to the King', as he liked to style himself.[1] Salt was a big source of tax income for his master, but the existing works were scarcely palatial. Ledoux, never one to think small, imagined this relatively humdrum commission to be the centrepiece of a complete utopian neoclassical worker town, Chaux, designed on a circular plan. All that got built was the first phase, but that (now restored) is impressive enough, a palatial sequence of buildings laid out in a very large semicircle. Some of the buildings are ceremonial, some administrative, residential or military. The two buildings flanking the Director's House are where industry meets agriculture, neoclassicism meets the vernacular. They are expressed as enormous barns with big tiled roofs and strangely compressed classical porticos. Each 80 metres long by 28 metres wide and 20 metres high, these are unusual stylistic hybrids. The main thing, though, is the overall concept of the Royal Saltworks – not just a factory but a complete industrial complex, expressed with all the architectural bravura of an aristocratic country house or palace.

As the mill owners had to build homes to attract their workforce, this resulted in some well-designed housing, sometimes with workshops and gardens included. But as early as 1804 the poet and artist William Blake (1757–1827) wrote of 'dark Satanic mills' in his poem 'And did those feet in ancient time' (most commonly known today as the hymn 'Jerusalem') and some certainly were, particularly those cruelly exploiting a ready supply of orphan children. More paternalistic mill owners had greater regard for the wellbeing of their workers, who were mostly drawn from rural poverty and so enjoyed a rise in living standards. Some tried to establish ideal communities, like Robert Owen (1771–1858) at New Lanark in Scotland. Like a socialist Ledoux, Owen imagined, but never fully built, his industrial utopias, either in New Lanark or at the grid-pattern New Harmony, Indiana in the United States. Despite such idealistic failures it became common for the larger mills to spawn not only housing but schools, churches, refectories, infirmaries and parks.

The mill builders and their architects grappled with more than social engineering. Using iron and brick or clay-pot vaults to make supposedly fireproof mill buildings was a technology that later transferred to office blocks and museums, while the freestanding iron frame was the technology that made the skyscraper possible. From that point on, the challenge for factories was more to accommodate changing production processes: first the Fordist production line, later automation. The other side of industry, upstream of production, is research, often including laboratories and requiring a more refined approach from the architect (see the Salk Institute, p. 109).

The robot has replaced many human assembly workers but by no means all. Factories have long been large, super-flexible spaces in which any process can happen. They can be, and often are, banal sheds. But if there is a brand to promote, then the architecture of the factory can reflect the values of the brand, and can even aspire to landmark status, as shown by Apple or BMW.

1 Ledoux referred to himself as 'architect to the King' both in his correspondence and in his drawings.

Shrewsbury Flaxmill Maltings

Ditherington, UK, 1796–7; restored 2017–22

ARCHITECTS: CHARLES BAGE (1751–1822)
WITH WILLIAM HAZLEDINE (1763–1840)

STYLE: GEORGIAN FUNCTIONALIST

A building only five storeys high would never be called a skyscraper. But the flax mill at Ditherington outside Shrewsbury in the English county of Shropshire is the building that, its supporters like to claim, introduced the technology that made skyscrapers possible. It is the world's first fully iron-framed building, every floor stacked one above the other on remarkably slender and delicate cruciform columns. From outside it may look conventional enough with its brick walls and slate roofs but inside is another story.

This was where a new industrial need – a large, fireproof, mechanised, steam-driven, multi-level factory for making linen thread – was answered by a new industrial process and a new transport infrastructure. The first ever cast-iron bridge had been built across the gorge of the upper River Severn, 24 kilometres away, between 1779 and 1781. Cast-iron columns were just starting to be used in buildings such as churches, where good sightlines were important, and in some early factories in Derbyshire. In Shrewsbury, ironmaster William Hazledine then went one further: if iron columns were good, then why not add cross-beams to make complete iron frames for buildings?

The world's first iron-framed building as restored in 2022. Foreground greenery marks the course of the original canal.

The ancient art of joining column and beam, done here in iron to make the building frame.

His friend, the self-taught architect and local businessman Charles Bage, was also one of the four partners pooling their resources to build the mill. The main partner, John Marshall (1765–1845), had previously built timber-floored linen mills in Leeds, Yorkshire. These were still the relatively early years of Britain's factory boom, but the coal that the mill needed (Marshall's earlier mills had been water-powered) was delivered by a canal running right alongside, linking to collieries further east. The canal had been authorised to be built by Parliament in 1793. Also invaluable for bringing local iron ore to Hazledine's foundry, the canal effectively made the economics of the mill work. Canal and factory opened in the same year.

Shropshire is known now as a largely rural county, but with coal and ore to be had there, it was also a formidable Georgian industrial centre, commemorated today in the open-air museum at the appropriately named town of Ironbridge. It was a time of rapid advance, when fortunes were made by those canny enough to see the opportunities and able to raise the capital to get going. A relatively impoverished rural workforce was rapidly enticed into the new mills – especially women and children. The demand for linen was increased by the wars England was fighting, with military uniforms driving the market. The flax mill at Ditherington was therefore the right building in the right place at the right time. At 55 metres long by 11 metres wide and five storeys high, it was designed for a specific set of processes in the linen-making trade. To go higher would not have been especially efficient, given the materials that had to be moved, while being a long building made more sense. It was a 'groundscraper'.

The linking of columns and cross-beams into a framed structure might seem obvious enough – timber-framed buildings going back to medieval times were structurally not so different – but textiles factories had a bad habit of burning down, what with frictional heat from the greased machinery, the use of naked flames for lighting and the inflammable materials being made. Even airborne dust could ignite explosively. Bage and Hazledine made their building as fireproof as was possible by the standards of the day. Floors were made of shallow brick 'jack arches' springing from the iron cross-beams beneath, levelled above with graded rubble that was then floored with tiles. Window frames and doors to each floor were also of cast iron, so there was little to burn.

The Shrewsbury Flaxmill was not yet quite a proto-skyscraper because its brick walls worked in a hybrid way with the iron frame as part of the overall structure. It was not until early in the twentieth century that lightweight cladding was introduced, so making the outer skin of buildings separate from the frame carrying the weight and by extension making possible glass-skinned buildings. However, by the late nineteenth century, buildings with iron exoskeletons and infill brickwork were moving in that direction (see the Moulin Saulnier cocoa mill, p. 103).

By the mid- to late nineteenth century this mill typology, with floors full of cacophonous, oily, dust-generating machines, powered either by water or steam, was near-universal in industrialised parts of the world. America was especially quick to take it up, from the 1790s, thanks to industrial espionage. The young Samuel Slater (1768–1835) from Belper, Derbyshire, having worked in the mills there, memorised the details of the patented cotton-spinning machinery, emigrated to Rhode Island, and there in 1793 set up a copycat cotton mill – now known as Slater Mill in Pawtucket, the first National Historic Landmark in the USA. Coming only 17 years after America's Declaration of Independence, this was a big risk for Slater, who was dubbed 'Slater the Traitor' back home in England and was a notoriously hard taskmaster to his employees in the United States.[1] He prospered mightily and was a multimillionaire by the time he died in 1835.

Slater may have taken the secrets of the cotton-making machinery to America but his departure pre-dated the development in building technology represented by the Shrewsbury Flaxmill. That too was rapidly and enthusiastically adopted across the Atlantic and drove the expansion of American cities. As for the original in Shropshire, the flax-spinning industry had declined by the end of the nineteenth century and the building was converted to form the core of a large maltings – part of the beer-brewing process. That use lasted for a further century until 1987, whereupon it fell into disuse and near-dereliction. Its significance was quickly realised and it has now been restored to something close to its original appearance as a mixed-used development of office and studio space and apartments, with its own visitor centre acting as a museum of itself.

1 Neil Heath, 'Samuel Slater: American Hero or British Traitor?', BBC News Nottingham, 22 September 2011.

Moulin Saulnier Cocoa Mill

Noisiel, France, 1869–72

ARCHITECT: JULES SAULNIER (1817–1881)
WITH ENGINEER ARMAND MOISANT (1838–1906)

STYLE: TECHNO-HISTORICIST

This is a building with a shiny wrapping like a chocolate bar, an advertisement for its product, designed as a wholly functional factory beneath its eye-catching, iron-framed, glazed-brick exterior. Drawing its power from the rushing water beneath, it spans a branch of the River Marne at Noisiel, a town on the eastern edge of the Paris conurbation. It is only a small part of a large factory complex, which today houses the headquarters of the Nestlé foods conglomerate. As built, it was the work of the Menier chocolate company and it was more than just a factory, it was part of a complete model worker town.

In 1824, Jean-Antoine Brutus Menier (1795–1853) – unqualified pharmacist and teenage veteran of Napoleon's army medical corps – was doing well enough in his entirely unregulated manufacture of medicinal powders to move out of Paris and buy an existing mill at Noisiel. The tiny settlement on the Marne had been a milling centre since medieval times. Chocolate, being regarded as medicinal, was one of his products, consumed in liquid form or used to coat

Simultaneously both advanced and backward-looking in design, this 19th-century mill is a built advertisement for the product made within.

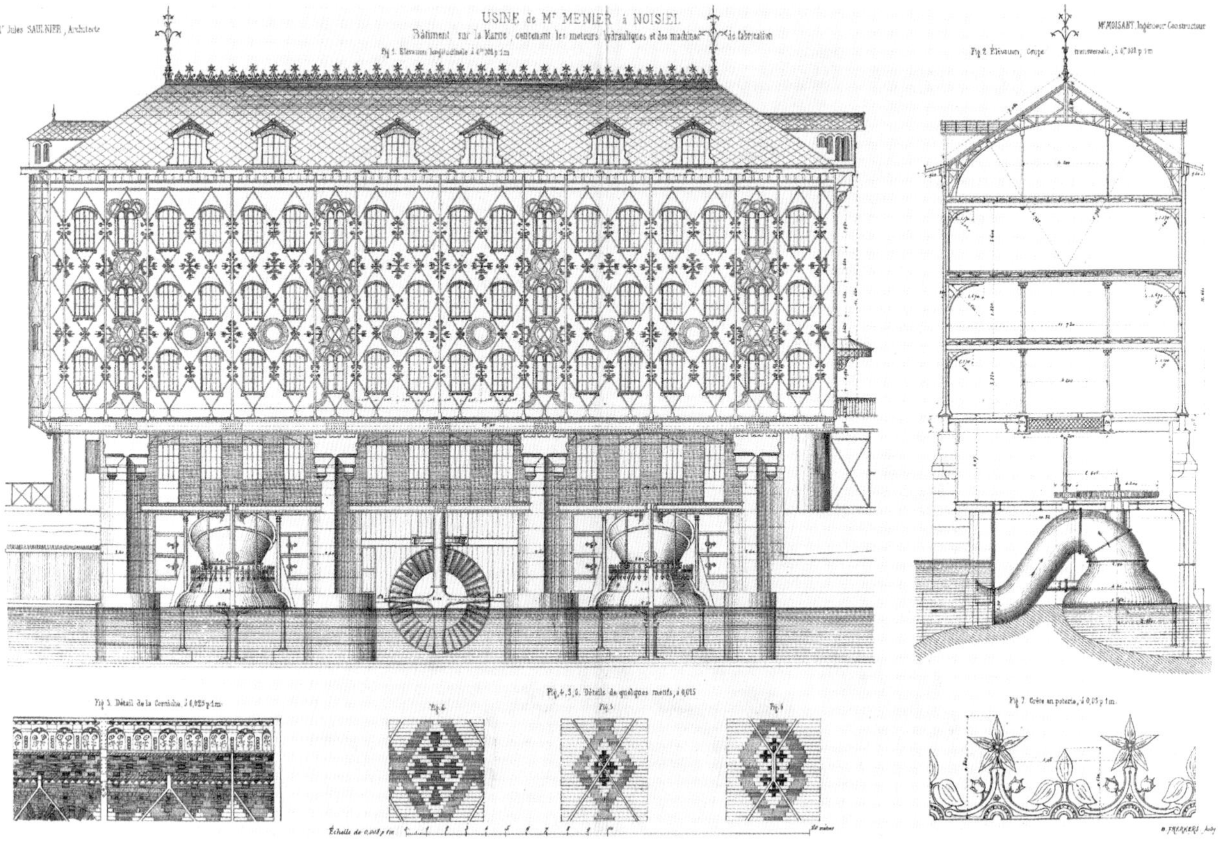

Section and elevation drawings at the time of construction make its ingenious structure clear, with tuba-like water-powered turbines below.

bitter pills. At Noisiel in 1836 it is said (although this is subject to debate) that he invented the first consumable solid chocolate bar, a product that he sold in an attractive, yellow-paper wrapper. Three years later Menier finally passed his pharmacy exams. However, he later sold the medical side of the business and became the founder of a family dynasty that was to be the biggest chocolate brand in France, perhaps even the world.

It was his son, Émile-Justin Menier (1826–1881), who oversaw all of this. He invested in cocoa estates in Nicaragua and sugar beet fields and a refinery on the Somme. He expanded the company production and distribution to London and New York while modernising production at Noisiel. This culminated in the new mill across the Marne, the milling processes on each floor powered directly via gears from the enclosed Girard water turbines beneath. Menier's chosen architect, Jules Saulnier, provided the company with another first which, like the chocolate bar, is inevitably disputed: the world's first iron exoskeleton building.

If the Shrewsbury Flaxmill Maltings (see p. 100) was the world's first iron-framed structure, it did not express that structure externally. Saulnier's mill looks far from high-tech – its form is traditional and its glazed-brick decoration, incorporating cocoa-bean and flower motifs, harks back to an earlier era – but he, or rather his young structural engineer Armand Moisant (a celebrated rival to Gustave Eiffel), made the whole building rock-solid with a delicate but strong iron exoskeleton. He set this braced four-storey box on a rigid platform of iron beams, in turn supported above the river on just four pre-existing stone piers from an earlier mill. Given the involvement of Moisant and given that this was a time of rapid technological advance in transport, it is no surprise that this structure is a variant of bridge engineering. Inside, it even includes suspension-bridge elements, in that the top floor is suspended on iron rods hanging from the roof trusses. This allowed a column-free floor below for the greatest possible flexibility of use (see cross-section, p. 104).

In appearance, however, the mill is more like a chateau. As was characteristic in this time of great industrial expansion, its modernity is dressed in heritage clothes, though some see also the influence of orientalism in the patterning of the facades. At the time, some critics felt that it was an impure concoction, looking as if a defective masonry building had been reinforced with metal. 'The ironwork appears to have been added later', said German architect Konstantin Lipsius.[1] By no means. Saulnier and Moisant organised the structural frame to be an intrinsic part of the decorative scheme, a very modern concept which cunningly also conveyed the look of medieval brick diaper-work. And like medieval timber-frame buildings, the glazed bricks within the frame are merely infill, bearing none of the main structural load.

This synthesis of architecture and visible structural engineering was indeed pioneering. When High Tech finally arrived as a full-blown architectural style a century later, the decorative potential of such external cross-bracing was fully exploited by architects such as Skidmore, Owings and Merrill (SOM) in their John Hancock Center tower in Chicago (1969), and in very different vein by Richard Rogers (1933–2021) and Renzo Piano (b.1937) in their Pompidou Centre in Paris (see p. 148).

Other fine factory buildings by other hands on both sides of the river soon joined Saulnier and Moisant's mill. In common with earlier cotton mill complexes, it was necessary to provide homes for the workers in the mills. In Noisiel these duly arrived in the form of handsome, generous houses laid out on a grid of streets named after members of the Menier family. Again, like some of those early cotton mills, the town was effectively the property of the mill owners who provided most facilities and essentially ran it. Indeed, the mayors of Noisiel formed an uninterrupted line of Menier chocolate magnates right up to 1959, by which point, held back by two World Wars (which had advantaged the chocolate makers of neutral Switzerland and elsewhere), the Menier brand was in decline and was later sold. But the building remains as a historic monument to a time when manufacturing, architecture and engineering marched in step to create a masterpiece.

1 Konstantin Lipsius in a speech of 1878 to the Confederation of German Architects and Structural Engineers, cited by Konstantina Demiri in 'Corporate Image: Consolidation of Pioneer Architecture with Innovative Structure', *International Journal of Engineering Technology*, Vol. 2, No. 2, May 2013.

The Van Nelle Factory Complex

Rotterdam, Netherlands, 1925–31; restored 1998–2004

ARCHITECTS: LEENDERT VAN DER VLUGT (1894–1936) AND ENGINEER JOHANNES BRINKMAN (1902–1949) WITH MART STAM (1899–1986)

STYLE: INTERNATIONAL MODERNIST

It is extraordinary to think that the Van Nelle factory, such a beacon of modernism, is getting on for a century old. Historic modernism, now with its own specialised repair and restoration techniques, is a relatively recent concept. After all, if kept in good order (a big *if*, as they can be high-maintenance) these buildings still look fresh, anything but 'historic'. And yet this factory is now a UNESCO World Heritage Site.

This would have amazed its original architects who – consciously designing for the future – had little idea how far into the future their buildings would go, or how they would be regarded by successive generations. As far as Van der Vlugt and Stam were concerned, they were simply building in a new way for new and better times. This was not just building as efficient production tool: it also marks an attempt to improve the lot of factory workers through a well-ventilated, well-daylit factory with good staff facilities.

Van Nelle is a brand name dating back to the eighteenth century, associated with tea, coffee, tobacco and rice products, staple trading commodities for the Dutch and their empire. Its director Cees van der Leeuw (1890–1973), a humanist, artist, socialist and theosophist (a very popular religious cult of the time), initiated the project. He saw it as his duty to improve people's lives and architecture was to be part of that mission in the form of a state-of-the-art adaptable factory complex. His architects were equally committed to the new ways.

If the Shrewsbury flax mill (see p. 100) was a pioneer of iron buildings that still looked conventional from the outside, and the Menier factory (see p. 103) disguised its advanced frame-construction technology with nostalgist trimmings,

The smoke shows coffee roasting in progress: the factory complex in the post-war years.

Van Nelle today: its history as a modernist 'daylight factory' making it a UNESCO World Heritage Site.

the Van Nelle factory cast off these vestiges of the past and leapt into another era. Its frame is reinforced concrete – often a favourite of the modernists because of its mouldability and strength. Previously solid walls have dissolved into large window strips, a trick made possible by the simple expedient of placing the octagonal columns holding the building up inboard of the edge of the floor slabs. The 20-hectare factory complex is a horizontalist hymn to the resulting 'curtain wall', 220 metres long, divided into the four key buildings of different heights, interrupted by three staircase towers. As with its Shrewsbury ancestor, it was placed alongside a canal, where raw materials were unloaded by crane from barges: but it was also handily sited for roads and railways.

The traditional manufacturing practice was followed of delivering raw materials to the top floor and then moving them down or between the buildings as the processes continued through to packaging and dispatch. Tobacco products needed the most work, so that section, the main building, is eight floors high. Coffee needed five floors and tea needed three. Five covered conveyor-belt bridges (now walkways) in steel and glass link the buildings at various angles to the later dispatching hall. This pragmatic solution, hardly 'designed' at all, gives the whole composition great energy. There is also a curving office wing and – the crowning architectural gesture – a circular tea room is placed on top of one end of the tobacco building like an airport control tower.

Men and women were segregated on arrival and took showers before starting work, something previously unheard of. Cleanliness and health were obsessions. The key tenets of early modernism have been described as 'light, air and openness',[1] a tripartite belief system that first emerged at the start of the century in tuberculosis sanatoria. Rickets, a disease caused by lack of exposure to sunlight, was also commonplace and may also have informed these ideas. The roots of modernism also explain why buildings influenced by this style can sometimes look clinical: they were intended as a visible expression of healthy living. As with many office buildings of the period, however, the windows were

The tea room when first built: a belvedere set high on the prow of the building.

arranged so that the workers could not see out and get distracted when seated at their work.

Very consciously conceived and designed as a model industrial complex socially as well as architecturally, it embodies the values of a certainly paternalistic but caring family-run firm. Not everyone liked this. In 1933 the socialist critic R.N. Roland Holst (1868–1938) wrote: 'The factory is perfect, but the sight of people working in it nonetheless upsets me: work has here been reduced to the deadliest degree of intensity ... it is a palace of mechanised exploitation.'[2]

There was a bit of an unseemly credits tussle between Van der Vlugt and Stam. Both were young men making a name for themselves in this revolutionary kind of architecture, but Van der Vlugt, being a partner in the firm along with the even younger engineer Johannes Brinkman, gave the orders. Stam, however, had greater exposure to avant-garde architecture from his earlier work in Berlin and contacts with post-revolutionary 'constructivist' Russian architects and artists. He was Van der Vlugt's right-hand man for exactly one year, shortly after the outset of the project in April 1926, and while it is not known who did what, it is likely that Stam brought much of the constructivist drama to the design. Between them they achieved an architecture that goes beyond functionalism to attain a real civic quality.

The company continued to take great pride in its showpiece factory until the firm and its brands were sold and asset-stripped in the 1990s, the fate of many such venerable concerns. The factory ceased working in 1996 but by then its value was recognised and rather than being swept away for housing or commercial sheds, as tends to happen with many such former industrial sites, it was carefully restored as a multiple-occupancy office, studio and events building. It is now also something of a tourist attraction.

1 Paul Overy, *Light, Air and Openness: Modern Architecture between the Wars*, 2008.
2 Cited in Joris Molenaar, *Brinkman and Van der Vlugt Architects: Rotterdam's City-Ideal in International Style*, 2012.

Salk Institute for Biological Studies La Jolla, California, USA, 1959–65

ARCHITECT: LOUIS KAHN (1901–1974)

STYLE: BRUTALIST

This is the most refined and ambitious building ever to be associated with the pharmaceutical industry, though it is equally at home in the education sector. Dr Jonas Salk (1914–1995), a reluctant celebrity virologist since his 1955 invention of the first safe, effective vaccine against the crippling, often fatal disease polio, told his architect that he wanted his new research institute to be a place 'worthy of a visit by Picasso'.[1] What drove Salk was the conviction that there should be no barriers between science, industry and the arts. Coincidentally, it was a joint appreciation of architecture that later brought him into contact with one of Picasso's long-term former mistresses, the artist Françoise Gilot (b.1921). She and Salk married in 1970.

Salk's great fame in the late 1950s made it possible for him to establish and raise finance for an institute for molecular and cellular biology aimed at new and younger scientists. This was to be a pharmaceutical research complex but, Salk announced, it would be more than just a set of large labs. This was to be a modern Socratic academy: a place where all disciplines could come together

The infinity view out to the Pacific, accompanied by the sound of water gurgling in the central rill.

It looks collegiate, but behind these academics' rooms are ranges of large research and development laboratories serving the pharmaceutical industry.

and converse. 'We cannot be certain what will happen here, but we can be certain it will contribute to the welfare and understanding of man', he said.[2]

The Estonian-born architect Louis Kahn was central to this outlook. Salk chose his architect the moment he had a site to build on, 11 hectares at La Jolla near San Diego, overlooking a scrubby canyon leading to the Pacific Ocean. The site was gifted following a local referendum. The mayor was a polio survivor.

Kahn was a great and meticulous architect and teacher, not a flashy or public figure like his revered older peers Frank Lloyd Wright or Le Corbusier. A late achiever who only started to receive large-scale commissions after the age of 50, he had nonetheless recently designed something Salk was very interested in: the Richards Medical Research Laboratories at the University of Pennsylvania, Philadelphia. The laboratories included beautiful biological research labs grouped in glazed corner pavilions amid dramatic towers of stairs and vents. Kahn was convinced that scientists worked in some ways like artists, effectively in studios, a viewpoint that was music to Salk's ears. He met up with Kahn at the Richards labs and hired him immediately.

Salk drew inspiration not only from artists, but also from monks. His reference, far from labs and industry, was the thirteenth-century hill-town monastery of San Francis at Assisi, Italy. This sequence of buildings culminates in the courtyard heart of the monastery, commanding the bluff high above the Umbrian plains. Kahn, whose knowledge of historic architecture was second to none, had been there, studying and sketching it 30 years previously.

Not everything that the two men imagined got built. But the ideas, distilled down into the eventual building, made such a very powerful piece of architecture that it became, and remains, world-famous. Its power comes from the highly charged 'empty' courtyard at its heart, aligned with the setting sun to the west. As you enter this travertine-marble courtyard through an orange grove at the landward end, it and the trickling rill of water running down its centre seem to lead to nothing but the horizon. Does it stand on the edge of a cliff? Not quite. It steps down to a more intimate courtyard overlooking the canyon at the far end. There are 16 more secretive sunken areas, mini-courts, to be found: private places for conversation and study.

The ultimate break-out space: grab your surfboard and head for the sea.

The multi-level arrangement is sophisticated but in appearance sublimely simple. It is a rectangular layout. Two laboratory blocks – plainly but beautifully finished in smooth pale concrete, kept column- and clutter-free by wide-spanning trusses every other level – march down each outer edge. These blocks are linked via walkways across the inner range of those sunken courts to join eight little towers, containing studies for the scientists, running down each side of the central courtyard, each with an angled look-out towards the sea. It is this space – in line of descent from Moorish courtyards as much as the arcade-surrounded space of the monastery at Assisi – that people come to see. It has no obvious function but to delight the senses. Leaving it open to the horizon is a masterstroke. The proportions of buildings and spaces are just so. Nothing feels wrong or out of place. The materials – marble, smooth and finely textured concrete, large panes of glass and teak for window frames, doors and panelling – are beautiful. The play of light and shade on the surfaces across the day and seasons was as carefully planned as everything else.

For all of these reasons, Kahn is perhaps the ultimate architects' architect, and this his best building. Today, the previously bare flat roofs are covered in photovoltaic solar panels, which are invisible from the ground. It was enlarged in the mid-1990s with a pair of big entrance buildings that defer madly to Kahn, but have little of his spatial adroitness. Still, the expansion is proof of the success of Salk's original concept. Several Nobel laureates have graced its doors.

Salk has a college-like appearance but is attached to no university. In its laboratories, seldom photographed internally for reasons of commercial confidentiality, scientists develop cures or treatments for cancer, dementia and diabetes, among many others. Given the size of the worldwide pharmaceutical sector, the applied science practised here is of immense value. True to its cross-disciplinary origins it can also be deemed to be academic and, in its generous planning, civic. In its numinous way, remembering St Francis, it is humanism's answer to religious buildings too.

---

1 Alessandra Latour (ed.), *Louis I. Kahn: Writings, Lectures, Interviews*, 1991.
2 'History of Salk', Salk Institute website, www.salk.edu/about/history-of-salk.

Shenzhen Energy Ring

Shenzhen, China, 2016–2022

ARCHITECTS: SCHMIDT HAMMER LASSEN ARCHITECTS AND GOTTLIEB PALUDAN ARCHITECTS

STYLE: ECO-TECH

A power station as a civic building open to the public is an unusual proposition. But the city of Shenzhen, part of south-east China's Pearl River Delta megalopolis, took the idea seriously enough to run an international competition to find architects to design it. The Shenzhen Energy Ring is the result: a very large showpiece industrial building, which people are invited to visit. It is the world's largest waste-to-energy plant, the kind of usually smelly building that used to be as off-limits to the public as a sewage works. It is designed by architects better known for cultural buildings such as libraries and museums.

The economic liberalisation of China from the late twentieth century onwards led to massive urbanisation. The commensurate demand for power added to often severe air pollution in parts of the country, as more low-grade, coal-fired plants came online. As the world's largest economy with an affluent urban society, China also produces vastly more consumer waste than it used to, not all of which can be readily recycled. Hence the arrival of a waste-to-energy plant such as this. They have become common worldwide but never previously at such a scale.

The architect's main move was to take a building type that is usually rectangular – determined by the linear nature of fuel feed/boiler/steam turbine/generator rigs – and instead to make it circular. A tapering angled steel-lattice drum, clad in burnt-orange-coloured aluminium blades, houses the conventional power station equipment layout, which is reorganised to be more compact. This leaves a lot of space around the edges, used for some of the secondary functions of power plant, which are often separated out. So, refuse trucks arrive through a tunnel and drive straight into the building to replenish enormous fuel bunkers, and around half of the main floor area is given over to the equipment cleaning the flue gases after the fuel is burnt. The public areas slot into all of this. Your arrival is theatrically managed: you enter the building via a bridge rising from ground level, curving in between the twin chimney stacks, thence through a portal in the facade. Inside you find an education centre and exhibition over three levels, plus a walkway overlooking the works, from which you can peer into the enormous waste hoppers.

The project is an example of the internationalism of architecture at this level. The lead architectural practice, Schmidt Hammer Lassen, is a Danish firm, itself part of a larger American company. The firm's Shanghai-based director, who was responsible for designing the building, is another nationality again: in this case, Scottish-born Chris Hardie (b.1977). His concept, he explained, was for the power station 'to act as a resource to educate everyone from school children and community workers to city and district leaders on the processes required and the importance of managing and reducing waste'.[1] The original brief he was given envisaged the education centre some distance

OPPOSITE
Sitting in the hills outside Shenzhen, the scale of the site is indicated by the five-storey circular hotel, front left.

away from the plant: he persuaded the municipality to incorporate it into the plant itself.

This is design at an enormous scale, akin to the largest airport terminals. Set in a hollow among wooded hills some distance from the city, the steel latticework exoskeleton of the building is a kilometre in circumference and 67 metres at its highest point. The chimneys rise to 100 metres. This pedagogical power plant processes 5,000 tonnes of waste per day, generating 600 million kilowatt hours of electricity annually: a typical capacity for a large conventional power station but unusually large for this type.

The tilted disc of the plant's roof, 286 metres in diameter, itself doubles as a photovoltaic solar-power array, large enough to provide a decent extra contribution to the city's energy demand. This roof is also accessible to the public, with a 900-metre perimeter walkway around it. Those subsidiary functions that did not fit inside the main building are expressed as satellites orbiting the mother planet. One is a hotel with a courtyard garden for visiting engineers. Others contain cooling towers for the steam turbines, which in turn drive generators in the main building.

The inclusion of a cultural-buildings architect as lead designer is clear not only in the unusual shape of the building – its artfully composed metal carapace designed to vent surplus heat naturally and the twin chimney flues offset towards the front (a more basic design would tend to centralise them) – but also in its educational mission to be a museum of itself. It is designed to an international green-building standard at high ('gold') level, meaning it helps fight carbon emissions and climate change.[2]

Given which, it is worth considering the pros and cons of alternative power sources. You can certainly question the eco-credentials of such waste-to-energy plants – burning is burning, after all, however well controlled and filtered – but if the alternative is landfill, it makes sense as part of the energy-generation mix. Generating electricity is a traditionally dirty industry and a huge emitter of carbon dioxide (burning fossil fuels or, increasingly controversially, wood pellets), or it leaves relatively small but intensely deadly amounts of nuclear waste that require careful stewardship as far into the future as it is possible to imagine. Wind and solar power are highly effective and benign but come with their own issues concerning the materials and energy used in making and disposing of the equipment. They also need efficient power storage to balance fluctuations in output – or to be balanced by other forms of generation such as this. The longed-for goal of clean waste-free nuclear fusion is not yet commercially viable, though it is getting closer. Hydroelectric plants require dams and tidal barrages that can adversely affect the ecology of entire regions.

The world's largest energy-from-waste plant is also an educational visitor attraction.

So, when it comes to generating the electricity we all depend on, nothing is perfect, though some methods are considerably better than others. At the Shenzhen Energy Ring the process is laid out for you, at full scale and in real time, to examine and ponder on. Part of its aim is to point out the profligacy of non-recyclable waste. Were it to succeed in reducing that to virtually nothing, it would be redundant.

1 Conversation with the author, April 2022.
2 The green-building ratings standard, LEED (Leadership in Energy and Environmental Design).

66

Transport

If a transport system works successfully, the designed experience may be both efficient and, in some instances, exciting. But from a time well before the railways, it has always been something else as well, and that something is to do not with movement but, rather, with stopping. The *caravanserai* (traveller's resting places) of the ancient Asian and North African trade routes such as the fabled Silk Road, medieval European coaching inns and their Far Eastern equivalents, such as the Japanese *ryokan*, which date back to the eighth century, were all about the break on the journey.

The architecture of transport buildings can relate to the more glamorous features, passed while at high speed – a mighty bridge, say – but it is more likely to be to do with the incidentals of travel: processing of people and goods, security checks, eating, drinking, shopping and the maintenance and preparation of fast machines. A large transport terminal or interchange is a very complex place with a mix of many uses, from industrial to retail. The task that architects, engineers and designers face is to try to make all that complexity seem simple.

The architecture periodically has to play catch-up with the technology, or to choose between available technologies. Engineering becomes key, although this can go awry. The English engineer Isambard Kingdom Brunel (1806–1859) might have got it right with his Great Western Railway, his bridges and some of his ships, but he got it entirely wrong when he decided on the technology of the 'atmospheric railway' – trains powered from a pneumatic vacuum tube – for his 32-kilometre South Devon Railway. It worked, but not for long because it was absurdly high-maintenance and prone to failure. Had the system succeeded, the world's railway architecture would have featured, not puffing steam locomotives, but instead, sizeable trackside air-pumping houses every few kilometres.

Similarly, the architects of inter-war airports faced a dilemma. Airships aside (never very common), should they cater for land planes or flying boats? Each had its merits. For a while, many airports were sited and designed so as to accommodate airliners either with wheels or floating hulls. New York's 1939 La Guardia airport, by architects William Adams Delano (1874–1960) and Chester Holmes Aldrich (1871–1940), with its art deco flourishes and Marine Terminal, is a case in point.

One by one, the alternative technologies tend to drop away, along with their associated buildings: there were never any great hoverports anyway. Monorails (suspended railways where the trains hang from a single rail carried on gantries rather than sitting on two rails on the ground) are forever the future that never quite arrives. Although perfectly practicable, only a handful of proper examples for regular passengers have ever been built, the most famous being the Schwebebahn at Wuppertal in Germany dating from 1901. This is used as an everyday metro system, sailing over streets and river alike, with a variety of

The Schwebebahn monorail in Wuppertal, Germany, as seen in 1910. The monorail was designed by Carl Eugen Langen (1833–1895) and constructed between 1897 and 1903. With updated hanging stock it still runs today.

elevated station buildings. There are two such more recent urban lines in Japan, but generally cities plump for trams or underground metro systems instead.

The buildings and structures associated with transport span the architectural and engineering spectrum for two reasons: the way the infrastructure itself impacts on our towns, cities and countryside, and the buildings it generates. Canals gave rise to pleasingly functional bridges, warehouses, small homes for workers and occasional wonders such as aqueducts, tunnels and staircases of locks. Shipping needs its docks and dockyards and container terminals. Railways continue to use advances in engineering to enable some spectacular structures along the line as well as at the stations and termini (see Chhatrapati Shivaji Terminus, p. 123). But for all the magnificence of the best railway terminals, the arrival of the original railways into the world's cities was often brutal, creating swathes of demolition and societal divisions, hence the coining of the pejorative phrase 'the wrong side of the tracks'.

Convenience aside (we all use them in one way or another, even if we just sit at home and order goods online), modern roads are the most difficult to love. Though there is a geometrical beauty in a well-designed motorway intersection, noise and pollution mean that few would elect to live next to one. Electric vehicles reduce one type of pollution, but little of the noise (mostly generated by tyres which, like brakes and the road surface itself, send off dust particles). The buildings that spring up along such roads are the node points of today's commerce, clusters of vast distribution warehouses (see Magna Park, p. 220) approaching the size of small towns.

Exceptions are to be found, however. A bridge such as the Millau Viaduct in Central France, a rhythmic sequence of masts and taut cables leaping from one side of a steep river gorge to the other and curving as it goes, is a match for any of the structures produced by earlier transport technologies. Opening in 2004, its design a collaboration between structural engineer Michel Virlogeux (b.1946) and architect Norman Foster, it was still, at the time of writing, the tallest bridge in the world. It is something of a visitor attraction in itself and the motorway rest area next to it is designed as much as an observation gallery for the bridge as for all the usual facilities. Such places, often basic elsewhere, are designed to a very high standard in France.

The century-long history of air travel is especially fascinating. Aside from the development of the air terminal and the landing field over time, this is an infrastructure of the air, and a very visible one. At peak there can be as many as 20,000 planes aloft globally at any one time, though the average is half that. The vapour trails criss-crossing the sky, the sight and sound of the planes circling above your head – in the populous parts of the world and plenty of the less populous ones too, it is rare to be in a place where this transport method does not impinge somehow. On the few occasions when air travel shuts down altogether there is a discernible change in our sense of our surroundings.

Whatever the mode of transport, it is the beginnings, interchange points and ends of journeys that most require the architect's attention. Transport buildings continue to evolve to suit new patterns of trade and movement of people. A generation of architects (Foster included) who grew up with science-fiction stories is now designing spaceports for super-rich tourism. Orbiting space stations are now quite old (late twentieth-century) technology. Studies have been done into ways to build settlements on the Moon and Mars as the termini of interplanetary travel.

One great paradox remains, and this comes back to air travel. So much investment goes into the development of large airliners and their military equivalents that the planes themselves can last longer – much longer – than the buildings that serve them. The sinister Boeing B52 bombers first introduced in 1952 are predicted, with refits, to still be flying in the 2050s. Once you have a century-old flying machine, you have something more permanent than many buildings and just as much part of our visual culture.

The Canal du Midi Southern France, 1666–81

ENGINEER(S): PIERRE-PAUL RIQUET (1609–1680) AND FRANÇOIS ANDRÉOSSY (1633–1688)

STYLE: FUNCTIONALIST, NEOCLASSICAL

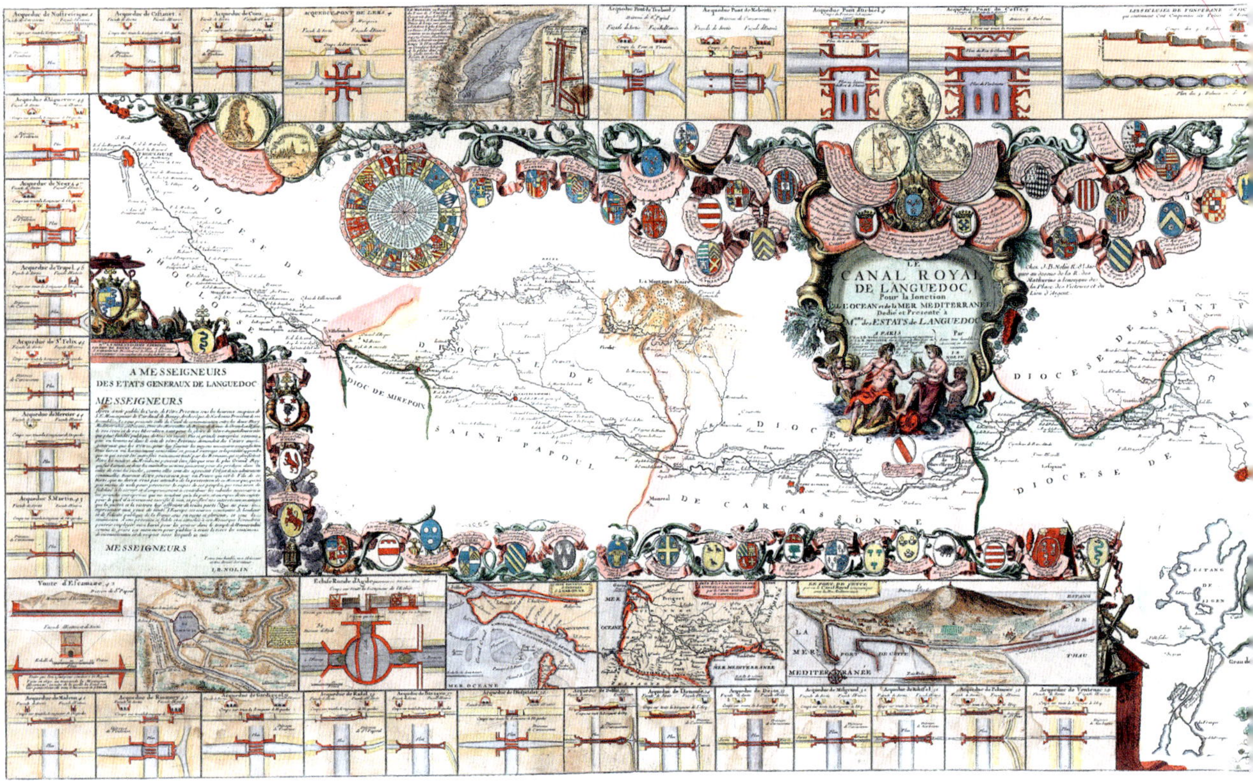

In 1666, the 'Sun King', Louis XIV of France (r.1643–1715), issued a royal decree from his palace at Versailles via his First Minister of State and public-works supremo, Jean-Baptiste Colbert (1619–1683): a canal was to be built to join two seas, Atlantic and Mediterranean. This would have a double benefit: it would bypass troublesome Spain with its notorious pirates and, in the process, it would open up the interior of *la France profonde* – deepest rural France – to development, providing transport for its goods. Colbert was a great moderniser.

The idea was the brainchild of the self-taught engineer Pierre-Paul Riquet. Riquet was a native of Béziers, which was on the route of the 'Two Seas Canal' (his working title). He was an independently wealthy salt-tax collector for the king, and was made a baron to further ensure his loyalty. Riquet was to sink most of his fortune into the project, reducing the cost of it to the State in exchange for ownership of it as a personal fiefdom. He stuck to it, linking the two oceans by water from Toulouse in the west to Sète in the east on a route first considered by Roman military engineers, later by Leonardo da Vinci (1452–1519).

ABOVE
A celebratory map of the Canal du Midi, produced in 1697, just a few years after opening. The map shows diagrams of every significant engineering structure on the route.

ABOVE RIGHT
The staircase locks at Fonserannes showing the characteristic oval shape determined by Riquet. They are drawn in plan and section at the top of the map, fifth from right.

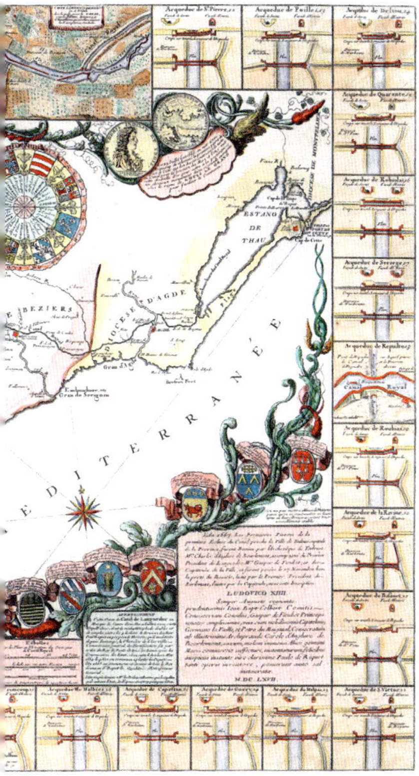

Riquet made it happen a century before the start of what is commonly regarded as 'the canal age', from the mid-eighteenth to the late nineteenth centuries, which was mostly about transporting heavy materials such as coal, stone, lead and iron. The Canal du Midi, in contrast, was an agrarian undertaking: as well as wheat it was to convey wine, cloth and salt for export. But the basic engineering ideas pre-existed. Canals and their associated engineering works were not a new idea: Pharaonic Egypt had them.

Another tax collector, from the Chinese Song Dynasty (960–1279), Qiao Weiyue, is credited as having built a 'pound lock' – two sets of gates set in the canal a short distance apart that, by letting water in at one end and out at the other, can raise or lower boats. That was in 984 and the principle holds true today. In Europe locks gradually arrived in the fourteenth and fifteenth centuries, generally on river navigations. But Riquet took canal engineering a step further, allowing the canal to traverse difficult terrain, rising to a watershed of 190 metres above sea level and down again, while finding the water to supply it in what was and is quite an arid region. To do this he built the largest dam in Europe to make a reservoir, the St Ferréol basin, some 32 kilometres away up in the rainy Montagne Noir range to the north, and ran a feeder stream to his canal from there.

A linear transport corridor is evidently not a building, although buildings always feature. But the Canal du Midi was built on a grand scale and with a great sense of style befitting its royal patronage. Riquet and his assistant Andréossy evolved a visual language for the canal that combined rugged masonry engineering for locks, bridges and wharf-side buildings, with occasional touches of sculptural flamboyance. The locks are of an unusual oval shape (rectangular is more common), which help define the particular character of the canal. Large basins were made at points along the route, expanding into a broad lake at Castelnaudary. In the face of much scepticism, Riquet built the world's first canal tunnel at Malpas, a circular three-way lock at Agde and a 'staircase' of linked locks cut through solid rock at Fonserannes.

At 57, Riquet was an old man for the time when he started, and knew he had to move at pace. He organised and paid his workers (many of them women) well. The whole route, from the river Garonne at Toulouse to the Mediterranean lagoon of the Étang de Thau near Sète, a distance of almost 230 kilometres, opened only 15 years after work commenced. Not all his plans came to fruition: his idea to line the canal with crop trees such as mulberries (for silk worms) or willows (for basket-weaving) did not work. But shelter from the sun and wind was necessary. Eventually, the fast-growing *platane* or plane tree, grown for firewood before coal became commonplace, was planted alongside the canal. Along with other species such as oak, lime and chestnut, there were eventually 200,000 trees lining the route.

At the summit of the canal at Naurouze, where bubbling mountain waters arrive to feed it, there is an obelisk commemorating Riquet. He had died aged 76, two million livres in debt, just a few months before his great venture opened. The name he knew it by is also recorded: 'To Pierre-Paul Riquet, Baron Bonrepos, author of the Two Seas Canal in Languedoc.' Engineering, architecture and landscape thus developed together. The canal has been partly updated since at intervals, typically with later aqueducts built to carry it across rivers it originally crossed on the level. Financially, it was never a huge commercial success, so escaped having its character wrecked by over-enlargement. In consequence, this waterway survives, fully navigable, as an early infrastructural marvel, way ahead of its time. It showed what could be done: conceptually, the Suez and Panama canals started here.

At Castelnaudary the canal broadens into a lake, acting as an inland port and reservoir combined.

Chhatrapati Shivaji Terminus

Mumbai, India, 1878–88

ARCHITECT: FREDERICK WILLIAM STEVENS (1847–1900)
WITH ENGINEER RAOSAHEB VAIDYA (D.1900)

STYLE: GOTHIC REVIVAL/INDO-SARACENIC

An exuberant fusion of Western and Central Asian architectural motifs, this is one of the grandest railway stations in the world.

Some two million people a day, alighting from a thousand trains, pour through the doors of the astonishing architectural confection (originally called the Victoria Terminus) that is now the Chhatrapati Shivaji Terminus in Mumbai. Back in the late nineteenth century this was the British Raj in action: building railways and station buildings with seemingly endless imperial glory in mind. At a glance – though it is hard to take it all in at a glance – it could be some great museum or even a palace.

The Raj – direct rule of what is now India, Pakistan and Bangladesh from 1858 to 1947, succeeding a century of notoriously buccaneering, sometimes brutal rule by the East India Company – was a big employer of young British men and their families. Indeed, the British elite school system pretty much existed to produce such rulers of Empire. Stevens was one such, a promising architect-engineer from Bath who sailed out in 1867, aged just 20, to take up a post in the newly minted Indian Public Works Department. After nearly 20 years there, the Victoria Terminus, close to the docks, was his last project for the Department before setting up in private practice in Bombay. It was a triumphant way to bow out of public service.

The golden era of grand railway station design yields immense surviving architectural riches. How do you choose between this, London's St Pancras, Amsterdam and Antwerp Central, Helsinki, New York's Grand Central,

Washington's Union Station, among many others? In the end, the Victoria Terminus is here because it is such an extraordinary work by a lesser-known designer, and because of the way it reflects the patrician British attitude to this most cherished part of the vast domains of the Queen-Empress after whom it was named.

On the one hand, it is a munificent civic gift and a wonderful gateway to and from Mumbai; on the other, it is – like the later government buildings of New Delhi by Sir Edwin Lutyens and Herbert Baker (1862–1946) – a statement of imperial power. This was the head of the Great Indian Peninsula Railway leading to the interior, east to Calcutta (now Kolkata) and later to Madras (Chennai) and Delhi. It was used by the ruling classes and the general populace alike – though usually on different trains and from very different, segregated waiting rooms. In the drawing office, however, English and Indians worked together: Stevens's engineering assistant was Raosaheb Vaidya and his supervisor was M.M. Janardhan.

Where George Gilbert Scott's (1811–1878) great Gothic frontage to St Pancras Station in London was a hotel, Stevens's even more over-the-top equivalent is a railway building for public use and company administration. As a passenger you therefore get to see and use more of the building, in particular its extravagantly lofty booking hall, which is a riot of tall polychromatic vaults, the fever dream of a Victorian architect reimagining Scott for the tropics. Meanwhile, the railway company officials used a spectacular staircase to the upper levels that was more generously proportioned than its London equivalent. Externally, the building is arranged with wings flanking an entrance courtyard, the overall architecture serving as a fusion of European Gothic Revival and Indian details, especially the open loggias (high-level arcades) providing shade and ventilation across the entire frontage. This architectural fusion was official policy for public buildings, intended to reflect the Anglo-Indian nature of government itself.

At its centre an octagonal tower erupts, rising to a segmental dome topped with a 4-metre statue. You might expect this to be Queen Victoria, but no (her statue was elsewhere, and later removed). It is 'Progress'. She, along with the Imperial lion and Indian tiger standing either side of the entrance court, were by sculptor Thomas Earp (1828–1893). Overall, the building bristles with turrets, spires, pinnacles and is richly decorated with sculptures, many emanating from students at the city's school of art run by John Lockwood Kipling (1837–1911), father of the poet and great story-teller of the British Empire, Rudyard Kipling (1865–1936). The materials were the best available, from India or overseas, from Aberdeen to Italy. So overwhelming was it, in fact, that at its opening the Vicereine, Lady Dufferin, disdainfully remarked that it was 'much too magnificent for a bustling crowd of railway passengers'.[1]

An oddity about the terminus is that it is unusually sited: not across the head of the tracks, as was often the British way, and not on the long side, as was more common across Europe, but a combination of the two. This monumental gateway building is arranged parallel with the tracks, but set forward of where they end. So you enter through the front and then take a left turn through the lavish interiors to get to the platforms behind. There are side entrances as well. Unlike St Pancras, there is no virtuoso trainshed beyond the terminus building, though the long interlinked iron-and-glass canopies are serviceable enough. The main terminus building was the public concourse and where the money was spent, and lavishly so.

As for Stevens, he left four years before it was completed (upon which he was paid a 5,000 rupee bonus by the Great Indian Peninsular Railway Company, the

The vaulted ticket hall more than rivals that of London's St Pancras Station (dating from 1868).

equivalent of more than £54,000 today). He enjoyed a flourishing career in the city he had come to love. Towards the end of his life – cut short by malaria in 1900 – he designed an actual maharajah's palace in Mehsanah in much the same style, which exists to this day. His engineer colleague Raosaheb Vaidya went on to design the city's extravagantly decorated Taj Mahal Hotel, opened in 1903 after his death. Stevens also added to the surroundings of Victoria Terminus, designing another of the city's great Victorian set pieces right opposite: the 77-metre-tall Municipal Corporation Buildings (1884–93), home of the city council, with a central tower and dome even more ambitious than that of the station. It is possible that, had he remained in England, he could have become one of the most famous architects of his generation. Then again, perhaps he needed the extraordinary stimulus, opportunities and talented colleagues of India in order to achieve his potential.

1 See Michael Satow and Roy Desmond, *Railways of the Raj*, 1980.

Fiat Tagliero Service Station

Asmara, Eritrea, 1938

ARCHITECT: GIUSEPPE PETAZZI (1907–2001)

STYLE: FUTURIST/STREAMLINE MODERNE

Grounded but ready for take-off: the 15-metre canopies of the Fiat Tagliero garage strongly resemble wings.

Petazzi, it is said, had to pull a gun to make sure this little masterpiece was built the way he intended. Nobody else in the Italian Fascist colonial enclave of Asmara at the time believed that its 15-metre wings could be self-supporting: local officials insisted they should be propped at the ends and at first they were. The story varies: in one version Petazzi threatened his builder with the gun, in another he stood on one of the wings and threatened to kill himself unless the supports were removed.

Such drama, but as a talented architect-engineer he knew his cantilevered structure – one where such long projections are safely counterbalanced – was just fine. There are two rows of six pillars like wing struts each side to provide stability, tucked in tight alongside the centre. These connect to six tapering roof beams running from one side to the other, so the whole structure is locked together. The little garage has shrugged off time, neglect and war damage and is now privately owned, but it is officially protected as a heritage asset along with other contemporary buildings dating from this European intrusion into Africa.

It might seem quixotic to choose such a tiny building to represent motor transport, but the filling station/garage was for a long time one of the most numerous and familiar building types on earth and is only now being challenged by more diffuse electric charging networks. This one was built in the years when car ownership was an elitist affair, especially in this part of Africa.

It resembles a stubby monoplane poised for take-off, so the imagery is all wrong for ground-based transport. Various airports in the inter-war period, including Birmingham in England, had spawned winged buildings in this manner to shelter arriving and departing planes, so perhaps Petazzi saw this as a calling card for future airport clients. He appears to have been influenced by the Italian Futurism movement of just before the First World War which glorified the architectural and artistic potential of power production and transport, although he was only a child at the time. This he blended with the Streamline Moderne of later years, which was an aspect of art deco – more expressive, more decorated, less functionalist than mainstream modernism. Moderne provides a licence for strictly unnecessary folderols.

Its delicacy is made possible by its refined structural engineering, apparent from above.

In fact, this building is highly practical as well. Those broad wings provided the necessary shelter from sun and rain in this mild but drought-prone tropical climate. Beneath the wings, which extend backwards behind the central building, vehicles could fill up and be worked on. The relative lack of columns to collide with is a virtue in this context. The central section, like the control tower of an airport, contained the garage's office on the upper level and the payment counter and shop down below. Between the floors, a continuation of the 'wings' forms a canopy running round the nose of the building to provide extra cover. The metal-framed glazing is not quite a modernist ribbon, being given narrow vertical panes, the better to wrap round the tight curve of the frontage but continued along the flat sides as well.

So, what was a simple enough brief – there is not a lot of complexity to a garage/filling station – in Petazzi's hands yielded maximum aesthetic results. It is a tiny landmark building, surmounted with a nicely proportioned tower, crowned with twin flagpoles. The names of the Fiat motor company and the garage owner – Tagliero – form part of the architecture, which has already been restored once, in 2003.

It was built at a convulsive moment in the history of African colonisation. In 1889 Italy had taken over the various existing kingdoms of the region that found themselves strategically placed on the shipping lanes leading to the then-new Suez Canal. Their regional governors started to re-plan Asmara as a European-style capital between 1913 and 1916 on essentially apartheid lines: the south and west of the expanding city was for Europeans only, although the centre was allowed to be mixed. This policy was reinforced when Fascist dictator Benito Mussolini (1883–1945) came to power in Italy in 1922, and in 1933 he declared that there should be a new 'European Zone' built there. He used his Eritrean colony as a launchpad to invade neighbouring Ethiopia in 1935 and Asmara became the manufacturing centre of what was, briefly, imperial Italian East Africa, regarded by Mussolini as part of his new Roman Empire.

Building began apace according to a 1938 masterplan by Vittorio Cafiero (1901–1981), expanding the earlier one. For whatever reason, the dominant style came to be an art deco-ish Moderne. Unlike Hitler, Mussolini did not reject modernism in favour of neoclassicism, but in Italy it was kept fairly austere. In this colony, however, a freer style, to some extent adapted to the climate, prevailed.

It was a brief and unusual architectural experiment: when the Second World War came, British troops drove out the Italians as early as 1941 and administered Eritrea and Ethiopia until the start of the 1950s. Then came an uneasy federation between the two countries until Ethiopia's Emperor Haile Selassie (1892–1975) annexed Eritrea in 1962, ushering in a 30-year war made even grimmer by famine. Independence only finally came in 1993, although, at the time of writing, Eritrea is ruled by a one-party militaristic state with a seeming president for life.

Against extraordinary odds, therefore, but no doubt helped by attention and money being directed elsewhere, this late-1930s Italian enclave survived, its boulevards and grand cinemas well-used. Its merits as a remarkable part of relatively recent history are recognised, not least by UNESCO. This little garage would be an unlikely survival in most places, but here, existing buildings are not lightly thrown away. It may be turned into an architecture centre: in its curious way it could almost be a pavilion at the Venice Biennale, so it might suit that role well. It awaits a new generation of Eritrean architects and conservationists to emerge.

Washington Dulles International Airport

Washington, DC, USA, 1958–62; extended 1996

ARCHITECT: EERO SAARINEN (1910–1961)

STYLE: MODERN EXPRESSIONIST

The original Dulles Airport Terminal, now lengthened in an identical style.

It all looks so simple. Just a single, large, upward-swooping aerofoil roof, an obvious and gracefully achieved metaphor for flight. So many of the world's airports since have copied this model. Dulles Airport Terminal in Washington, DC was designed to handle the new breed of jet airliners at a time when the jet age was still very young and piston-engined Lockheed Super Constellations ruled the long-distance routes. It has proved to be one of the world's most durable and adaptable airport buildings.

Finnish-born architect Eero Saarinen came to America with his family in 1923. The ability to create extraordinary transport buildings was clearly in his blood. His father Eliel (1873–1950) was also a famous architect, winning the competition to design Helsinki's Central Railway Station in 1904 (finished 1919), a national showpiece with a remarkable central arch flanked by giant pairs of statues holding spherical lamps. That composition is completed by a mighty offset clocktower. It was coming second in another high-profile competition, for the skyscraper HQ of the *Chicago Tribune* newspaper in 1922, that gave Eliel his calling card to America. His son Eero joined his father in business towards the end of the latter's career and then – in the decade until his own untimely death – blossomed into a remarkably original modernist architect, rejecting the functionalist International Style for something far richer and more expressive.

The younger Saarinen specialised in wide-spanning structures and designed two extraordinary airport buildings, the other being the TWA Flight Center (1956–62) at New York's Idlewild – later John F. Kennedy – Airport. That building has a structure of interlocking shells that made Saarinen, as a judge for the Sydney Opera House competition at the time, see a kindred spirit in Danish architect Jørn Utzon (1918–2008), whose winning design he championed (see p. 173).

But the TWA terminal was designed to be complete in itself. As passenger numbers and facilities increased, it could not grow with them and it is now a hotel foyer. In contrast, Washington Dulles (named after President Eisenhower's Secretary of State John Foster Dulles) is an open proposition. Saarinen designed it with future expansion in mind, at both ends. In the early years this seemed hopelessly optimistic as the airport was slow to attract custom. Saarinen's two-level terminal, over 180 metres long by 60 metres wide, was at first echoingly empty. As the air industry expanded, it had plenty of capacity to absorb the passengers. Finally, in 1996 Saarinen's far-sighted plan came to fruition and the terminal was 'stretched' approximately 100 metres at each end, exactly to his original design. You have to look very carefully to see the joins. Thus stretched, its outward-leaning colonnade is now 31 bays long, each bay with its concave glazed wall 12 metres across, with a half-bay overhang at each glazed end. It runs east–west, meaning that the loftier glazed side faces north, away from the runways.

The whole immense roof is a suspended catenary structure, like fabric lightly tensioned between leaning poles. Saarinen and his engineers designed it to look that way too: the tapering angled columns do not just rise to meet the edge of the roof, instead passing through holes in the canopy, then curving back to delicately grasp its edge. It is an act of architectural and engineering showmanship. Further refinement consists of a curving row of piercings in the canopy above each bay, echoing the geometry of the curving glazed walls. Inside, there are no columns in this immense volume: it is the ultimate flexible space and so has been easy to reconfigure on multiple occasions.

Modern though it seems with its up-up-and-away roof and huge areas of glazing, there is one thing that the original terminal did not do: plug itself directly into planes via air bridges. This was quite deliberate. Early jets were very noisy, emitting high-pressure blast and fumes. Designers hadn't figured out how best to handle them close to buildings, especially as their numbers grew. So Saarinen came up with an ingenious solution, the 'mobile lounge', and promoted it in a film made by his friends and former colleagues Charles (1907–1978) and Ray Eames (1912–1988). Made by Chrysler with the Budd Company, each mobile lounge was 16 metres long, 5 metres wide and just over 5 metres tall. Each could take up to 102 people. You would walk on through doors on the airside of the

The roof is hung and tensioned between rows of outward-leaning columns, giving a sense of weightlessness.

main terminal building, most of you would sit down, and the lounge would trundle off to your 707 or DC-8 or Comet parked at a safe distance. At the plane, the lounge would rise off its chassis like a lift, bringing you up to the level of the plane doors, which it would connect to via a deck. With later variants for bigger, widebody planes, this system continues to be used for outfield departures. In consequence of this original design decision, Saarinen's Dulles terminal stands pure, unsullied by sprouting tubing. Standing right behind, on the airside, is his control tower, distinctly pagoda-like and providing the vertical element in his composition. In that sense it is not so very different from the clocktower on his father's railway terminus in Helsinki 40 years prior.

In the end, however, this idea was not to be the future. The direct plug-in passenger tube returned and, where the plane is parked remotely, passengers generally just take a conventional bus, climbing stairs to board the plane.

Inside, not a single column interrupts the space of the expanded concourse.

Saarinen's concept of the mobile lounge as a detachable, adjustable chunk of real building was beguiling but in truth never fully realised. Today, Dulles has opted for an underground shuttle connecting the original terminal to later ones.

In his early days as an architect in the 1950s, Frank Gehry (b.1929; see Disney Hall, p. 176) worked for architect William Pereira (1909–1985) on the 1958 iteration of Los Angeles Airport. Even then, in the days before intense airport security, he recalled in an interview in 2003, airports were becoming fiendishly complex propositions and he and his colleagues were wrestling with them all. 'Then all of a sudden Saarinen did this very simple thing and blew us all out of the water.'[1]

1 Interview with the author at Bard College, New York, April 2003. See also Hugh Pearman, *Airports: A Century of Architecture*, 2004.

Yokohama International Port Terminal Yokohama, Japan, 1995–2002

ARCHITECTS: FOREIGN OFFICE ARCHITECTS (FARSHID MOUSSAVI (B.1965) AND ALEJANDRO ZAERA-POLO (B.1963))

STYLE: DIGI-TECH

This is another story of two young architects catapulted to stardom with a famous competition win (see Pompidou Centre, p. 148). An early digital-age building at a time when most architecture was still drawn by hand, a fusion of transport terminal with landscaped public space in Japan's second largest city, it also demonstrates what an international occupation architecture can be.

Iranian-born Farshid Moussavi and Spanish-born Alejandro Zaera-Polo, having trained respectively in the UK and Spain, met in America at the end of the 1980s when both were doing master's degrees at Harvard University's Graduate Design School. They went on to work in the architectural hothouse of Rem Koolhaas's radical firm OMA in Rotterdam (see CCTV Headquarters, Beijing, p. 92), got married and set up their own practice in London in 1993. The name they chose for it – Foreign Office Architects (FOA) – was their wry acknowledgment of their diverse backgrounds.

Very soon they entered and, against the odds, won the competition for Yokohama's enormous new international shipping terminal: there were more than 660 entries. Yokohama is a teeming port city at the south-eastern end of the megalopolis surrounding the deep-water Tokyo Bay. This was to be the complete rebuilding of the existing late nineteenth-century Ōsanbashi Pier, an enormous task. Moussavi and Zaera-Polo moved to Japan for the eight years it took to bring to fruition. They had barely turned 30 when they won: architecture is a tough profession with a long training in which you are considered young if you are under 40.

A shipping terminal combined with a place of public promenade, the uses intertwining.

The lozenge-shaped cross-section of the building informs the architecture at varying scales throughout.

With youth comes nerve. What they set out to do was test a theory in real time and full scale: could they generate the design for such a building like this entirely from its circulation pattern of people and vehicles? At the same time, could they fuse a large private covered space (the part where vehicles come and go and passengers are processed) with an even larger public open space on top of it, with water all around and large boats, from cruise ships to excursion boats, docking alongside? 'We had been involved in the past in designing transportation buildings and we were very interested in them precisely because of the brutal limitations they have', the pair wrote once the project was successfully built.[1] Chief of these brutal limitations – and this applies to all transport buildings – is indeed circulation. Certain areas just have to be given over to certain functions for the rapid and efficient movement of people and vehicles. 'Usually a transportation building works as an input-output device, with very clear orientation: departures and arrivals. We were more interested in exploring the possibility of a transportation infrastructure that could operate less as a gate, as a limit, and more as a field of movements...'[2] The couple looked at conventional piers – you walk straight along them to the end, you either get on a boat there or you walk straight back, how boring. Why not devise a looping circulation system instead? In fact, multiple, interlaced loops?

Their second design move was to avoid making an 'icon', a landmark. They wanted nothing that would stand out on the skyline. They didn't want it to look like a gateway or a significant object at all. This was to be an anti-Sydney Opera House. The building was to be as flat as possible, to seem to be nothing more than an area of ground that would somehow be able to process thousands of people, cars and ship movements all year round. It is a very big object, 450 metres long, 70 metres wide and up to 15 metres high. A building squashed flat, perhaps, but on this scale not so flat as to rule out cavernous spaces inside.

It is a steel-framed, column-free double-decker arrangement. Its cross-section, visible at the ends, is lozenge-shaped. Down below under cover is a 400-car parking lot, and all the facilities needed for arrival and departure, customs, immigration and quarantine: there is an immense main hall with origami-like pleated vaults, a noble space with a no doubt intentional belly-of-the-whale feel to it.

The folded-plate vaulting of the main passenger hall, a noble space.

Up on top, meanwhile, is an urban park, highly geometric, arranged on all manner of interconnecting levels with multiple forking paths. Mostly taking the form of boardwalk timber decking but including grassed areas, it is an undulating landscape, reminiscent of wind-sculpted sand dunes and very tricky to design: the architects called an early design attempt 'a lasagne of warped surfaces'.[3] All around its edges run the flat wharfs for the ships to dock. As at air terminals, moveable covered walkways extend out from the sides of the building to meet the ships: domestic one side, international the other.

Obsessing about the details as good architects tend to do, FOA made the glazing of the sides as frameless and recessive as possible, to keep clean lines. There are kilometres of balustrading on the top deck, which had to be delicate: they were designed with minimal V-shaped supports and metal mesh inspired by fishermen's nets. Surface materials are few and good: timber, glass, metal.

The worlds of the Sunday-afternoon family stroll and of travellers coming and going cannot intersect much, both for security and customs reasons. As at an airport, you are in a different realm once through passport control or (for domestic journeys) the ticket gate. But long gentle ramps connect the levels so there is visual contact: you can wave. There is also a public hall overlooking the sea at the end.

The creative and personal relationship of Moussavi and Zaera-Polo did not survive beyond 2009: they went their separate ways with their own firms and academic posts and that was the end of the FOA phenomenon. While it lasted, the collaboration burned very brightly. The Yokohama International Port Terminal was one of architecture's significant moments – as with the Pompidou Centre or Walt Disney Hall (see p. 176) – when new technology made it possible to design and build in a way never done before.

1 Albert Ferre Losa and Michael Kubo (eds), *Phylogenesis: FOA's Ark*, 2003.
2 Ibid.
3 Ibid.

Museums

In 1683 Elias Ashmole (1617–1692) – English lawyer, state official, astrologer, natural historian and antiquarian – supervised the packing and dispatch of 26 large wooden chests from his home in Lambeth, to travel by barge up the River Thames from London to Oxford, where he had scholarly connections with the university. The river navigation was primitive and prone to delay at the whim of watermill owners, but the rutted, bandit-prone roads between the two cities were worse. The chests contained the collection that would form the basis of what was the world's first purpose-built public museum.

That museum – the Ashmolean – was based on the collection of Ashmole's Lambeth neighbour John Tradescant the Younger (1608–1662), who had continued his father's work as a botanist and collector of 'rarities' from around the known world: some real (a stuffed dodo from Mauritius), some fanciful (a piece of the True Cross and the egg of a Phoenix). The Tradescants displayed their collection in a fashionable 'cabinet of curiosities' that was more extensive than most, and their house with its many natural history specimens became known as 'Tradescant's Ark'. Unusually, it was open to the paying public at sixpence a time.

Ashmole had catalogued the 'Ark'; the younger Tradescant had bequeathed it to him and he in turn gifted it to Oxford University. The collection was given on the condition that the University construct a building in which to house it. This they duly did, adding their own material and, significantly, making it a public building. Possibly designed by Sir Christopher Wren, although quite likely not, it was ready five years later when Ashmole's precious chests arrived by wagon from the wharf. This proto-museum building was derived from the familiar form of a large house, precisely because it was in a domestic setting such as the Tradescants' that such 'curiosities' were originally shown. That first building can still be seen today on Broad Street, immediately to the right of Wren's Sheldonian Theatre. It is now the Museum of the History of Science since the expanding Ashmolean moved in 1845 to its present home in a refined neoclassical building on Beaumont Street, designed by the architect Charles Cockerell (1788–1863).

Although the Ashmolean was the first purpose-built public museum, collecting and displaying artefacts is a human instinct that far pre-dates its construction. Wealthy private collectors in Renaissance Italy began to make galleries to display their paintings and sculptures in the sixteenth century (see the Uffizi in Florence, p. 140). In 1539 one collector, Paolo Giovio (1483–1552),

Interior of Lina Bo Bardi's São Paulo Museum of Art, Brazil, opened in 1968. Within this enormous, clear-span space, works of art are displayed on sheets of glass set in concrete blocks.

called his collection in Como a *Musaeum*, a term meaning 'home of the muses', which dates back to the library in ancient Alexandria. It was only later that 'museum' came to mean a building rather than its contents, while 'gallery' came about because that was the name often given to the long rooms of grand houses where sculpture came to be displayed. By extension, a gallery is a room in any kind of museum, whereas in Europe it also means the complete building, housing art rather than artefacts. North America uses 'museum' for both.

Museums and galleries today are among the most prestigious commissions that any architect can receive: places reflecting the glory of their contents. Lina Bo Bardi's (1914–1992) São Paulo Museum of Art (1957–68) in Brazil is conceived as a civic space as well as one of cultural enrichment. We visit such places to see objects that have a strong cultural and rarity value, and which can convey an extraordinary amount of information about a person, place, event, time or technique. We go because we are in search of original examples of beauty, skill and knowledge. We go because curators have gathered works from around the world, which are seldom, if ever, seen together outside of special exhibitions, and we remember that experience. And we go because often the place itself – the container and display medium for the objects – is a high-value object that we can appreciate and enjoy.

The early museums housed mixed collections of everything deemed rare and valuable: books, objects (both man-made and natural) and art. A library was often also a museum and vice versa, just as today's 'presidential libraries' combine public exhibition with archives. In some areas, specialisation crept in – fine art and sculpture in one kind of museum, historical artefacts in another. Later, objects were further categorised by period or type: so, natural history, anthropology, craft, design and science became separated out, first into their own sections, then into their own buildings. Museums exist of single artists and people, of social history, of political movements, of place, of gender.

Nor is it even necessary for the objects collected to have any great age: a new museum of modern art, say, can be generated from living artists. Science and industry museums are often 'hands-on' – we operate equipment in order to understand it. Many traditional museums now make it a point to collect from the present as well as from the past, which means making some interesting judgement calls as to what will be deemed important in years to come.

As this building type developed, architects began to introduce innovations – natural indirect daylighting from above for picture galleries arrived in the early nineteenth century (see Dulwich Picture Gallery, p. 144) and while it was soon commonplace to protect delicate museum objects from too much light, it was only in the later twentieth century that interior climate controls for heat, light and humidity became more widespread. Gradually, the buildings became largely windowless, inward-looking places, both to control light and to provide more display space. Today, windows framing strategic views out are making a comeback. Meanwhile, the desirability of having a museum café or restaurant became apparent in the mid-nineteenth century. Henry Cole (1808–1882) of London's new Victoria and Albert Museum included a tea room and, later, larger restaurants, as he had noticed how successful these were at the Great Exhibition of 1851 in the nearby Crystal Palace.

Permanent collections aside, the great museums of the world are forever exchanging objects for temporary exhibitions, a process which often includes conservation as a quid pro quo for the loan. Behind the scenes at the museum, the conservation spaces are akin to laboratory complexes. The great public museums also need to have industrial-standard goods-intake, processing and dispatch facilities. To keep the people coming and the tills ringing, a top museum will have enough gallery space to be able to open the next temporary exhibition while the previous one is being dismantled. The existence of public museums thus guarantees, or at least greatly extends, the lives of the precious objects and gets them seen in a way that the private collections from which they originated did not.

However, museums can also be controversial. How did they acquire their collections? Were other cultures ransacked? How did the donors and philanthropists paying for the museums come by their money? Is acknowledgement of past wrongs enough, or is restitution required? This argument will not go away, especially where it concerns the museums which are effectively the repositories of vanished empires and genocidal regimes. A rebalancing of where, and what kind of, objects are housed in museums is thus underway. With original objects increasingly being returned to their places of origin, precision-made copies – previously avoided for anything other than artefacts which could not be moved – have become much more acceptable. This does not change the power of the curated collection. Museums offer a concentrated awareness of what we are capable of as humans beyond the everyday.

The Uffizi Florence, Italy, 1560–83

ARCHITECTS: GIORGIO VASARI (1511–1574) AND BERNARDO BUONTALENTI (1531–1608)

STYLE: MANNERIST

It is not unknown for an office building to become an art gallery, but it is one of those curious architectural facts that one of the *first* office buildings – the Uffizi in Florence, after which the type is named – also became, after two centuries, the first public art gallery, which it has remained ever since.

Giorgio Vasari designed the Uffizi for his client Cosimo I de' Medici (1519–1574), Grand Duke of Tuscany. Cosimo wanted a building to house the Florentine magistrates (the officials in charge of the city-state's industry and trade) and soon also the administration of the Grand Duchy itself. It was an annexe to the Palazzo Vecchio, Florence's centre of power. Vasari was also an artist and critic and he understood how the city was used by its people. Thus he designed the building in two long narrow halves either side of an open street, with covered arcades at their bases. Treated this way the street becomes an elongated *cortile* or courtyard, open at its north end where it branches off at one corner of the

The central *cortile* of the Uffizi, looking south towards the inhabited triumphal arch, with the river beyond.

Piazza della Signoria, and semi-enclosed at its southern end via a Venetian-style Doric triple archway where it meets the bank of the Arno. Two linking levels above this arch join the ends of the wings.

Vasari made the most of the opportunities to exploit perspective set up by his plan. This far into the Renaissance, architects were starting to have fun with the motifs of classical architecture, and so 'Mannerism' – in which the elements are juggled and exaggerated – was born. Vasari designed the two halves of his building with pronounced eaves and cornices on three levels, the cornices projecting round the inset columns of the facades. This strongly rhythmic linearity leads your eyes straight to the focal point of the southerly arch.

At a higher level in two senses, it does not end there. Rulers of the times were constantly in danger of assassination and Cosimo wanted to be able to move safely and discreetly between his workplace of the Palazzo Vecchio and his family home, the Palazzo Pitti south of the river. The Uffizi building lay on this route and so he commanded the making of a private link, literally a safe passage. Built in just five months in 1565, the 'Vasari Corridor' is a truly remarkable thing: a high-level enclosed walkway, kinking this way and that as it proceeds from the Palazzo Vecchio, passes through the Uffizi gallery, pops out of it and runs along the north bank of the Arno, takes a sharp left to continue right across the Ponte Vecchio, clambers round the outside of the Manelli Tower, grafts itself onto the church of Santa Felicita, punches through and past various houses and finally terminates, via the Boboli Gardens, in the Palazzo Pitti. The Vasari Corridor is a kilometre long and free of any unruly citizens or potential assassins. To keep the air sweet, Cosimo had the smelly butchers' shops on the Ponte Vecchio removed and replaced with goldsmiths.

Art, always present, became formalised when Francesco I (1541–1587) succeeded his father in 1574, the same year that Vasari died. Vasari's successor architects, including the aptly named Buontalenti, designed private galleries on the top-floor loggia of the building for the Medici collection of painting and sculpture: something made easier by the fact that Vasari had designed an adaptable, iron-reinforced structure with no fixed room sizes. The heart of this treasury of art and objects became the lavishly decorated octagonal 'Tribune' gallery of 1581–3 designed by Buontalenti. The most valuable pieces in the collection were, and still are, displayed here.

Under successive Medici rulers, more and more of the Uffizi was given over to house their art until 1737, when the dynasty, its authority crumbling and with no direct heir, expired. The widow of the last Medici Grand Duke was Princess Anna Maria Luisa (1667–1743), who bequeathed all the family possessions – art and treasures included – to the State of Tuscany on the proviso that it must remain in Florence 'as an ornament of the State, for public utility and to attract the curiosity of foreigners.'[1] Thus, in 1769, the gallery was opened to the public:

other European nations later duly followed this example of a public art museum. Today, the galleries in the fine rooms on the *piano nobile* and loggia of the Uffizi with their magnificent ceiling frescoes, the renovated Vasari Corridor with its collection of self-portraits, and the Palazzo Pitti it connects to, are all treasuries of art and sculpture, both in themselves and in what they contain.

This is all evidence of the Renaissance approach to art and life, the adaptability of buildings over time and, of course, the power of patronage. It also demonstrates the power of power itself. At the centre point of the Vasari Corridor atop the Ponte Vecchio, the original small windows suddenly give way to a row of large ones. These were inserted on the orders of Mussolini in order to impress Hitler on a visit in 1939. The Führer was awed enough by the treasures and architecture of the Uffizi and the bridge to order his generals not to destroy the Ponte Vecchio when they later retreated from the advancing Allied forces. It was the only Florentine bridge to be spared.

1 The 1737 'Family Pact' of Princess Anna Maria Luisa, cited in the Uffizi's online history, www.uffizi.it/en/the-uffizi/history.

Inside, the gallery works are displayed in a somewhat quixotic hang, with paintings interspersed among the sculptures.

Dulwich Picture Gallery

London, UK, 1811–14

ARCHITECT: SIR JOHN SOANE (1753–1837)

STYLE: STRIPPED NEOCLASSICAL

The west side of the gallery with its central mausoleum, rebuilt after wartime damage.

Some wealthy people finance an art gallery, some want to be commemorated in a mausoleum, but few find themselves magnificently interred among the pictures. It is fortunate for us, and for architecture generally, that Sir Peter Francis Bourgeois (1753–1811), Royal Academician and art collector, achieved exactly this. He and his two best friends ended up in what became the prototype of the modern art gallery. Its exquisite restraint, with classical details stripped back to the minimum, is admired by traditionalists and modernists alike.

In 1807 Bourgeois had inherited the art collection of his friend and business partner, the art dealer Noel Desenfans (1741–1807). In his will, Bourgeois bequeathed this and his own collection to his friend's widow, Margaret Desenfans (1731–1813). Margaret knew of Bourgeois's desire for the collection to go on public display and, honouring her friend's wishes, gave the collection to Dulwich College in south London. Dulwich College also had an art collection and Bourgeois had wanted the three collections to be displayed together. His will included £2,000 for the purpose of refurbishing the galleries at Dulwich College. Margaret also donated £4,000 to what became a much larger project.

Bourgeois's friend, John Soane, was his pre-selected architect. Soane had previously designed Bourgeois a mausoleum for Desenfans, built next door to

The sequence of top-lit galleries became the inspiration for other art galleries and museums worldwide.

their home in Charlotte (now Hallam) Street, in what was then bohemian North London. Bourgeois, Desenfans and Margaret had all lived there together. It is possible that the idea of the Dulwich mausoleum within the gallery building came from Soane himself, who discussed it with the dying Bourgeois. In any case, there was no delay: the day following Bourgeois's death, Soane was on site in Dulwich, measuring up.

A further oddity was that Soane was asked to include six almshouses (charitable homes for the elderly) for a number of women who were already housed in a wing of the college. As for the collection itself, that was conventional but valuable: the men had originally assembled most of it to make a national collection for King Stanislaus II Augustus of Poland (r.1764–1795) who unfortunately fled into exile in Russia in 1795 before taking delivery or paying them. As neither the Russian nor British governments were interested in taking it on, this left them with a lot of Old Masters on their hands.

Everything about this story is strange and that includes the architect and his highly distinctive architecture. Soane's work is more cerebral than the more conventional output of the day and often has a somewhat detached, unearthly feel to it. The result of the curious mixed-use commission in Dulwich was, however, a triumphant success. Soane designed not only a little jewel of a building on a very tight budget but also invented a building type: the top-lit art gallery. The handling of daylight – especially indirect light – was Soane's speciality and his particular genius, evident on his buildings ranging from private houses to the Bank of England. Dulwich brings this talent into the service of art. Pretty much every art museum designer since has gone on a pilgrimage to Dulwich.

The gallery sits in a small park next to the original school and chapel. It is 49 metres long on a single lofty level. Its design is at its most original on its west front, where you find three projecting wings – one at each end plus the mausoleum in the centre rising to a lantern tower with curved roof. Soane later chose a variation of this form for his own tomb in St Pancras churchyard, while in 1924 the design was borrowed directly by architect Giles Gilbert Scott for his classic red British telephone box.

Between the wings on the west side Soane tucked his replacement almshouses, later converted to extra gallery space. Behind those you see the higher roofscape of the main run of galleries with their glazed lanterns. The way Soane juggled these elements – expressing them as separate pieces within a greater whole – is masterly, especially given that he was using humble yellow stock brick as his main material, with minimal decoration and very restrained white Portland stone dressings.

The entrance is on the eastern side, where what you mostly see are Edwardian and late-1930s extensions by Edwin Thomas Hall (1851–1923) and Harry Goodhart-Rendel (1887–1959), both men deferring to Soane so successfully that most people assume these parts are by him. The upshot is that the expanded plan of the gallery became much more symmetrical. The way Soane had left it, a tall arched arcade (later obliterated by the extensions) ran along the east facade with an entrance door directly into the central gallery. Later buildings of 1999 by Soane aficionado Rick Mather (1937–2013), including a restaurant, form a deferential low, bricky entrance cluster to the park.

Inside the main building, it is still Soane's original sequence of galleries – square at each end and in the centre, with two oblong galleries either side of that – which commands attention. Each gallery opens into the next via a tall round-topped arch, forming a long perspectival sequence. The way the walls angle in at high level to support the (much modified) roof lanterns is a pleasure in itself. It is here and in the smaller east galleries that the treasures of the collection are displayed, while temporary exhibitions tend to be in the almshouse galleries.

And then there is the mausoleum, which is separate from the main circulation but opening off it, a mysterious presence bathed in dim light through Soane's favourite yellow glass. His minimalised neoclassical detailing here reaches a peak of refinement. Between the polished dark red Doric columns, beneath a shallow plaster dome, the three sarcophagi of the original friends and donors are gathered, as if in conversation. But in a final, perhaps apt, twist, their bones are all jumbled up. This was the result of the gallery being half-demolished on its western flank in 1944 by the blast from a V-1 flying bomb which hit the road outside. Fortunately, the art collection had been evacuated to Wales.

Even at a time of acute building material shortages in the immediate post-war years, the Dulwich Picture Gallery was treated as a cultural priority and – after much argument – pieced back together pretty much as it was, reopening in 1953 with a new eastern entrance porch (again very Soanian). No doubt this kind of reconstruction would be done more carefully today – look closely and you can spot the rebuilt areas – but despite this and the earlier extensions and alterations down the years, the spirit of Soane, Bourgeois and the Desenfans survives along with one of the great buildings of the world.

Pompidou Centre Paris, France, 1971–7

ARCHITECTS: RENZO PIANO (B.1937), RICHARD ROGERS (1933–2021) AND GIANFRANCO FRANCHINI (1938–2009) WITH ENGINEER PETER RICE (1935–1992)

STYLE: HIGH TECH, 'BOWELLIST'

'Ciao, vecchio!' began the voice on the phone from Genoa. 'Hello, old man! Are you sitting down?' It was Renzo Piano (aged 33) calling his friend Richard Rogers (aged 37) in London to tell him some incredible news.[1] Their little, impoverished firm of hippyish architects had just won the biggest international architecture competition of the day, for the French national arts centre or 'mediathèque' in central Paris. There had been 681 entries and they were the most unlikely of winners. Rogers had not wanted to take part in the first place but had been outvoted by Piano and Rogers's ex-wife Su (b.1939), herself a partner in the firm. Piano recruited fellow Genovese architect Franchini to help with the competition design.

What they built over the next six years (on the site of 1930s slum clearances used as a surface car park) marks a defining moment in modern architecture. Nothing like it had been seen previously, and with a few notable exceptions – mostly by Rogers – not much like it was seen subsequently. It is the most extreme example of the High Tech architectural style, which mostly consists of buildings that do indeed celebrate their technology and the way they are put together, but not usually in such an exuberant, even postmodernist, way. The term 'Bowellism', which was coined to describe the Pompidou Centre style of architecture did not really catch on any more than the style itself did, but it more accurately describes the way the building displays all its guts – the pipes and ducts, elevators and escalators that service all large modern buildings – on the outside, rather than hidden away inside. Its bolt-together steel structural frame is equally exposed on the outside, with the glass skin of the building set behind it.

The Pompidou Centre marked something else beyond its maverick, even perverse, styling, however: the arrival of a new generation of architects, and a more lightweight way of building. If the 1960s had been mostly about heavyweight concrete, a strong strand from the 1970s onwards would be component-based clip-together architecture, the parts usually specially made and sourced from manufacturers worldwide.

The building was named after the French President Georges Pompidou, who had commanded its construction in 1969. He had given his blessing to the winning design but died before it was complete. It is a multi-purpose cultural building, which invited a new kind of architecture. It brings together a museum of modern art, a large public library, cinema, auditorium, shops and an adjacent contemporary music centre. To these Rogers and Piano added the ingredient that made the building an enormous popular success: abundant public space inside and out. They devoted a large part of the site to a sloping public piazza. Indeed, around 20 per cent of those who visit do nothing more cultural than to take the ride on the escalators in their transparent tubes, overhanging that piazza and snaking their way across the main facade to the top with its viewing platform. This was a particular mission for the architects, who resisted the lure of monumentalism. They later said: 'We were like schoolchildren, sticking our tongues out at the

A multi-functional cultural building with a unique presence in predominantly low-rise central Paris.

examiners'.[2] Imbued with the spirit of protest that had almost led to a new revolution in France in 1968, their aim was to break down barriers to the public. For its first decades this ride to the top was free, but not since the Pompidou Centre's first big refurbishment at the end of the twentieth century.

The Pompidou Centre – which occupies the space of a conventional long rectangular box very unconventionally – faces the piazza, turning its back on the main street it was built on. That street frontage, however, gives you the full coloured-pipes impact, each colour being a code: blue pipes are air-conditioning ducts, green ones carry water, yellow contain electrics, red signifies people-movement – escalators and elevators. Big, white, metal funnels, distinctly nautical, ventilate a car park beneath the building. It was designed and built in the early 1970s but is very much a product of 1960s thinking in that it was conceived as a flexible, adaptable building that could change its configuration whenever necessary. It has column-free interiors thanks to a system of 48-metre-long steel trusses spanning from side to side, strong enough to take the huge weight of a public library. This, coupled with the fact that all the pipes are on the outside, makes the reconfiguration of the inside spaces relatively straightforward.

Rogers said that they wanted a place 'as free as possible from the constraints of solid architecture'.[3] As with all radical new buildings, the architects could not achieve this alone. Piano and Rogers depended on the Irish engineer Peter Rice of Ove Arup and Partners, the firm that had earlier made the seemingly impossible Sydney Opera House buildable (see p. 173). Rice came up with the tensioned, cross-braced structural system with its characteristic cast-steel 'gerberettes' as linking pieces. This made the vast internal 'shelves' of floors imagined by the architects possible and provide what Rice described as 'a large loose-fit frame where anything could happen'.[4] However, one idea got ditched: originally, the floors were meant to be able to move up and down as well.

A key part of the interior design is the enormous 'forum' area inside the entrance, overlooked by an open gallery, from which people move out, up and

The deeply layered facade is given further dynamism by the escalators snaking across the front.

The main lobby, a covered forum for visitors, was conceived as an extension of the sloping open piazza outside.

down to all the various parts of the building. This lofty civic space might seem a little oppressive at times, with all the exposed pipework overhead: demands on space caused by a height limitation ruled out an atrium or central lightwell. This huge circulation space does, however, anticipate another building type, the large airport terminal halls that both Rogers and Piano later designed, having become two of the most in-demand architects in the world.

The building was controversial, of course: its industrial appearance on the main street with all those pipes led to the inevitable 'oil refinery' jibe. Its immediate and continuing popularity overcame that: more people came to visit this than the Eiffel Tower. Like the Tower, it is as if a very large Expo or World's Fair building has become permanent. Today, the Pompidou Centre has also become an official historic monument, which carries an irony: a building designed to be supremely adaptable (and high-maintenance) is now regarded as aesthetically inviolable. Some of those functional coloured pipes are now purely decorative.

1 Bryan Appleyard, *Richard Rogers: A Biography*, 1986.
2 Piano and Rogers speaking in the 1997 documentary film, 'Le Centre Georges Pompidou', as part of the series 'Architectures – Achievements in Modern Architecture', Films Media Group.
3 Ibid.
4 Peter Rice, *An Engineer Imagines*, 1994.

Ningbo History Museum Zhejiang Province, China, 2004–8

ARCHITECTS: AMATEUR ARCHITECTURE STUDIO (WANG SHU (B.1963) AND LU WENYU (B.1966))

STYLE: SYMBOLIC, 'ARCHITECTURE PARLANTE'

Resembling an ancient fortress, made of the rubble of demolished villages and bamboo-moulded concrete, the Ningbo Museum speaks of the history of its region.

A historical museum in a new part of a city, built out of the rubble of the villages demolished to make way for it: the Ningbo History Museum is a commentary on, and an antidote to, the rapid urbanisation of China in the late twentieth and early twenty-first centuries. It was designed by architects based in the region who are very much not in love with the kind of glossy international super-tower world that now comprises so much of the larger Chinese cities.

Ningbo, a historically important large port city, sits south of Shanghai, where Hangzhou Bay opens into the East China Sea. The large, wealthy industrial centre of Hangzhou at the head of the bay – southern terminus of the extraordinary 1,500-year-old Grand Canal system, which connected it to Beijing some 1200 kilometres away – is where Wang Shu and Lu Wenyu base their studio. They named their firm 'Amateur Architecture' as a tongue-in-cheek way to differentiate themselves from the architects who for decades have been transforming China in its flight from rural life, without any feel for history or context. So it was a considerable coup when in 2004 this resourceful but small outfit won the international competition to build the Ningbo History Museum.

The bamboo-imprinted concrete continues into the cavernous interior.

There is an obvious link between what the museum does – which is to exhibit and interpret the rich history of the city area from Neolithic times some 6,000 years ago through all the dynasties since – and how it is made – which externally is largely out of the recycled bricks and tiles of much older buildings, combined with the bamboo-moulded concrete construction typical of the region. The reference is a clear enough reproach, since the demolition of the old villages took place as a precursor to what was then the latest wave of the southerly expansion of the city. As a result, this building, far from being a historical remnant in the old centre, is placed on a formally planned grid in parkland, part of a new cultural quarter. Here, the architects defiantly placed their museum as a built manifesto of sustainable construction carrying memories of the past.

The imagery is multivalent – in its rough, unexpectedly angled walls you can see a fortress, a ship, mountains and, in the way the recycled materials are organised in colour fields towards the top, distant landscapes of the kind the architects often cite as an inspiration. Wang Shu has described it as 'architecture as mountains', as if it were geological.[1] Within it are architectural interpretations of valleys, caves, lakes and hills, linked by meandering paths and so making an inside-out landscape of its interiors. But the museum is also, in its use of materials that would typically go to landfill or to the foundations of roads, an architecture of salvage. Using found or scavenged materials for buildings is an activity as old as the human race: Wang Shu and Lu Wenyu practise a sustainable form of Chinese vernacular architecture which acts as a commentary on generic international styles. Being a cultural building designed to evoke its subject matter, it can also be regarded as an example of 'architecture parlante' or 'speaking architecture'.

Pierced by many small windows framing particular views, it is strangely scale-less. From the outside you would not know how many levels it contains, but it looks like more than it is. Inside, it is no smoother, the rough tactility of the place continuing on all surfaces, in places daylit from above. You can clamber all over it inside and out, with openings connecting the two. There are, of course, the usual permanent and temporary exhibition zones but – rather like the wholly different 'kit-of-parts' Pompidou Centre in Paris (see p. 148) – it has a purely civic function. It works as a place to promenade or explore in itself, irrespective of its headline function.

At first Wang Shu had wanted to be an artist or a writer, but was also fascinated by his father's carpentry, and on entering architecture, unusually chose to spend a lot of time with construction workers, learning how buildings were made. The couple's first commissions after they set up Amateur Architecture Studio in 1998 were refurbishments and conversions of homes. As their buildings grew larger, the celebration of handicraft continued. They

As you move up within the building, you emerge into broad open spaces and steep slopes recalling hillsides.

tend to refer to all their buildings as 'houses' in the broader sense: everyday, unself-conscious buildings rather than self-consciously 'architectural' ones are their declared aim. Well, up to a point: their cultural and educational buildings in particular, such as this museum, might not be glittering precision-made objects but they have enormous architectural presence, and most certainly stand out from the background.

A perfect building has to stay pristine. A deliberately imperfect one does not. It can crumble and erode and we don't mind. Architects are usually very concerned about the durability of the outer skin of their buildings but here, if it needs to be patched, that would be cheaply done – no shortage of demolition materials, after all – and would merely add to its character, making what is in one sense an artificially aged building into one that is actually visibly ageing.

Is this anti-iconic architecture, then? Not really, but it is a richer kind of iconography. It is seen politically as being true to the illustrious origins of modern China at a time when coincidentally the official attitude towards architecture is moving to a less internationalist approach. Thus, it has become very influential in China among other architects who are paying respect to the merits of the past in both new and restoration projects.

1 'China Today: Wang Shu & Lu Wenyu, Ningbo History Museum', GA Document, 112, 2010.

Smithsonian National Museum of African American History and Culture

Washington, DC, USA, 2009–2016

ARCHITECTS: FREELON ADJAYE BOND + SMITH GROUP (KEY ARCHITECTS SIR DAVID ADJAYE (B.1966) AND PHIL FREELON (1953–2019))

STYLE: SYMBOLIST

A memory of Africa on Washington Mall, signalled by its 'crown' of perforated, bronzed-aluminium cladding.

'I'll never forget watching the Smithsonian National Museum of African American History and Culture rise near the White House, that bold bronze statement in a city of marble, and then having a chance to step inside and feel how this Ghanaian British architect helped tell a uniquely American story', said former American President Barack Obama in 2021. 'That was genius, pure and simple.'[1]

By the generally slow-burning standards of most architecture careers, Sir David Adjaye – Tanzanian-born to a Ghanaian diplomat father, based (at the time of writing) in London, New York and Accra – has had a meteoric rise. His first built project other than one-off houses (mainly for artist friends) was a public library in East London in 2005. Three years later he and his American colleagues won the competition to design this new museum on the last available large plot on Washington's National Mall, the broad stately park flanked with state and cultural buildings and memorials stretching from the Capitol in the east to the Lincoln Memorial in the west.

The museum stands on the key intersection, overlooking the obelisk of the Washington Monument, where an axis of parkland and gardens at right angles to the National Mall leads a short distance north to the White House. This was a

Inside, the feel is more conventional than the exterior suggests, with a glass and steel structure opening the space up visually to its surroundings.

project mooted for nearly a century in various forms and finally realised during Obama's two presidencies. Adjaye, by then in demand internationally, found himself dining at the White House. He had properly arrived.

His experienced collaborator Phil Freelon, Philadelphia-born of African American origin, was himself a relatively rare example of a black architect in a white-dominated profession when he started out. Within the sizeable group of consultants that inevitably attend such big projects, the two of them kept the design concept strikingly intact. Such a building would be unusual for anywhere, but certainly for Washington Mall, lined as it is with the very conservative neoclassical buildings of the city of marble.

Instead, Adjaye gave them a building symbolic of a different culture. Its outward form of three ornate bronze aluminium tiers is inspired by a 1930 sculpture by the artist Olowe of Ise (1873–1938), namely a veranda post carved in the form of a wooden figure wearing a tall tiered headdress. Adjaye, an indefatigable traveller and recorder of cultural artefacts, found it in a museum in Munich. Olowe was of the Yoruba tribe of West Africa, source of the majority of the slaves traded to America. The sculpture is an antidote to the very different columns of the neoclassical buildings of the slave owners. So the very shape of this museum is symbolically highly charged, while its colour recalls the superb bronzes of the ancient Kingdom of Benin, looted by British colonialists when they violently overthrew the kingdom in 1897.

It is not necessary for the casual visitor to the museum to know such references: it is enough that in consequence the resulting building stands out as it does. Adjaye did not want to fit in politely here, even if the height of the building is comparable with the other museums along the Mall. Just one block along from the forbidding abstract-classical facades of the 1964 Smithsonian Museum of American History (which clearly did not tell nearly enough of a key part of the history), he wanted to make a statement. In fact, he wanted the exterior to be of real, solid bronze but the thought of supporting the weight of such massive outward-leaning panels – the angle being the same as the capstone on the Washington Monument – alarmed the risk-averse construction overseers, hence the aluminium compromise. There are always compromises in getting a large cultural – or any – building built.

You enter the museum beneath an enormous, full-width, slightly uptilted canopy on the south side of the building, which extends over a pool, so creating that favourite device of many architects, an 'outdoor room'. Given the queues that often form outside in all weathers, this is a valuable feature. From there you move through to a large entrance atrium, rising over three floors, giving access to the various exhibition levels above and below, and finally you reach the rooftop terrace. Inside, it becomes apparent that within the filigree bronze carapace is a more conventional glass, steel and concrete building, engineered to allow for column-free exhibition spaces. These range from early history and the horrors of slavery at the bottom, to cultural exhibits at the top.

Many museums go for a windowless 'black box' approach to exhibitions, which allows for optimum lighting of, and concentration on, the exhibits, keeping direct daylight away from fragile materials, but at the expense of a certain amount of disorientation: where are you in the building, relative to the outside? This attitude is changing – daylight can be successfully filtered to conservation levels while still allowing you to see out. Here, the exhibitions are largely internalised but views are carefully framed at points throughout the building so as to capture the surrounding monuments – especially the Washington Monument, which acted as a partial spur to the design. The architect's job is, at its most basic, to provide an adaptable container for exhibition design by others, which will change over time. And that is the important thing. Here, however, the architecture of the building itself expresses a great deal of what the museum is about. As with the Ningbo History Museum (see p. 152), it symbolises its subject matter.

1 From President Barack Obama's video message on the occasion of David Adjaye receiving the RIBA Royal Gold Medal for Architecture, 2021.

The geometry and symbolism of the Washington Monument is acknowledged in a framed view.

VIRTVTI AC GENIO
OLYMPICOR ACADEMIA THEATRVM HOC
A FVNDAMENTIS EREXIT
ANN MDLXXXIIII

Performance

There is a tradition dating from the theatre of the Italian Renaissance – which was the first time that theatres had been built in the West since ancient times – that the building itself must be able to represent the whole world. This is the flipside of Shakespeare's 'All the world's a stage'.[1] As a concept, it is logical enough. If, at its best, the power of theatre can transport us to wherever the playwright chooses – even the magical, non-existent 'coast of Bohemia' of Shakespeare's *The Winter's Tale* – then the scenography of the theatre, as well as the set design and lighting, can ease your journey there.

So, Andrea Palladio's Teatro Olimpico (1580–85) in Vicenza, northern Italy, brings the outside world in. Palladio based his theatre on the classical *odeon*, or enclosed theatre, an example of which, with a timber, tent-like roof, was known in Athens as early as 435 BCE. Like the much larger open-air amphitheatres of the time (see Epidauros, p. 164), it has curving tiers of benches focusing on the visual and acoustic sweet spot, along with an architectural 'stage house' behind, to be used during the action. The cloud-dappled, blue sky above in Palladio's theatre is, however, a *trompe l'oeil* painted on the ceiling.

In fact, everything within the theatre plays with reality. If you are inside, but also somehow outside, how is it that the rear of the stage, itself seemingly a building, reveals through its arches city streets lined with other internally lit buildings, stretching away into the distance? This turns out to be a false-perspective, painted plaster-and-timber stage set representing ancient Thebes, designed by Palladio's fellow architect Vincenzo Scamozzi (1548–1616) who took over on the project following Palladio's death in 1580. Dating from the opening production of *Oedipus Rex*, this remarkable set has remained ever since, the supposedly temporary scenery as old as the permanent building housing it.

Shakespeare's equally famous lines, addressed by his Chorus alter ego directly to the audience, discuss the limitations and possibilities of a theatre building as container of worlds:

> Can this cockpit hold
> The vasty fields of France? Or may we cram
> Within this wooden O the very casques
> That did affright the air at Agincourt?'[2]

Of course we may. 'Piece out our imperfections with your thoughts', as the Chorus goes on to say.[3] The form of the building helps, of course: all theatres

The Teatro Olimpico in Vicenza, Italy (opened in 1585), is a thoroughly Renaissance reinterpretation of the buildings of the ancient world and contemporary with Shakespeare's rough timber theatres in London.

since the very first have been designed to direct your view to the action, making the audience–actor connection as direct as possible. The embracing form of the 'wooden O' (see Shakespeare's Globe, p. 167, first built only a few years after Palladio's in Vicenza) took this a step further, bringing the actors and audience into close proximity. This could be the theatre of intimacy as well as spectacle.

For a big, purpose-built theatre or opera house, the architect has to design three different worlds. Audiences inhabit front of house and the auditorium; beyond the stage actors have their own domain, from 'green room' lounge area to changing rooms and rehearsal stages; and finally there is the world of industry. A large theatre – especially a repertory theatre, hosting changing but repeated productions – has elements of the factory about it. Scenery and costumes are made and repaired. Whole sets can be constructed to slide on and off, descend and ascend, and these sets need to be warehoused. Meanwhile, the mechanisms for changes of scenery and vertical movement result in the hard-to-ignore fly tower rising above the stage to erupt through the roof.

For music venues – whether for full symphony orchestras, lavish musicals, rock concerts or opera – the hall must be commensurately large but with everyone, wherever they are seated, able to hear clearly: the architect must work even more hand in hand with the acoustician. For concert halls, an acoustically reliable form is the shoebox shape, as originally derived from the state rooms of palaces. Fan-shaped halls are less good, unless they are Richard Wagner's (1813–1883) Bayreuth (see p. 170). There is much to be said for the more broken-up 'vineyard' configuration, such as Hans Scharoun's (1893–1972) Berlin Philharmonie (1956–63). Here, an audience on various levels surrounds the orchestra rather than seeing and hearing it from a distance. The acoustics of a full house tend to be different from a half-empty one: there are now techniques to make an empty seat of equivalent sound absorbency to a human body.

The architect has to consider varying audience sizes in theatre design, too: not so much for acoustic as for emotional reasons. Playing to a tiny audience in a large, open space is off-putting both for actors and audiences. Traditional, tightly packed, vertically stacked urban theatres with several levels and a stage behind a proscenium arch can flatter the actor: a small audience lining the edge of each level looks almost like a full house. Against that can be set the dramatic power of having an audience surround three sides of the stage ('thrust stage') or all the way round it ('in the round'), though in those cases there is generally no way of concealing how many or few are attending. The tight seven-sided, three-level, in-the-round Royal Exchange Theatre in Manchester, England (1974–6) by designer Richard Negri (1927–1999) and architectural practice Levitt Bernstein manages to achieve both size (800 seats) and intimacy.

With variations, the principles of designing a building for stagecraft apply worldwide. The venerable tradition of the highly stylised Noh theatre in Japan dates back a millennium, first emerging from ritualistic performances at Buddhist temples, later becoming a more secular form of refined entertainment with its gorgeous costumes and masks, precise choreography and music. By the fourteenth century it had assumed the form it takes today. Originally, the audience would have been outside, gathered round a rectangular, roofed stage resembling an open-sided summerhouse, which the actors reached via a raised gangway. Nothing has changed except that this arrangement now sits within a much larger auditorium: the summerhouse is always still there, the rows of audience seating organised to face its two main sides.

Performance buildings can become enslaved by their form and their equipment, which is why, at times, directors and their architects and designers go back to basics and put on the play right there in the barn, or the abandoned factory, or library, or museum. This looser approach is often formalised into the highly adaptable 'black box' theatre, with its adjustable seating or no seating at all, and usually very little by way of props or scenery either. Theatre and church share much, especially this: the buildings can be very grand and expensive but it is the people who make them, and they can go anywhere for the performance and the experience. How that experience is shared and shaped, however – that is what brings the architects and designers into the limelight.

1 Shakespeare, *As You Like It*, Act 2, Scene 7. Thought by some to be the play that opened the new Globe Theatre in 1599.
2 Shakespeare, *The Life of King Henry V*, Prologue, 1599.
3 Ibid.

Theatre at Epidauros

Greece, Fourth Century BCE

ARCHITECT: POLYKLEITOS THE YOUNGER (ACTIVE FOURTH CENTURY BCE)

STYLE: HELLENIC (ANCIENT GREEK CLASSICAL)

Theatres come into existence for all kinds of reasons, be they civic pride, rivalry, or the drive of individuals on a mission (as we see with Wagner's Bayreuth Festspielhaus: see p. 170). In the case of the remarkable theatre of Epidauros on the eastern side of the Peloponnese peninsula of southern Greece, we have a god to thank.

The god, Asklepios, son of Apollo (a multi-talented, radiant role-model), was deity of medicine and healing. The modern symbol of medicine, a staff entwined with snakes, is also Asklepios' logo, since a wise snake taught him much of his knowledge. This knowledge was considerable and powerful: Asklepios could both cure people of their ills and bring them back from the dead. Accordingly, the temples built to Asklepios were places of healing and pilgrimage – remarkably akin to health spas – and one of the main ones, known as an Asklepion, was built in ancient Epidauros, his place of birth. So, Epidauros grew large and populous and needed cultural, as well as religious, buildings to keep everyone happy. By tradition, if not certain fact, Polykleitos the Younger,

Built outwards in two phases by the Greeks and Romans, Epidauros has intriguing acoustics and a superb natural setting.

The entrances to the wings are shown, with the foundations of the largely vanished *skene* or stage house visible bottom right.

son of a famous sculptor, provided both. Once he had done his cylindrical *tholos* at the Asklepion, with its circlets of delicate exterior and interior columns (purpose unknown, possibly a tomb), he turned to the theatre.

Amphitheatres had become quite the thing since the flowering of Greek drama, both tragedy and comedy, in the hands of playwrights from Aeschylus (c.525–c.456 BCE) to Aristophanes (c.446–c.386 BCE). Their makeshift stages, often no more than a cart drawn up in a city square, next became formalised into what we can regard as one of the earliest forms of permanent theatre design (the other being the much smaller covered theatres known as *odeons*, thought to have been for music performances). The great increase in scale of the amphitheatre suggests that the nature of the productions was changing. Architects had to respond to this: lacking artificial amplification, how was everyone to hear?

The theatre at Epidauros had space for 5,000 people on its curving stone benches, arranged in 34 tiers in a bowl set into the hillside, so the sightlines were superb. Two centuries later, the Romans added another 21 tiers, following the same exact geometry to fan out much wider. This raised the capacity to some 14,000, which is much larger than any modern theatre or concert hall but well short of a typical modern enclosed arena.

These large Ancient Greek/Roman theatres (broadly similar in form to each other, like the temples of the period) were not enclosed and there are no surviving examples of acoustic-amplification aids, though everything has been suggested from actors wearing megaphonic masks to the strategic placing of large empty vases to act as passive amplifiers. Traditionally, Epidauros is noted for superb acoustics: if you go there, they like to demonstrate how far even a small sound carries from the centre spot, assuming calm conditions. The British archaeologist Sir Mortimer Wheeler (1890–1976) declared in 1958 that 'the

Greeks were past masters at acoustic contrivance ... even a stage whisper could be picked up by the furthest spectator with the cheapest ticket.'[1]

There have been various theories surrounding this and much research by acousticians – is it due to the pitch of the slope against which the tiers are set, the curving geometry of the bowl, or the direction of the local prevailing winds? There is some evidence that the size, shape and spacing of the limestone benches, combining to form a concave ridged shell, helps acoustically by reducing the frequency of background noise. Some sceptical acousticians contend that the sound quality is really not that good, rather we just like to pretend that it is. Nonetheless, Epidauros fares better sound-wise than most other amphitheatres of the period and performances are frequently held there to audience satisfaction. Whatever the cause, it may well have been happy accident rather than brilliant design.

Epidauros combines what, in modern terms, are two kinds of theatrical layout: the proscenium stage, set in front of the rows of seats, and the 'thrust stage', which extends out into the auditorium with the seating wrapping around it. In the theatrical tradition of the Ancient Greeks, the shallow stage, or *proskenion*, reached via ramps to either side, was the place from where actors declaimed. Behind the stage was the *skene*, or stage house: a structure with windows and doors for the actors to appear at. This also may have had an acoustic-reflection quality. Finally, in front of and lower than the stage with the lowest tiers of seating wrapped round it is the circular 'orchestra' area – for dancing and chorus-declaiming rather than acting. Music was included. The centre point of the orchestra is the point of convergence of the radiating tiers of the whole theatre and so, you would assume, would be the ideal place for an actor to stand, so there is another mystery. Scene, orchestra, proscenium: just as today's stadia are not so different from the Roman Colosseum, so the terms we use in today's theatres are in direct line of descent from the Greek, in addition to the physical layout (entry and exit routes through the auditorium, for instance, are deftly handled at Epidauros). Later, particularly in cities with space at a premium, the equivalent of that second outer tier of seating at Epidauros was brought forward and raised as a second deck or several decks or 'circles', so bringing more of the audience closer to the stage. For that, we had to await the invention of slender cast-iron columns in the eighteenth and nineteenth centuries CE.

It is impossible in such a sprawling open-air theatre for an audience member to share the space and breathe the same air as the actor. It is not intimate at all. But in the embracing bowl of Epidauros, with its seemingly unique atmosphere, you can, nonetheless, make eye and ear contact. You are participating in a shared event.

---

1 Sir Mortimer Wheeler, speaking on 'Armchair Voyage: Hellenic Cruise', BBC Series, 1958.

The Globe Theatre

London, UK, 1599–1614; reconstruction 1971–97

ARCHITECTS: RICHARD BURBAGE (1567–1619), PETER STREET (1553–1609), THEO CROSBY (1925–1994) AND JOHN ORRELL (1934–2003)

STYLE: VERNACULAR

As rebuilt, 'Shakespeare's Globe' (opened 1997) is a successful, if often conjectural, recreation reflecting 1980s archaeology and scholarship.

Richard Burbage was the son of carpenter turned actor-manager James Burbage (c.1531–1597). He followed his father onto the stage, where he was to become celebrated as the leading man in the plays of his friend William Shakespeare (1564–1616) and his contemporaries. In this line of work carpentry was a craft he had much need of, and not just for stage scenery. Everyday buildings in Tudor England (and some grand ones too) were made mostly of oak columns and beams, jointed and pegged together, the frame then being made weathertight with materials ranging from wattle-and-daub (basically mud mixed with chopped straw plastered over thin wooden strips) to brick, often laid in herringbone pattern. Roofs could be thatched or tiled. So, when the first 'modern' British theatres were built, this was the technique used.

The first purpose-built theatre in London (as opposed to adapted existing buildings such as inn courtyards, halls and barns) is thought to have been the polygonal building simply called The Theatre. This was built in Shoreditch, north-east of London's perimeter wall, in 1576 by the older Burbage, possibly with the assistance of apprentice carpenter Peter Street. Come 1599, a lease-renewal dispute with the site owner led the younger Burbage, his brother and a gang of workmen to dismantle the building one night and subsequently transport its components south of the Thames to Bankside. There, they reused the pieces to make part of a larger theatre that they named the Globe. Street, by then a successful builder, was much involved. This move brought Burbage's acting company, the Lord Chamberlain's Men (William Shakespeare among them as both playwright and actor), to what was already an emerging entertainment district. Along with other nearby theatres such as the Rose, the much larger Swan and later the Hope, plus lower forms of entertainment such as cock-fighting and bear-baiting venues, this district was no less louche and edgy than its Shoreditch predecessor.

So, here was a case of creative reuse, but the Globe burned down in 1613, to be rebuilt the following year with some modifications. In this guise it survived until it was closed down by the Puritans in 1642, being demolished a few years after that. Its form, and that of many of its companion theatres from the days of The Theatre onwards, has become instantly recognisable – the broadly cylindrical shape made of tall wooden bays, together forming a three-storey circlet of galleries with thatched roof: Shakespeare's 'wooden O' as mentioned in the section introduction. These surrounded the standing-only circular courtyard known as the Pit, open to the sky. Into the pit projected a 'thrust stage' – meaning the audience could surround it on three sides. The stage, too, had a roof and, like its long-distant Ancient Greek ancestors, a 'stage house' at the back, with doors and windows for actors to appear at and to arrive and depart. The stage house also served to house the musicians. Hatches in the stage and roof (known as the 'heavens' and painted to resemble the sky) allowed other entry and exit options.

For all its familiarity via more or less fanciful artists' impressions down the centuries – and some influential experiments from the 1940s to the 1960s by another actor-manager, Tyrone Guthrie (1900–1971), to build auditoria with thrust stages akin to those of Shakespeare's day – there was very little accurate documentary evidence as to what the Globe looked like, especially inside. Until late in the twentieth century there was no archaeological evidence either. What

Intimacy was provided by the enclosing galleries of costlier sheltered benches and the thrust stage, which was surrounded by the 'pit' where the 'groundlings' stood in the open.

It was common for performances to move indoors in winter. The tiny Sam Wanamaker Playhouse (opened 2014) in the Shakespeare's Globe complex is based on designs of the later Jacobean period.

was its exact shape if not circular, for instance? This became of crucial importance for Sam Wanamaker (1919–1993), the American actor-producer who, in 1970, discovered a memorial plaque on the approximate site of the Globe in Southwark, at that time an industrial part of town. Wanamaker dedicated the rest of his life to reconstructing Shakespeare's Globe and he succeeded, though both he and his architect, Theo Crosby (1925–1994), died before it was complete.

Just in time, with the design well advanced, an archaeological dig took place in 1988–9 on part of the original Globe site exposed by demolition. This revealed a section of its foundations, just enough for the whole plan geometry to be extrapolated. The Globe had been a 20-sided polyhedron about 30 metres across. Wanamaker, Crosby and theatre historian and consultant John Orrell (1934–2003) adjusted their design accordingly and continued – not on the original site, which was not available, but on the riverside nearby. The Globe had been built further back from the river's marshy margin, which is now embanked with a riverside walkway. They could recreate the building, but never its edgeland surroundings.

The nearby rival Rose Theatre was also excavated at this time and provided further clues. Much else was trial and error. Where were the columns holding up the stage roof placed? How big and high was the stage? Being an actor himself, Wanamaker got Shakespearian actors in to try out various configurations – what worked best for a set-piece speech, what for a whispered aside and so on. The process was presumably not so different from the original: we know that the actor-managers of the time often altered their theatres according to circumstances.

Thus, the third version of the Globe since 1599 was finally built, as faithfully as the sketchy historical and partial archaeological information allowed. It is, therefore, a mix of scholarship and fruitful conjecture. It required some juggling with modern-day building codes, especially given that it had the first thatched roof in London since the nineteenth century, but the construction techniques of its superstructure are authentic enough. Opened in 1997, it is now a fixture on the London theatre scene, with excellent directors and productions from the outset. Busy though it can get, it only holds around a third as many people as it would have originally – we are bigger people now, and we have space-consuming fire escape routes that the Elizabethans did not.

Being part open to the weather, the Globe was, and is, a summer-season theatre; in winter the Elizabethan actors decamped to indoor premises in adapted buildings at Blackfriars, across the river. The modern Shakespeare's Globe complex includes such a place, the frequently candlelit Sam Wanamaker Playhouse, which opened in 2014. Based on unbuilt seventeenth-century theatre plans by architect John Webb (1611–1672), and so arguably more authentic than its summertime sister, this highly decorated little timber auditorium has wonderful acoustics, especially for music.

Bayreuth Festspielhaus

Bayreuth, Germany, 1872–6

ARCHITECTS: RICHARD WAGNER (1813–1883), GOTTFRIED SEMPER (1803–1879), OTTO BRÜCKWALD (1841–1917) AND CARL BRANDT (1928–1881)

STYLE: NEO-VERNACULAR, CLASSICAL

'I am pondering the most daring of plans', wrote composer Richard Wagner to a friend in 1850. 'I would like to build a theatre out of planks here, bring the most suitable singers to join me, and organise everything necessary for this special event, so that I can be sure of the best possible performance of the opera.'[1]

Wagner, already eminent following the success of his operas *The Flying Dutchman*, *Tannhäuser* and *Lohengrin*, was starting work on the myth-based cycle of operatic dramas that became *Der Ring des Nibelungen* (the *Ring Cycle*). Obsessed with the idea of this cycle as a total work of art, or *Gesamtkunstwerk*, he was unwilling to have it performed in just any opera house or theatre: he wanted to design the building as well, so that it would become part of the overall experience. One idea he briefly explored was a temporary wooden barn-like building that would be ceremonially burnt down, along with his score, after just three performances of *Siegfried*, the opera that was later to become the third in the *Ring Cycle* of four.

Temporary or permanent, there was a problem. Having taken part, along with his friend the architect Gottfried Semper, in the violent abortive attempt at a republican pan-German nationalist revolution in Dresden in 1849, Wagner was banned from the German states and had fled into exile. He was pardoned in 1862 and his luck changed when a new King of Bavaria inherited the throne at the age of 18. Ludwig II (r.1864–1886) was a Wagner obsessive, fantasist and builder of castles. He became Wagner's patron, invited him to Munich, paid off his debts and eventually loaned him most of the money to build a new theatre just to perform the *Ring Cycle*.

Semper had drawn up designs for an opera house for Wagner in Munich, but the composer found himself driven out of the city following the scandal of his affair with a prominent, much younger, married woman, Cosima von Bülow (1837–1930), daughter of composer Franz Liszt (1811–1886) and the future Mrs Wagner. Besides, there were too many other cultural distractions in Munich. So, Wagner alighted upon the town of Bayreuth in north-eastern Bavaria. It already had an opera house (which still exists) but that was all wrong for his ambitions. The eager municipality gave him the land on a gentle hill to build a new one. Dusting down Semper's plans, calling on the innovative stage designer Carl Brandt, adding his own ideas and using Otto Brückwald as tame architect to follow his orders, Wagner built his theatre made of 'planks'. It is still one of the largest timber structures in the world.

At this time, interest in the civilisation and culture of Ancient Greece was high, and Wagner saw his opera-drama cycle as a modern equivalent of the *Oresteia* tragedies of Aeschylus. For Munich, Semper had explored the idea of a modern fan-shaped auditorium based on a Greek amphitheatre (see Epidauros, p. 164) and Wagner, Aeschylus in mind, agreed.

An audacious timber construction, Wagner's theatre was designed as a perfectly tuned instrument for the performance of his operas.

It is a large opera house designed for summer festivals, lacking most of the public spaces we associate with nineteenth-century opera houses, such as the sumptuous Palais Garnier in Paris (1861–75, and so broadly contemporary with Bayreuth), which is much more about socialising and personal display than attending to the performance. Wagner's Bayreuth is the exact opposite of that: it is entirely about the Immersive performance.

The auditorium is much the same capacity as the Palais Garnier at a little under 2,000. It and its large stage fills most of the building. Ancillary spaces at the rear were the minimum necessary for the performers although later rear extensions have made productions easier. The paying public is far from being cosseted, however, although a grander neoclassical entrance portico was added to the timber-and-brick edifice towards the end of the nineteenth century, and today a low restaurant block sits alongside the building. From outside, perhaps its most successful architectural move is the fly tower – something architects have long struggled to integrate successfully into their buildings. Here, it is confidently handled as a pitched-roofed pavilion with a large Diocletian (semi-circular) window, looking out over the arriving pilgrims like a giant's eye.

Wagner made a number of innovations here apart from forgoing audience comforts. He introduced the idea of putting the audience in darkness so that all attention would be focused on the brightly lit stage. That stage was given added importance by means of a double proscenium arch, emphasising its depth and

No distractions: sound and vision are concentrated via the double proscenium arch and orchestra cowl.

height. Acoustically, it is tremendously good and this is due largely to another innovation from Wagner. He did not want the orchestra to be seen (not wanting the audience's attention to stray from the stage) nor did he want the singers to have to compete with the orchestra. His solution to both issues was to build a curving timber cowl above the deep, sloping orchestra pit. This conceals the musicians and throws the sound to the back of the stage, from where it bounces forward into the auditorium.

The auditorium is itself odd to modern eyes, its flanks being interrupted by short projecting walls terminating in classical columns. These were devised by Brandt as a way to deal with the wedges of space left either side of the fan-shaped seating plan. You can enter the auditorium via doors between these walls but their effect on the overall sound still baffles modern acousticians. Not that this matters: performers, critics and Wagner aficionados agree that the place is tuned just right for the ten operas regularly performed here.

Wagner will always be a controversial figure. He held anti-Semitic views and his German nationalist ideals and narratives played into the hands of the Nazis: he was Hitler's favourite composer. His own descendants, who are still involved in the Bayreuth Festival, have disowned this side of his character. For the aficionados of his work the music triumphs over everything: it is quite simply glorious, especially at Bayreuth. Architecturally, the building is unique. This low-budget 'temporary' timber-framed building, the outcome of one person's extraordinary determination and charisma, has lasted nearly a century and a half. And during every festival season, two fire engines are stationed outside, just in case.

1 Letter from Wagner in Zurich to his friend, the Dresden artist Ernst Benedikt Kietz, in 1850, cited by the Richard Wagner Scholarship Foundation, www.richard-wagner-stipendienstiftung.de/en.

Sydney Opera House

Sydney, Australia, 1956–73

ARCHITECT: JØRN UTZON (1918–2008)
WITH ENGINEER OVE ARUP (1895–1988)

STYLE: MODERN EXPRESSIONIST

It could have been so much better. An odd thing to say perhaps about what is the most instantly recognisable modern building in the world, a symbol of Australia, an acknowledged masterpiece. It is the image that counts. Unless you are in a society cut off from all global communication, you will know this building, be able to name it. Yet only a very tiny fraction of all those who know what it is have ever been there. It could be completely empty, derelict even, and this would not have the slightest impact on its communicative power: building as logo.

It could have been so much better if its Danish architect, Jørn Utzon, who won the competition in 1957 at the age of 38 (regarded as young in this demanding profession), had known how on earth to build his beautiful and highly conceptual charcoal sketches. Eventually, working with the London-based engineer Ove Arup, they came up with a workable solution: each of the famous arched hoods forming the roofs of the opera-house complex was to be a section of a sphere. Computer mainframe power in the form of the Ferranti Pegasus

A national symbol as much as a performance venue, the Sydney Opera House (though initially sketched by hand) was the first computer-calculated, 'icon' cultural building.

In the main orchestral hall the interiors were completed by other architects. They have recently been acoustically improved.

Mark 1 arrived only just in time to crunch slowly through the alarmingly complex engineering calculations – this was the first building in the world to harness computers in its design – but crunch them successfully it did. Without it, the necessary calculations by hand would have taken a further ten years.

It could have been so much better if costs had not spiralled, if Utzon had not been frozen out by a philistine, populist minister of works and, in 1966, forced to resign and leave the project, never to return. This caused uproar and was a particular shame because it meant that the opera house was finished by others, so that the interiors as they turned out were not as Utzon intended. But this is, in the eyes of the world, not really a problem. Well over a million people attend performances at this multi-auditorium venue every year, and they mostly do not know how it might have been different. Meanwhile, the rest of the world sees only the photography and video. For them the image of the shimmering ceramic-clad shells – or are they sails, or hulls, or monks' cowls, or the gaping mouths of whales or sharks? – in the waterside setting of Bennelong Point, close to the great steel arch of the 1932 Sydney Harbour Bridge, is enough. Previously there had been only wharfs and a large tram depot on the site.

Utzon was interested not only in geometry but also (following the lead of another architect he much admired, America's Frank Lloyd Wright, see p. 86) in the architecture of ancient cultures such as the Mayan complexes of Central America with their ceremonial platforms or plinths. His opera house places the pale shells of the main roofs on just such a massive plinth, approached in Mayan fashion by a broad, awe-inducing stair. Within this podium a lot of the activity of the complex takes place. At a glance, or from a distance, however, the eye does not particularly take it in. Though perhaps this lower half of the building is brutalist in its use of precast concrete, it is also recessive in its pinkish-buff coloration. A plinth, having to support something, can never be the main event: here, that is of course the shells/sails of the roofs, which cleverly absorb the lumps of the fly towers. It may be a horizontalist composition, but it rises very high too. The biggest shell is 65 metres tall.

The largest volume is a 2,679-seat orchestral concert hall. The slightly smaller one, flanking it at an angle and given an identical exterior treatment, is the 1,500-seat Joan Sutherland Theatre, which houses opera and ballet. There are three other theatre spaces in descending size and configuration, and plenty of cafés, restaurants and shops, this being a tourist destination. The main restaurant to one side of the podium stairway is a freestanding miniature version of the opera house, itself with shell roofs, vital to the overall composition. And, of course, given the period this was designed and built in, there is a large underground car park.

The shells are made of framed concrete ribwork with infill panels, the whole then tiled in a subtle interlocking chevron pattern of white and cream. They rightly attract most attention, but not enough is said about the glazing to the fronts of the shells. Perhaps this did not turn out quite as elegantly as Utzon had intended, but it is still a virtuoso way to terminate the large foyers to the auditoria, looking out across the Harbour or back to the city. The bronze-glass walls, V-shaped in plan, drop down from the arches, then curve outward like thumbnails, then fold back in on themselves beneath so you can see downwards as well as outwards. This glazing alone is a considerable engineering challenge and the steelwork is beefy. Looking out from there is like being on the bridge of a huge ship, another nautical reference.

Utzon, you might think, would be a broken man after being effectively expelled from his own project, and he can certainly be blamed for some serious design difficulties such as the workable sizes of the two main auditoria, which were not as capacious as required. However, most of the notorious overspending on the project took place after he left. He got on with his career, he won all the major awards. There is a happy ending of sorts. Later generations felt sorry for how he was treated. Towards the end of his life, the Sydney Opera House Trust invited him to advise on redesigning the interiors. He never returned to Sydney but with his son Jan (b.1944), he set to work and the improvements started to be made.

Detail of the geometric glazed tiling on the concrete shells.

When Utzon died in 2008 he received a state memorial service in his opera house. The building pioneered techniques and an aesthetic that led the way for the turn-of-the century explosion of 'icon' buildings, or 'shapeism' as some call it. That is not necessarily a good thing, but then again – despite its troubled birth – nothing has ever eclipsed Utzon's Sydney Opera House as the realisation of a uniquely original architectural idea that everyone can somehow relate to.

Walt Disney Concert Hall

Los Angeles, USA, 1991–2003

ARCHITECT: FRANK GEHRY (B.1929)

STYLE: DECONSTRUCTIVIST

Frank Owen Gehry is an undemonstrative, if sometimes curmudgeonly, person who makes very showy buildings. In that sense he is unlike the dandified Frank Lloyd Wright with his cult of personality (see Johnson Wax building, p. 86), but at points there are similarities. Like Wright, he achieved relatively late-in-life success with startling compositions that are uniquely his. However, there is no school of Gehry, unless it is the free-form way of designing that was initially called deconstructivism and morphed into demonstrative 'icon' buildings.

While there is no 'form follows function' to this kind of architecture, Gehry (who uncharacteristically voiced himself as a cartoon character in an episode of *The Simpsons* spoofing this very building) is a surprisingly practical architect. This practicality behoves a man who began his working life as a truck driver and who spent the early part of his architectural career working for the Austro-American shopping mall architect Victor Gruen (1903–1980; see p. 204).

Gehry, as a child, encouraged by his grandmother, used to play by making model buildings and cities out of scrap bits of wood from his grandfather's Toronto hardware store. The love of humble materials stayed with him when he became a practising architect and his own first house in Venice, California, was a noted exercise in junk bricolage, using corrugated metal sheeting, chain-link fencing material, raw plywood and so forth.

Gehry wanted to make more radical shapes in architecture than conventional techniques would allow, however. What came to his aid in the 1990s was his adoption and adaptation of computer-aided design techniques borrowed from the aerospace industry: essentially, this was the ability to scan a hand-made model to make a virtual model, and to use the resulting data to directly make the components of the building. This was a moment of liberation for Gehry, who was never himself computer-literate but made sure he employed plenty of people who were.

The Walt Disney Concert Hall – so named because it was majority-funded by Walt's widow Lilian (1899–1997) and the Disney Company, among many

The 1990s saw a new generation of computer programming, drawn from aerospace technology, which made Frank Gehry's more daring concepts (see his 1991 sketch, facing page) buildable. The first of these was the Walt Disney Concert Hall.

others – was chronologically the first of Gehry's spectacular large-scale cultural buildings to be designed this way. The long delays it encountered meant that it was overtaken by the slightly later design that made him world-famous, the titanium-clad Guggenheim Museum Bilbao, which opened in 1997 and which shows Gehry's gathering confidence in its more fluent composition. We are over-accustomed to 'icon' buildings these days but at the time their impact was immense. For all the promise of Gehry's earlier career, nobody had seen anything to compare with these.

The Gehry method is often to stand his billowing forms – reminiscent of sails, ribbons, fish and cloudscapes – well proud of the underlying functional parts of the building, which are deliberately clunky, and visible through the interstices. For him the skin of the building is a visually kinetic affair, frozen movement – in the case of the Walt Disney Concert Hall done in stainless steel. One concave mirror-shiny section turned out to be focusing the sun rather uncomfortably on the pavement: it had to be made matt-finish.

Though his buildings can be very beautiful, his was never the pursuit of elegance. He understood the desire for cultural landmarks, saying once, 'Public buildings deserve to have a certain level of iconicity and personality. Historically, that's what makes them define the cities and communities they're in.'[1] Then again, Gehry applied his style (which evolved, and later at times took on a more orthogonal aspect) equally to non-public buildings such as residential and commercial blocks. In more subdued domestic form, the Gehry approach made one of the most satisfying Maggie's cancer care centres in Dundee, Scotland, which opened in 2003.

The Walt Disney Concert Hall is the home of the Los Angeles Philharmonic Orchestra and – with acoustic design by Gehry's frequent collaborator Yasuhisa Toyota (b.1952) – it sounds excellent for the more traditional symphonic repertoire, perhaps less accommodating for more radical music: a slight disconnect between its visual and aural character. Gehry let rip on the interior as much as the acoustics would allow. It is something of a compromise between the 'vineyard' style of terraced auditorium – as demonstrated by Hans Scharoun's 1963 Berlin Philharmonie, where the audience wraps around the orchestra on multiple levels – and the more conventional shoebox shape, with the former winning out visually. You cannot avoid the visual focal point of the interior, which is Gehry's arrangement of the square-section wooden organ pipes, caught as if at the moment of an explosion in the works or a chaotic collapse.

As so often with such late-running, cost-escalating projects (the Sydney Opera House being a prime case in point, see p. 173), attempts to save money led to rather less lavish public circulation areas than were originally intended: the whole experience of concert-going is usually as much to do with what goes on outside the auditorium as inside it. But no matter: the popularity of the Walt Disney Concert Hall proved to be as much of a stimulus for the regeneration of what had become a decaying LA Downtown as the Bilbao Guggenheim had been for that city, or New York's High Line linear park (by Diller Scofidio + Renfro, see p. 244) has been for the meat-packing district of Manhattan. An empty monument is not enough: such buildings have to work for the people who use them, providing the footfall and demand to spark further regeneration.

1 Interview with the author, published in the *Sunday Times*, 13 July 2008.

Gehry kept control of the interior of the symphony hall, right down to the arrangement of organ pipes.

Religion

Architects, whether people of faith or not, must understand and respond to the practices of the religious communities they serve. These must be expressed through functionality, symbolism and something intangible: a sense of something beyond the building, something unseen and, even if not understood, evoked.

There are many fine religious buildings from architects who are not believers, or not in the same faith or denomination as the building they are asked to design. The secular Jewish American-Estonian architect Louis Kahn (see the Salk Institute, p. 109) designed churches, synagogues and a mosque. Spanish architect Rafael Moneo (b.1937) admitted to being a lapsed Catholic when designing the new Roman Catholic Cathedral of Our Lady of the Angels in Los Angeles (1996–2002). Sited right next to a sunken freeway with a public plaza on the other side, this is one of the better recent large places of worship. Moneo contends that a cathedral is a public institution more than a place for practising a religion and, indeed, this is how most of us treat them.

On the other hand, the British architect Basil Spence (1907–1976) was a person of deep conventional Anglican faith. He wrote about how his competition-winning design for the new Coventry Cathedral (1950–62) – which both preserved and replaced elements of the previous Blitzed cathedral – resolved itself in a vision while he was, somewhat bathetically, knocked out by anaesthetic in the dentist's chair. In the same year (1950) the edgier Swiss-French architect Le Corbusier could tell his priest-client, 'I don't care about your church, I didn't ask you to do it. And, if I do it, I'll do it my way. It interests me because it's a plastic work. It's difficult.'[1] By 'plastic', Le Corbusier meant moulded or free-form rather than orthogonal (see Ronchamp chapel, p. 194). His discourteous and seemingly non-believing response did not bother his highly sophisticated client in the slightest. The result was, and is, a masterpiece that has a greater spiritual feel to it than plenty of more conventional churches.

Spence had one thing in common with Corbusier: both at the time were tiring of International Modernism, and were returning to an architecture of greater mass and fluidity. 'I was bored with the stretched glass skin over a frame, and I was much more interested in the plastic expression of a natural material like stone ... I would have a punctured stone wall of great simplicity enclosing the altar', wrote Spence.[2] His inspiration (when not divine or dental) was the great brick medieval cathedral-fortress of Albi in south-west France. Coventry maintains links with several other cities largely destroyed by war and rebuilt in hope, principal among them Dresden in Germany, which in 1994–2005 finally rebuilt (in faithful replica, incorporating some surviving stonework) its bombed eighteenth-century Lutheran Frauenkirche.

In Syracuse, on the eastern side of Sicily, stands a cathedral with an impressive baroque frontage built in the white stone of the area, of much the

Gaspare Fossati (1809–1883), *Interior of Hagia Sofia, Istanbul*, hand-coloured lithograph, published 1852.

same age as the original Frauenkirche. But behind this veneer is a building some 2,200 years older: a Greek Temple of Athena, dating from 480 BCE. Its original fluted Doric columns, although replaced on the front, are part-buried in its flanks and are clearly visible from both inside and out. In its time, as empires came and went, the building has also served as a mosque. Such changes of religious usage also happen because of migrancy patterns. In London's East End, for example, is an eighteenth-century Huguenot Protestant chapel, which later became a synagogue, and most recently a mosque. The building has had to adapt considerably, but then it was capable of adaptation.

When it comes to the design of places of worship there is plenty of common ground. The ancient classical religions were conducted by a priesthood, with the public kept well away: the temple was the home of the deity or deities in question, or sometimes a place of sacrifice (in the Inca and Aztec civilisations of Central and South America especially, human sacrifice). Those not in the priesthood would gather outside. In the three main monotheistic religions of Judaism, Christianity and Islam, the public were gradually accorded greater participation as time went by. A place for preaching or reading from was required: *bimah*, pulpit or *minbar*. A visible focus of religious faith: the Ark, the altar, the *mihrab*, in Indian religions the *stupa*. Often there is a compass orientation, real or assumed: Jerusalem or Mecca, with east favoured even by some eastern religions as the direction of sunrise. Bell towers and spires evolved in mainstream Christian denominations, minarets in Islamic ones, domes in all three, a dome being an efficient and spectacular way to span a large space to house many people.

The key early example here is the Hagia Sophia ('Holy Wisdom') (532–560 CE) in Constantinople, now Istanbul. Originally a Byzantine cathedral, then a mosque, later a secular museum, it has since 2020 been a mosque again. It was designed for the Emperor Justinian (482–565) by mathematician Anthemius (474–534) and engineer Isidore (442–537) – both, according to one account, undercover pagans with a more ancient God, namely the Sun, in mind. Much rebuilt and strengthened soon after, following earthquake damage, it remains one of the great religious spaces of the world. With a width of 33 metres and a height above the floor of 55 metres, the dome is just part of a much larger sequence of sublime spaces roofed with foothills of other domes, the whole composition with its four later minarets appearing almost organic in form.

The home of the deity in Ancient Greek and Roman temples, the *cella* – a largely blank-walled but richly decorated structure set within perimeter colonnades – translated into the inner sanctum of the buildings of subsequent religions. In particular, this space translates into the chancel in churches, often including the choir, this section being east of the usual 'crossing' of transepts, frequently separated and visually filtered from the more public nave by the perforated partition of the rood screen. The stupa containing holy relics at the far end of Indian (especially Buddhist) *chaitya*, or prayer halls, is of similar importance and is often a separate building. Generally, in Buddhism, the temple complex is arranged to symbolically represent the entire universe or known world. Also in Buddhism comes an echo of the Hellenic practice of erecting huge likenesses of the deity. Buddha as saint or avatar is there, standing, seated or reclining.

The religious building was until quite recent times accorded prime importance in any city and would very often be the largest, highest and most richly adorned building of all, a testament of faith and a place of regular public assembly. Places of worship and buildings of state were, and often still are, closely linked. Groups who break away from established religions tend to adopt a different architecture: nonconformist Christian sects often opted for neoclassical buildings – the temple type – in preference to the pointed-Gothic persuasion of the established church. Today's evangelical groups colonise huge redundant cinemas or big cheap sheds on industrial estates with little overt symbolism other than billboard slogans.

While the adept handling of light and shade is vital in producing a meditative and spiritual atmosphere, any place of worship is also a place of performance, with the audience more or less involved, depending on religion, denomination or sect. The spoken and sung word, the sound of instruments and the need to see what is going on demand a visual and acoustic response from the architect similar to that of a theatre or concert hall, and in some traditions the most glorious music has been composed specifically for the acoustic qualities of these buildings.

---

1 Le Corbusier, 'Letter to Father Pierre Marie Alain Couturier', in Hugh Pearman, *Contemporary World Architecture*, 1998.

2 Basil Spence, *Phoenix at Coventry: The Building of a Cathedral*, 1962.

Angkor Wat Siem Reap, Cambodia, Twelfth Century

ARCHITECT: UNKNOWN, DIRECTED BY KING SURYAVARMAN II (R.1113–1150)

STYLE: KHMER ARCHITECTURE

A complete landscape rather than a single building, Angkor Wat represents the high point of the Khmer civilisation.

In 1586, the Portuguese explorer and friar António da Madalena (d.1589) made his way to the almost deserted complex of Angkor Wat. He later recounted to Diogo da Couto (c.1542–1616), chronicler of the Portuguese empire, that he realised at once that here had been a great civilisation, though he had no clue what that was. The buildings were a revelation:

> It is of such extraordinary construction that it is not possible to describe it with a pen, particularly since it is like no other building in the world. It has towers and decoration and all the refinements which the human genius can conceive of. There are many smaller towers of similar style, in the same stone, which are gilded. The temple is surrounded by a moat, and access is by a single bridge, protected by two stone tigers so grand and fearsome as to strike terror into the visitor.[1]

This is the architecture of mass, a 'temple-mountain' representing the homes of the gods.

Madalena was one of the first Western visitors to the greatest temple of what is now thought to have been the largest pre-industrial city in the world. The Khmer emperors had abandoned it a century before, most likely due to over-population, consequent ecological disasters and the threat from neighbouring powers. What Madalena saw was a place that was – unknown to the medieval builders of cathedrals and mosques working at the same time – the grandest religious centre of them all. Its builder was a warrior king, Suryavarman II, and his religion was Hinduism.

As kingdoms and empires come and go, such places can, over time, switch religions, as with those Greek temples that later became mosques and then cathedrals. In the case of Angkor Wat, after around a century the temple switched to Buddhism and so it has remained ever since. But its Hindu iconography – it is covered in rich and ornate carvings – was not altered.

Colonial expansion at this time by the later empires of the West began to reveal such wonders and unfamiliar architectures as Moctezuma II's (r. c.1502–1520) capital Tenochtitlan in what is now Mexico. As in the West, so in the East: though unlike Mexico, by the time the Portuguese traders and missionaries arrived in this part of south-east Asia there was no proud empire to trade with or conquer. The Khmer Empire had all but dissolved, but its built legacy was extraordinary.

The perimeter of this entirely symmetrical rectangular complex is roughly 1.6 kilometres long by 1.2 kilometres wide. Within that is a deep moat, itself

174 metres wide, through which a river gently flows, and which you cross on a bridge leading to a broad stone causeway advancing towards the complex between two large square reflecting ponds. Once inside the complex, a dense cruciform arrangement of galleries contains four smaller sacred ponds. At the centre stands the square temple, rising in three tiers to the top with its inner sanctuary and central conical tower reaching 65 metres. This is the apotheosis of the 'temple-mountain', familiar in Hindu architecture, in which the building symbolises Mount Meru, seat of the Hindu gods.

Surrounding this inner complex, with its four subsidiary corner peaks, are 'galleries', long buildings forming something akin to an immense rectangular cloister, only here enclosing the main religious building rather than being off to one side as in the European monastic tradition. These galleries, each a linear work of sculpture, represent foothills. In courtyards, both inside and out, are pairs of vertiginously raised buildings known as 'libraries', which are thought

Angkor Wat is richly decorated with relief carvings, especially in the 'galleries' surrounding the central complex.

to have been shrines. Beyond all this, the broad moat represents the sea. The whole complex is hierarchical, becoming steadily more sacred and so more exclusive as you work your way through it to the centre.

The Khmer Empire of south-east Asia was in a near-perpetual state of war with its neighbours, but Suryavarman was a great leader, military commander and strategist. He also, as such rulers tend to, wanted a monument, one grander than any by his predecessors. Angkor Wat, originally dedicated to Vishnu, is thought to have been intended as Suryavarman's mausoleum or funerary temple, in which case it is on a par with Egypt's Great Pyramid of Khufu (r.2589–2566 BCE). The Hindu faith cremates rather than buries its dead, but Suryavarman is there, carved in a detailed bas-relief in the south gallery, pictured surrounded by his court. The temple also appears to have been very carefully aligned with the rising and setting sun at various times of year, so it had a further astronomical significance.

Madalena and later visitors noted how massive and beautifully cut and fitted were the stones used to build the complex, which had been transported from a quarry 40 kilometres away by canal. Other buildings were of brick and timber, originally mortar-rendered and painted. Hindu temple architecture, as with that of all great religions, existed in its own recognisable evolving tradition and in this fertile region of Cambodia there had already been a three-century history of temple-building under previous kings. But with Suryavarman II's Angkor Wat (the name means 'city of temples') it reached a summit of magnificence in everything from its expansive layout to its sophistication of decoration, mostly depicting the epic stories of the Hindu faith such as the Ramayana and the Mahabharata.

Skilled though the Khmer builders were, unlike their colleagues in Europe and the Middle East at this time, they never developed a technology of wide-span arches and domes, or beams any longer than needed to allow an elephant or wagon through a main entrance. Indeed, they treated stone and wood much the same. There are no huge interior spaces, then, though many are certainly impressive and tall. The overall architectural effect is of one mighty building made of an accumulation of smaller units.

There is still much to learn about Angkor Wat. Where was the imperial palace? What lesser buildings were there? Suggestions of streets have been detected. Would these streets have housed a priesthood, civil administrators or both? This was the heart of a capital city at the peak of imperial power. It commemorates Suryavarman as much as Vishnu.

---

1 Account given by António da Madalena to Diogo da Couto, transcription discovered in 1947 by historian Charles R. Boxer, in Bernard-Philippe Groslier, *Angkor and Cambodia in the Sixteenth Century: According to Portuguese and Spanish Sources*, 1958, trans. 2006.

Portuguese Synagogue

Amsterdam, Netherlands, 1671–5

ARCHITECT: ELIAS BOUMAN (1636–1686)

STYLE: POST-RENAISSANCE CLASSICAL

With many of the long-established religions, for all their liturgical and architectural developments over time, certain elements of the faith translate into buildings in a broadly consistent way. From the houses of the Ancient Greek gods via cathedrals, mosques, Hindu, Buddhist and Sikh temples, there is a traceable visual continuity to each, even if the line occasionally jumps disconcertingly. With synagogues – externally rather than internally – things are different. Over long periods of Jewish history, this has been a religious community forced to move from place to place, driven by often state-sanctioned persecution. When allowed to remain in a given place, it has often been strictly segregated, as in Venice from 1516 to 1797, where the Jewish quarter's location in an area of iron foundries (foundry being *giotto* or *geto*) gave us the word 'ghetto'. In consequence, synagogues were often hidden away, in houses, on upper floors, in back lots. Not usually being associated with ruling elites meant that prime civic sites were generally not available. Even when a period of peaceful toleration led to settled, safe communities, there was very often the feeling of a need to visually fit in rather than proclaim religious difference with the majority population. Consequently – at least until the mid-nineteenth century when Moorish/Byzantine stylings revived strongly among newer communities – the architecture of synagogues was likely to be whatever the prevailing tastes were, wherever they happened to be.

It is rare, then, to find quite such a commanding building of its type in the seventeenth century as the Portuguese Synagogue in Amsterdam. This emerged

Entrance front of the synagogue, a large, relatively plain building with the merest hint of baroque classical detailing.

The often candlelit interior is one large space, architecturally divided into three parts by twin rows of full-height columns. Balthasar Bernaerts, *The Festival of Purim*, 1737. Coloured engraving after a drawing by Louis Fabritius Dubourg.

from the coalescence of a number of Sephardic Jewish communities who had been expelled from the Iberian peninsula by the Spanish after centuries of fruitful coexistence with the former Muslim rulers. They were obliged to emigrate rather than face mandatory conversion to Christianity or death at the hands of the Spanish Inquisition. Iberia's great loss was the gain of the Netherlands (who had thrown off the Spanish yoke), with its developing history of international trading and religious freedom.

In liturgical terms, any synagogue harks back to Solomon's Temple, as described in the Bible. It relates to other ancient temples in that there was a porch, a place of assembly and ceremony inside and then, towards the back, the 'holy of holies', the room containing the Ark of the Covenant, which held the tablets bearing the Ten Commandments and by extension was a direct conduit to God, or at least the 'name' of God. This derived from the ceremonial tabernacle, or tent, which covered the Ark at resting points after the Israelites' expulsion from Egypt, but also equates to the *cella* of ancient temples (such as the Parthenon, p. 16), which were essentially the innermost shrine of the god and where the essence of the god resided. The temple is also the ancestor of most Christian churches in the faithful's procession on arrival through nave and choir to the holy place of the high altar.

Bouman, though not himself Jewish, had previously worked on other synagogues and houses in the Jewish quarter of Amsterdam. His site for this *Esnoga*, in the Judaeo-Spanish language of its community, was then on the perimeter of the city, a watery landscape with canals where (as in Venice) buildings, including this one, had foundations built on deep wooden piles. He is thought to have taken the biblical description of Solomon's Temple as his starting point.

As expressed in the architectural language of the time, it is a very large, quite plain rectangular brick box organised into three sections on each facade, edged with full-height pilasters, each centre section projecting slightly. The handling of the corners where the pairs of pilasters are kept just slightly apart is adroit. There are three levels of windows, the middle-level ones being tall and round-topped in the manner of many religious buildings of the period. There are a lot of them: this is a building flooded with daylight by day and glowing like a huge lantern at night from the chandeliers (still real candles) within. There is some restrained baroque detailing at eaves-level. This was built by a large, wealthy and confident community but – size of the building apart – not an over-ostentatious one. Today, it is surrounded by a single-storey perimeter of later ancillary buildings that form an outer wall: once through that you are in an open courtyard in front of the main entrance.

Inside, two rows of four plain full-height stone columns with classical capitals and beams (entablatures) support the roof, thereby visually dividing the space longitudinally into three. Despite the galleries, it reads as one very large room from floor to triple-arched timber ceilings. The arrangement of Sephardic and other Orthodox synagogues, with men's seating facing across the space rather than along it (women here in a raised gallery) and with a centrally positioned raised *bimah* for the reader, rather than being set to one side as is usual in churches, might almost be said to have anticipated the liturgical changes in the Roman Catholic Church in the 1960s – when the ceremony started to involve the congregations much more and an in-the-round format started to be applied. It can also be noted that the broadness in plan of many such synagogues has something in common with the dimensions of many mosques, a result of the earlier Moorish symbiosis in Iberia as much as the stated biblical dimensions.

Amsterdam's *Esnoga* is a remarkable survival, particularly given the way the Netherlands was occupied by Nazi Germany during the Second World War. Those were the years of terrible danger, suffering and loss for the community. But it and its furnishings survived and its very valuable historic library, though sent to Germany, was returned after the war. One of Europe's oldest synagogues, it functions as it has always done, sparkling with thousands of candles.

Basílica de la Sagrada Família

Barcelona, Spain, 1883–present

ARCHITECTS: ANTONI GAUDÍ (1852–1926) AND SUCCESSORS

STYLE: *SUI GENERIS*

A frozen eruption in the cityscape of Barcelona, Antoni Gaudí's masterwork is scheduled for completion in the 2030s.

Gaudí is the only architect in this book to have their style described as '*sui generis*'. It is true that his colossal church in Barcelona has its origins in Gothic stylings. It is true also that it was heavily influenced by, and helped to define, the unearthly blooms of the European art movement generally known by its French name of art nouveau. It is equally the case that Gaudí was not alone in Catalonia in the later nineteenth and early twentieth centuries in producing buildings of fantastical richness and allusion, much influenced by Islamic precedents.

This was the time of a quest for a new national style for Catalonia, a style confusingly known as 'modernisme'. As with related movements with various names across Europe and America, modernisme was steeped in historic nostalgia and heavy symbolism, as seen through the bottom of a glass of absinthe. But only teetotal, vegetarian Gaudí took all these strands of architectural and religious yearning and synthesised them into one wholly extraordinary religious object: the Sagrada Família is a built vision.

Even during his lifetime, it seemed to be taking rather a long time to get built, by modern if not medieval standards. 'My client,' observed Gaudí, perhaps apocryphally, 'is not in a hurry.'[1] He certainly remarked that great churches conventionally take centuries to complete and that others contribute different styles. His 'client' meant God rather than the Roman Catholic Church: technically, his client was a local society of religious zealots led by a fiercely nationalist bookseller who desired an 'expiatory temple' to atone for the materialist sins of the modern world.[2]

It is not a cathedral: Barcelona already has one of those, with geese in its cloisters. The Sagrada Família is largely unofficial, its construction originally funded by private donations, later by ticket sales. It did not even have official permission to be built until 2018. It just happened, and went on happening. Although the church was consecrated as a 'minor basilica' by Pope Benedict XVI (b.1927) in 2010, when the nave roof was watertight and the first of what will eventually be several organs installed, at the time of writing it is not due to be finally complete until around 2032.

Construction has accelerated in recent years thanks to new engineering and computer-driven fabrication techniques, but you would not bet against it still taking somewhat longer. It has been delayed not only by its ascetic elderly architect fatally walking into the path of a tram in 1926, but also by wars, by politics, by pestilences and by unfashionability. But then again, its almost perpetually unfinished state is a great deal of its attraction. Many over the years, especially artists, have called for it to be left as a ruin. Will we love it so much when, instead, it moves from completion into a perpetual state of repair and restoration?

For all the extraordinary, colourful and wilful eccentricity of his houses, apartment buildings and parks in and around Barcelona, Gaudí was no mere stylistic innovator. He was also – up to a point – technically proficient, his main contribution being the development of the parabolic, or catenary, arch. His way to design these was to make upside-down models in which the arches were loops of chain or weighted string. The closer together the ends of the chain and the longer the chain itself, the taller and narrower the arch. These are pure forms, structurally sound. He viewed these hanging models in a mirror and photographed them as a foundation for his drawings, although he was always willing to change a building as it was built, tearing parts down and rebuilding according to whim. His clients mostly needed to be rich.

Gaudí inherited a building already designed as a conventional Gothic church by another architect, with building under way. That architect was sacked and when Gaudí took over he insisted on scrapping

The recent 'Passion' facade of the basilica, with controversial sculptures by Josep Maria Subirachs (1927–2014).

Seen as kitsch by some, as magnificent by others, the interior is an extreme stylised example of the organic forms inherent in neo-Gothic architecture.

the design and starting again, though using the existing foundations. It is relatively conventional if stubby in plan – nave with aisles, transepts, choir surrounded by an ambulatory in an apsidal end. Relatively short end to end, it is very tall, a forest of spires representing the key figures of the faith. There will finally be 18 of them and the tallest central 'Jesus' spire will rise to 171 metres, surrounded by four slightly lesser towers representing the Evangelists (gospel-writers Matthew, Mark, Luke and John). Set in front of this cluster is the spire representing the Virgin Mary. There are three main frontages to the church, the 'Nativity', 'Passion' and 'Glory' facades, each surmounted by four spires in total representing the 12 disciples of Jesus.

Then there is the ornament. Only the extraordinary 'Nativity' facade, alive with carved figures and with its four spires well under way, was reasonably complete at the time of Gaudí's death, and from that point things became complicated because Gaudí's archive of drawings and models, kept in the crypt on site, were wrecked during the Spanish Civil War. It took 16 years just to reconstruct the master model, and work on the church itself only resumed in the 1950s. By 2010 it was still only half-finished.

It was originally designed to be a colourful place externally, as Gaudí's other buildings are. There is some external colour but one senses it will never be quite so gaudy as Gaudí wanted. Nor was it by any means designed in all its details at his death, which means that his successors have had to quite freely interpret what imagery exists. Externally, it has tended to get less elaborate over time.

The Sagrada Família can be seen as hugely vulgar, kitsch even. But there are plenty of other churches that accusation could be levelled at. Gaudí in the end escapes the charge of vulgarity simply by being so very inventive, original and single-minded. One is almost surprised to find some more or less conventional Gothic windows in the nave, but it is as if some extraordinary organic force has erupted up through that. Inside, it is breath-taking and pretty much impossible to describe, except to say that it is like looking up from a tropical forest floor or coral reef. The tree-forest analogy is often made of Gothic architecture, but here, where the columns twist and branch as they rise, it is entirely apt. There are carved details for which you will find no name in a glossary of architecture, as if they were as yet uncatalogued species. The building belongs, perhaps, in a fantasy animation: but there it is, and it is real.

---

1 Reported by his architectural assistant and first biographer Josep F. Ràfols, *Antonio Gaudí*, 1929.
2 The bookseller was José María Bocabella (1815–1892) and the cult he founded in 1866 was the *Spiritual Association of Devotees of St Joseph*. 'Expiatory temple' was part of the original official name of the church: 'Expiatory Temple of the Holy Family'. The 'basilica' designation discussed in the text is now its official name.

Notre Dame du Haut

Ronchamp, Eastern France, 1950–54

ARCHITECT: LE CORBUSIER (1887–1965)

STYLE: SCULPTURAL PRIMITIVIST

The chapel on its hill is now part of a religious community including (left) a convent and visitor centre (2006–11) by Renzo Piano.

This out-of-the-way chapel, in a former mining area between the Vosges and the Jura mountains near Belfort, is a sublime, enigmatic object to approach and be in. It was also the stylistic bombshell of the post-war years. 'Le Corbusier' – the name and character assumed by Swiss-French architect Charles-Édouard Jeanneret-Gris – had been one of the pioneers of modernism in the 1920s and 1930s. The 'International Style', as this early modernist phase came to be known after an 1933 exhibition of that name at New York's Museum of Modern Art, was meant above all to be rational, functional, even anonymous. But Le Corbusier, ever restless, egocentric and as much an artist as an architect, was having none of that. He saw the commission for the Ronchamp chapel as a chance to try something new, very new. Instead of being rational it was to be spiritual and sculptural.

More than that, it is Le Corbusier's way of proving that modernism can play all the same aesthetic and emotional tricks that traditional religious buildings do. He was not a man of faith, though he had a sense of it. 'Every man has the religious consciousness of belonging to a greater mankind, to a greater or lesser degree', he said. 'I am not a pagan. Ronchamp is a response to the desire that one occasionally has to extend beyond oneself, and to seek contact with the unknown.'[1]

The 'chapel' is actually two chapels: one of the pulpits of the outdoor space, seen here, connects through to the second, interior space.

This chapel symbolised the recovery of France from the trauma of the Second World War and so the return of hope. There is no functional brief for that, only for the usual list of spatial requirements: nave, altar, pulpit, side chapels, confessionals, sacristy. There had been a much-altered and unlovely long-established pilgrimage chapel here, war-damaged but intact. It could have been patched up but the ambitious priest in charge of the project, the Dominican friar and patron of contemporary sacred art Marie-Alain Couturier (1897–1954), championed a move to something entirely new. He always trusted good artists, whatever their beliefs or none, agreeing with Corbusier that theirs is a parallel form of spirituality.

The resulting building is refined primitivism, a return to first principles. Non-symmetrical, it stakes its claim as being in descent from the very beginnings of architecture. It has something of the spirit of a Neolithic barrow about it and also something of the ancient temple. Corbusier liked to claim that there was no such thing as style, only approach, and that this went back to fundamentals. For him this was 'a plastic work', meaning moulded and pierced as if from clay.[2]

There is symbolism of course: the chapel as a vessel with a sharp prow (some see a pair of cupped hands). Its roof can also be seen as a boat, being a hollow construction between two thin shells of concrete separated and

The interior is a place of immense calm. The roof is seemingly floating and beams of light creep in from a multitude of small punched windows.

supported by concealed girders and beams. The eastern wall is pulled inwards beneath this oversailing roof, providing shelter outside for a separate open-air chapel with altar and two pulpits. The wall curls inwards at three points to form the side chapels. Invisibly, stones from the previous chapel are built into the north and west walls, south and east being new, though all have the same white-painted textured finish and so look the same. Salvaged stones are also used in a ziggurat (stepped pyramid) as the base for a pilgrimage cross a little further up the hill. For the chapel Le Corbusier used sprayed concrete as the surface finish, an experimental technique at the time.

A large square enamelled door on the south side (an abstract artwork in itself) leads you to the interior, which is all to do with the play of solidity, light and colour. The curving, unpainted concrete roof above your head, sloping gently from south to north, appears to hover on a strip of daylight. A multitude of small windows set in deep splayed apertures provides further illumination. These are in a mix of clear and coloured glass, some bearing gnomic words or phrases – emphatically *not* stained glass, Corbusier insisted, but we do not have to believe him. The polished floor follows the gentle slope of the hill down towards the slightly raised plain stone altar behind a curving, polished-iron communion rail. A concrete pulpit projects into the space from the priest's quarters built into the north-east side of the building, and a curving interior corner balcony leads to the outdoor equivalent. The simple timber and concrete pews are set at an angle to one side, leaving a lot of clear floorspace: at times of pilgrimage it can be standing room only. At other, calmer, times one can lose oneself in contemplation here.

Although one side of the chapel is the clerical rather than public area, from the outside this is a building with no unsatisfactory facades, only very different ones. Outside, the views across to the nearby mountains are tremendous: Le Corbusier had a gift of a site. It has become the centre of a small architectural and faith community, with a simple bell stand designed by French architect Jean Prouvé (1901–1984), and, arranged around the foot of the slope near the original single-storey entrance buildings, a new small convent by Italian architect Renzo Piano, which makes use of the chapel daily.

Pilgrims come in various forms, and you are as likely – perhaps even more likely – to encounter the architectural as the religious kind here. For both, this intense little building is a powerful device for concentration and contemplation.

1 Jean Petit, *Le Corbusier lui-même*, trans. Helen Walden, 1970.
2 Hugh Pearman, *Contemporary World Architecture*, 1998.

The Ismaili Centre Toronto, Canada, 2001–14

ARCHITECT: CHARLES CORREA (1930–2015)

STYLE: HIGH-TECH SYMBOLIST

The prayer hall's virtuoso, double-skin glass roof is aligned with Mecca.

Charles Correa was arguably India's greatest post-war architect, instrumental in establishing a distinct, historically informed style for the nation after independence. He went on to achieve international fame. He also had a particular virtue, according to an admirer of his, architect David Adjaye (see the NMAAHC, p. 156). He was, said Adjaye in 2013, 'someone who has that rare capacity to give physical form to something as intangible as culture or society.'[1]

For Correa, an Indian Roman Catholic, to design what is essentially a mosque in Canada at the behest of the Swiss-born Aga Khan, seemed wholly natural. Indeed, he had previously designed Hindu and Christian buildings. Equally natural was the fact that his faceted pyramidal glass and steel prayer hall is surely inspired in no small part by the Beth Sholom synagogue in Philadelphia (1953–9) by Frank Lloyd Wright (which itself, use of glass aside, referenced ancient Mayan temples). For Correa, the religion to which the building was aligned was unimportant; what mattered was Wright's masterly handling of light. In the secular world, Wright's Johnson Wax HQ in Racine, Wisconsin (see p. 86), was for Correa a 'Temple of Lux'.[2] In the case of the Beth Sholom synagogue, the handling of light is in the service of the numinous – a sense of sacredness, of spirituality. Light is a principal ingredient in all buildings but it takes on a particular, directed character in religious ones. Wright and Correa both embraced the mystical in their work.

The dome is a traditional feature of many mosques. A historical peak of cultural and technical achievement is the Sultan Ahmed, or 'Blue Mosque', in Istanbul (1609–16). Designed by Sedefkar Mehmed Agha (d.1617), architect to the Ottoman court, it has an ascending symmetrical sequence of domes from small to large, rows of minarets and of course the interior Iznik tilework that gives it its name. But there was no point, reasoned Correa, in replicating anything of that in the somewhat unlikely business-park setting, overlooking a busy freeway intersection, in Toronto's suburbs. 'You have to have the freedom to speak in your contemporary voice', he said at the time. 'You devalue that if you just make a cartoon version of history. There's no need to do golden domes.'[3]

So he avoided straight replication of the past, though some of the elements of the building, with its sequence of meeting, social and teaching spaces, deploy his take on traditional motifs, especially geometric patterning. The *muqarnas*, a traditional corbelled ornamental ceiling, is present and correct in simplified form as you approach the main hall or *Jamatkhana*, the place of congregation. So too is a geometric screen, though here made from delicate ribbons of steel. For the main prayer hall, he wanted to show how a modern lofty space could speak of the spiritual. A dome that is not a dome, rising from a circular stone podium, placed on the highest point of the site. He and the Aga Khan – with his outreach agenda for the Ismaili strand of Shia Islam – both saw light as key, glowing outward as much as inward. It is a beacon for the faith.

It has a structural skeleton of slender steel rods that are then sandwiched by layers of opalescent glass. The double skin reflects a lot of sunlight and provides ventilation against overheating: it is also a very strong structure, necessary against the heavy snowfalls of winter when the hall starts to resemble a mountain peak. A clear glazed slot in the prow of the hall is aligned with Mecca via the most direct route round the globe, which from this location means pointing north-east, initially towards Iceland.

The Ismaili Centre has its own entrance set in the sweeping curve of its entrance buildings beneath a timber and glass canopy. It is, however, one of a pair of buildings in a freshly landscaped setting that will take many years to fully mature. The other is the Aga Khan Museum, with a rich collection of Islamic artefacts from all periods and including a centre for performances, talks and other events. The museum is by Japanese architect Fumihiko Maki (b.1928). In its chiselled-box way it is as different as could be from the more organic shapes of Correa's contribution. These two set pieces face each other across a calm landscaped courtyard of planting and mirror pools. Again, this is a traditional motif of Islamic architecture, but in this case not expressed through enclosure, being instead an incident in elevated, relatively open parkland. The landscape architect for the project was the Lebanese architect Vladimir Djurovic (b.1976), so adding to the transnational nature of the project, which took 13 years from conception to completion. By the time it was finished, both Correa and Maki were well into their eighties.

There have been more radical attempts around the world to redefine the architecture of the mosque (not a term generally used by Ismailis) and some of them can be rather effortful. At the other extreme, wholly traditional new mosques are being built. The largest in the Arab world, for instance, has been built in the New Administrative Capital of Egypt, and opened in 2019. It can house 17,000 people and with its domes and minarets is broadly (and crudely) in the manner of the Fatimid architecture of the area. It was inaugurated on the same day as a new Coptic Christian Orthodox cathedral in the city.

In contrast with both of these, Correa's late-career contribution in Toronto was to start from scratch: to synthesise a long and complex history of mosque design into a few key elements where tradition and modernism play off each other. It was what he had been doing successfully for his entire career. While it was strange to meet this now-stooping tall and affable man in a Canadian suburb far from his normal Indian or European milieu, here was a fine conclusion to a career. 'This,' he said with apparent satisfaction rather than sorrow at its opening, 'is my last building.'[4]

---

1 David Adjaye speaking at the opening of the Charles Correa exhibition at the RIBA in 2013. Adjaye had designed the exhibition.

2 Conversation with the author, September 2014.

3 Ibid.

4 Ibid.

The elements of a traditional prayer hall, though conventionally arranged, are expressed in a determinedly non-traditional way.

Retail

No building type is in more of a state of flux in mature economies than the traditional shopping outlet. As online sales and rapid delivery to your door make physical browsing and buying an increasingly marginal activity, our town centres are rapidly changing. Such changes can be positive: department stores becoming modern-day souks for independent traders, or touchdown office space for self-employed people, or even city-centre housing. Individual shops change their use to artists' studios, or community or medical centres. Seen this way, the previous retail monopoly of our town centres is replaced with something more varied and interesting.

It will take some years for the process to complete. Even then it will not be total: a nimbler kind of shop will always be in the mix, because shopping is more than a transactional activity. It is a form of entertainment and social interchange. Those economies where prices are not fixed, and bargaining is the cultural norm, are less exposed, though not immune, to such changes.

Individual shop interiors tend to have short lives, though there are some historic survivals such as the eighteenth-century premises of wine merchants Berry Brothers and Rudd in London's St James's. However, wherever people gather to trade and sell goods, places are designed to contain that activity. These host buildings for shops have much longer lives. The Greek agora and the Roman forum were places of commerce as well as administration. The colonnades, or *stoa*, of Greek cities were where merchants laid out their wares under cover: in medieval times the market square became the equivalent and continues in that role today as a place for mobile traders.

From early streets of shops and market places to giant in town or out-of-town shopping malls is a logical progression, with an increasingly 'designed' overall experience. The development of ever larger sheets of plate glass in the nineteenth and early twentieth centuries made shopfront streets into places to browse and enabled streets to be covered to make arcades in cities such as Paris, London and, greatest arcade of them all, Milan (see p. 210).

The peak of retail architecture, pre-shopping mall, was the great period of the department store: the multi-level attempt to provide nearly everything you might want under one roof. From the mid-nineteenth century onwards these stores were a kind of shopping centre that was not arranged in linear fashion, so not a memory of the street. Brought into being by rising standards of living and disposable income, these were safe places, especially for middle-class women at a time when the streets outside could be hazardous and you might not wish to brave them alone. Department stores had washrooms, changing rooms, places to meet and eat. They would deliver the goods you purchased to your home. Accordingly, they proved

Au Bon Marché, from *Le Monde Illustré*, c.1875. This engraving shows the department store's then-new staircase, designed by Frédéric Lix (1830–1897).

very successful and, like hotels, competed with each other through architecture and design.

The 'Bon Marché' store in Paris of 1869–72 was designed by Jean-Alexandre Laplanche (1839–1910) and Louis-Auguste Boileau (1812–1896). It was later extended by Boileau's son, Louis-Charles Boileau (1837–1914), with the engineer Gustave Eiffel (1832–1923). Bon Marché set the tone for the great cities of the world: stores as grand as palaces, often with spectacular staircases and top-lit atria beneath decorative glazed roofs and as good to look at outside as in. Perhaps retail architecture never got better than that familiar, now declining, form: but as a type, across history, the architecture of selling and buying is much broader than that.

The covered shopping mall as a type was the development of the open shopping precinct – essentially a purpose-built pedestrianised street. These were characteristic of the post-war rebuilding of devastated European cities such as Rotterdam in the Netherlands and Coventry, England. The typology is, however, much older. The pedestrian shopping precinct known as the Pantiles in the spa town of Tunbridge Wells in southern England dates from 1638. Arranged on two 'walks', or levels, to take account of the slope of the land, and including an arcade for shelter, with a pleasing variety of buildings of different styles and ages incorporating housing and hotels, it is almost a perfect model of its kind.

The first fully enclosed multi-level shopping centre in the world was designed by architect Ralph Erskine in the port city of Lulea in northern Sweden. It opened in 1955. Still there, though much altered since, it was a logical attempt to move city life indoors during long, harsh, dark winters. Shortly after came an anti-urban type: the now familiar agglomeration of large, flat-roofed, air-conditioned shopping sheds surrounded by hundreds of acres of car park in a wide open space. Architect Victor Gruen's Southdale Center of 1956 in Edina, Minnesota, was the first such regional shopping centre. 'Regional' implies size: people drive to such places from a great distance.

Gruen was Viennese, an émigré to the United States in 1938 after Nazi Germany annexed his homeland. He later claimed, with justification, that he had been misunderstood. He was an urbanist, steeped in European culture, who had intended the Southdale Center to be just the first part of an effective new town, with everything provided, from houses to hospitals and schools and beautifully landscaped parks. None of that happened, but the architectural and commercial worlds took note of the commercial success of his stand-alone out-of-town mall with its 5,000 parking spaces and copied and enlarged it assiduously, everywhere, soon adding in leisure elements such as cinemas and theme parks as well. Far from being parts of real communities, they were isolated, car-dependent islands. Towards the end of his life Gruen ruefully told a conference of shopping-centre professionals in London, 'I refuse to pay alimony for those bastard developments. They destroyed our cities.'[1] What he wanted, and urged developers to build, continued to be the mixed-use urban model.

Such mall architecture, in or out of town, has for decades been determined by four things. The first is the overall size of the 'anchor stores' deemed necessary for the financial viability of the whole project and which are usually modern versions of department stores. Secondly, the required number of medium and smaller units to accommodate the usual tally of smaller familiar chain stores. Thirdly, the finely calculated dimensions of the pedestrian malls and node points between malls to make the place seem active but not overcrowded. Finally, all the car parking, surface or stacked, required for the shoppers and the turning circles and unloading bays of the long articulated trucks keeping the stores stocked. This is the model that is now under strain, though not everywhere.

Architects have a variety of different involvements in retail, from broad planning to fine detail. The design of individual shops is generally a matter of interior design, which is heavily linked to branding: Apple Stores, for instance, are notable in employing a sophisticated clean techno-design language appropriate to the products sold. At the less glamorous end of the retail process, architects are no less involved in the design and grouping of the enormous retail distribution warehouses that service our online orders, and such stores. At the large-scale level of an open precinct or mall, the architectural intent is in the overall framing: individual retailers have their own designers and want you to look at their stores with their separate identities. What the architect does in mall design is more to do with the 'public' aspects – movement of people, places to relax, the overall sense of space. The nature of older malls is to be inward-looking: it is often hard to think what one actually looks like from the outside. Some recent examples succeed in knitting themselves into the surrounding streets convincingly.

Somewhat unexpectedly, the largest example of any mall in the world at the time of writing is the Iran Mall in Tehran, opened in 2018. It has approximately 1.4 million square metres of commercial space, planned to rise to 2 million square metres in future phases. The first phase contains more than 2,500 shops. Particularly in extreme climates with great swings between hot and cold, dry and humid, such places offer the ultimate controlled environment, the corollary of which is massive energy consumption and carbon-dioxide emissions, which worsen the climate extremes. The desirable alternative of the naturally cooled mall, however, already exists in the form of traditional bazaars.

1 Victor Gruen speaking at the Third Annual European Conference of the International Council of Shopping Centres, London, 1978.

Grand Bazaar

Istanbul, Turkey, 1455–1791; last renovated 2016–19

ARCHITECTS: VARIOUS

STYLE: BYZANTINE/OTTOMAN

You know it, even if you think you don't. It filters into our consciousness through films (among them the opening scene in the 2012 Bond movie *Skyfall*, itself a knowing reference to Bond's previous visit in 1963's *From Russia with Love*), through novels, travelogues, magazines, board and video games, blogs and vlogs. Its domes, vaults, painted barrel-vaulted passageways and air of vivid, controlled chaos are familiar. One of the largest and oldest covered markets anywhere, Istanbul's Grand Bazaar is the ancestor of modern shopping malls and will most likely outlive them all.

This was always a place for merchants and craftsmen, especially in textiles, jewellery, leatherware, metalwork and woodwork. It was also a regional bourse, or exchange in gold, with prices fixed daily. Constantinople, as it was then called, was the centre of the Ottoman Empire from the moment Sultan Mehmet II (1432–1481), then aged just 21, conquered the city in 1453 following a highly destructive siege. This marked the final collapse of the once-great Byzantine Empire.

Mehmet set about rebuilding the city as a cosmopolitan, Muslim-ruled centre. Constantinople was sited at the intersection of trade routes between East and West and, as such, a place to concentrate this trade was needed.

The original multi-domed sections of the bazaar rise above the later, now restored ad hoc roofscape.

Mehmet built the first covered market or *bedesten*, a large rectangular building with 15 large brick domes and eight smaller ones. Located at the heart of the historic city, close to other civic and religious buildings, this was to be a secure place for traders in jewellery and precious metals. Nearly a century later, another similar *bedesten* was built nearby to specialise in textiles, covering about the same area but this time with 20 large domes.

That was the end of any kind of proactive planning for what became the Grand Bazaar. Rapidly new, closely packed streets were built between and around the two multi-domed buildings by ever-increasing numbers of traders. The narrow streets, piled high with goods, were often sheltered by tarpaulins, later timber roofs. With workshops and kitchens everywhere, fires were common, and it was an attempt to make the place less flammable that led to the covered streets being vaulted over in brick or stone from the early eighteenth century (stone vaults beneath timber roofs having long been a fire protection in medieval cathedrals and mosques). But such was the growth of the Bazaar that it had already reached what is pretty much its extent today a century before that.

Earthquakes, wars, civil unrest, neglect and unauthorised alterations have had their inevitable effect, but the Grand Bazaar has always been patched up

Inside is a maze of vaulted arcades where traders' booths open directly onto the street.

and periodically improved. The Bond stunt filming (motorcycle chase across the crumbling, leaky roofs) drew attention to the fragile state of the structure. A huge renovation of the many hectares of roofs with their traditional red pantiles, plus the foundations and drainage took place from 2016, section by section, with the Bazaar still in operation; the job was completed in 2019. In what is one of the most populous places in the world, they take a more eastern than western approach to such state-led projects: the trades are mobilised and the work is carried out relatively speedily, even under these challenging conditions.

Some figures: the Grand Bazaar covers some 31 hectares, has 61 covered streets and 21 entrance gates, is the workplace for some 30,000 people and its annual visitor numbers can surpass 91 million. Apart from all the traders' booths it includes mosques, cafés and courtyard inns, or *hans*, often containing workshops, which originally housed visiting traders and allowed them space to display their goods. More localised food markets are elsewhere in the city.

The oldest parts of the complex are roofed with the characteristically Byzantine shallow domes, absorbed by Ottoman culture.

This market was, and to some extent still is, an international trading centre for hand-crafted goods. While today, its customers are mostly the inevitable tourists, there are still plenty of workshops there making goods: it is not all tat and souvenirs.

The ancestor of the modern shopping malls it may be, but it is unlike those in two important respects. The modern mall tends to have a few broad covered thoroughfares, readily navigable. The Grand Bazaar, although organised on a loose grid pattern and roughly rectangular (with an offshoot to the north) is a mazy net of smaller streets. The individual 'retail units', as they are called in the jargon of the business, are mostly small, some very small, and not enclosed: the traders and their goods spill out in front of the booths, the better to proclaim the virtues of their wares, seize the attention of slightly panicked shoppers and try to clinch a deal before their rival next door or opposite gets there first.

The old *hans* with their courtyards perhaps provide some respite but the overall impression is of a great, highly active, press of people and things. The density is as much human as urban – and urbanistically, this is a very tightly laid-out place indeed, with none of the vehicle access, parking and service yards you find in any modern retail centre. Indeed, it is something of a mystery how all the goods get in there, until you realise that there is little on sale that cannot be carried or pushed on a trolley. In this immersive experience, buyers and sellers are on the same, human, scale.

Since it and its kind work very well, you might wonder why modern shopping malls are not designed along similar lines. One answer is that the goods sold here are mostly small, easily carried items. Another is that here you are looking at something that has evolved organically on the much tighter grain of old cities; it is by no means easy to replicate that from scratch, and today's building regulations would make it difficult, if not impossible. Nonetheless, such places hold lessons, the greatest of these being that high urban density is nothing to be afraid of.

Galleria Vittorio Emanuele II

Milan, Italy, 1861–78

ARCHITECT: GIUSEPPE MENGONI (1829–1877)

STYLE: NEO-RENAISSANCE

The retail malls of the second half of the twentieth century and early years of the twenty-first owe their beginnings to the covered arcades of European and American cities in the early nineteenth century, starting in Paris and London. Such arcades consist of commercial spaces – cafés, shops, bars – either side of narrow streets roofed with glass. These were different from the ancient forms of markets or bazaars, even when those too were covered, because the individual shops in arcades are themselves enclosed rather than being freestanding stalls. What could be simpler or more convenient than a covered street? Networks of them, sometimes forming routes through successive blocks, rapidly became established across most larger cities. By the time we reach the late nineteenth century and Milan's Galleria, however, the straightforward arcade had become something altogether more ambitious.

Milan in northern Italy was prosperous and highly civic-minded. Throughout the nineteenth century the municipality had wanted to give its fantastically ornate, marble-roofed, Gothic cathedral (inching towards completion after six centuries) a grander square to sit in. Gradually, plans emerged to do more: to extend the square into an arcade so monumentally large as to be a proper civic space in itself. A public, under-cover forum. Even better, it would link the cathedral square with the square of the La Scala opera house several blocks to the north.

This plan was put out to competition, eventually won by the young Giuseppe Mengoni. Milan had been liberated from Austrian rule in 1859. Following the long and complex struggle for Italian unification, Milan had emerged as one of the principal cities of the newly proclaimed 'Kingdom of Italy', under the king Vittorio Emanuele II (r.1861–1878). Plans for urban improvements were seen as a priority for the new administration, though bureaucracy and uncertainty delayed things starting until 1865. By that time, Mengoni, having toured the best examples in Paris and London, had developed a cruciform plan for his arcade, with two side wings leading in from flanking open streets. The intersection where they met was a very large octagon – so large, in fact, that a dome could be placed on top which, at 37 metres across, had a base the exact circumference of St Peter's Basilica in Rome.

The project was regarded as so important that the king himself attended the ceremony to lay the foundation stone. This was not just some commercial speculation. Although it was privately financed by an English firm set up for the purpose – the City of Milan Improvement Company Ltd – it was nonetheless seen as a proper new piece of open-access urban realm, dedicated to the fortunate public of the new Italy, with their king's name on it. This is in sharp contrast to most modern urban-scale developments where the owner companies have control over what might appear to be public space but is policed by private security guards and that can be shut off at any time.

The retail arcade in excelsis, with a central dome as broad as that of St Peter's Basilica (1506–1626) in Rome.

The scale of Mengoni's achievement is remarkable and still awe-inspiring today. It is certainly not one of the subtlest pieces of architecture: its interior facades are rather overdone when compared to the Renaissance precedents they refer to and its fresco-work beneath the main dome (symbolically representing the four continents) is verging on kitsch. At the time, it was seen as being the height of good taste; today, 'good fun' might describe it better. There is plenty of figurative sculpture everywhere, often of famous Italians in various fields, plus coats of arms and ornamental iron eagles to add to the already-ornate ironwork. Such visual richness was by no means confined to Mengoni or even to Italy, of course: this was a near-universal language of building ornament by the late nineteenth century across Europe and America, and it is certainly done with great vigour here. More is more.

Any doubts are defused by the boldness of the concept and the sheer size of it all. The main mall, originally lit by gas lamps, is 200 metres from end to end, the cross mall is 105 metres, both are nearly 15 metres across, the vaults are 30 metres high and the top of the dome is 47 metres above the floor. The buildings lining this covered streetscape are not miniatures, as in London's Burlington Arcade, say, but full-sized and containing a mix of uses.

Ground and mezzanine floors are for the retail world, including some of the best luxury shops and restaurants in town. The tall third floor houses offices, clubs, rentable space for events, design studios and the like. Finally comes a continuous row of balconies with three more floors above that containing apartments. Access to them is from rear courtyards, while getting goods in and out of the shops is done via a large basement level. It is very thoroughly thought through. It even originally had a little wheeled robot on tracks running around the dome which lit the gas lamps.

This is not a sealed environment: not only is it open at all four ends but also its glazed roofs and dome have 'raised hat' sections, keeping the rain out but letting air flow through. The barrel vaults and that St Peter's-sized glass dome take the technology that had developed throughout the nineteenth century, first in botanical glasshouses, then in railway termini and exhibition buildings such as Joseph Paxton's 'Crystal Palace' in London in 1851. By the time of the Galleria, the best available engineering and fabrication of this kind of architecture was in France. It was a French company that made the Galleria's wonderful roof.

Outside, Mengoni made another big gesture. The expanded new cathedral square suggested something monumental to lead into the Galleria. He turned to the Roman form of a victory arch, composed in three bays with the central

Looking down from the dome to the central octagon. Above the balcony level are apartments.

A Roman-style triumphal arch marks the entry into the Galleria from the cathedral square; this was also the site of its architect's tragic death.

entrance arch rising to the full height of the vaulted roof inside. The buildings to either side are set further back to emphasise it. The victory in question, of course, was the united Italy's defeat of Austria under Vittorio Emanuele II. At the other end, where the Galleria arrives at the La Scala square at an angle in one corner, Mengoni placed a lesser, but still huge, arch flush with the side of the square. Within that he put two smaller arches at an angle to each other in an apse. One of them goes into the Galleria, the other to a museum at one side. This resolved the awkward geometry, just: there's a sense of great effort.

The king and Mengoni were back for the grand opening in September 1867 and the place was an immediate success: people flocked to it, and have done so ever since. It was not finished, however, as work on the triumphal arch dragged on for a further decade. At the end of 1877, shortly before its completion, the 48-year-old Mengoni fell fatally from the scaffolding. Ten days later, the king who had inspired it all himself died, aged 57. So, neither saw the last stone laid, but what a tremendous monument to them both it is, and what a tremendous affirmation of civilised urban life.

Ljubljana Central Market Arcades

Ljubljana, Slovenia, 1934–44

ARCHITECT: JOŽE PLEČNIK (1872–1957)

STYLE: NEOCLASSICAL

Jože Plečnik's highly original neoclassical style defines the double-decker riverside frontage of the markets complex.

A covered market is a familiar thing, whether it is made of a medieval series of stone or wooden arcades, or a nineteenth-century iron and glass structure. This one is as different as it could be. Arranged to serve two open market squares behind, it is a very long, narrow building running along and incorporating the bank of the Ljubljanica river in the Slovenian capital. It is a neoclassical composition, somewhat Venetian in flavour. Here is a market with great civic impact that transcends its function.

Jože Plečnik was one of the greatest architects of the twentieth century, and until comparatively recently he was somewhat overlooked compared to his contemporaries such as Frank Lloyd Wright in the United States or Charles Rennie Mackintosh in Scotland. This was partly because of his more conservative style and partly because of where he was based. The political melting-pot of Central Europe meant that he worked variously in Austria, Czechoslovakia and his native Slovenia, which emerged from the collapse of the Austro-Hungarian

Empire in 1918 but did not finally achieve full independence from Yugoslavia, and with it a higher national profile, until 1991.

His market arcades in Ljubljana are an inhabited wall, some 300 metres long, linking three of the city's bridges. On the river side the building is two-storey, the lower level in rough (rusticated) stone dropping down to just above the water level, the upper level rendered in smooth mortar. Where it faces the street it is single-storey and just one room deep behind a pedestrian arcade.

Working at a time of economic depression, Plečnik was forever grappling to find funds as well as fighting off traffic engineers and rival architects. His imagination always went far beyond the resources available. Impressive though his waterside market is, it is smaller than he had originally envisaged. He wanted a matching market complex on the other side of the river, linked by a covered bridge. All that came of that was a little tobacconist's kiosk, even this with a basic classical portico. Any possibility of further expansion ended with the Second World War when Italy occupied the city. Remarkably, however, the first set of market buildings was built, albeit slowly, during the war.

The arcades are best approached from another Plečnik work, his triple-bridge ensemble fanning out across the river towards the old town. The market starts with a delicate little flower shop with a double portico, one sitting inside the other. Behind that is an open colonnaded hall for traders to set out their stalls, with a staircase turret projecting over the water just for the fun of it. And beyond that the main sequence of the market building begins, its rhythm of semicircular windows on the river side echoed by those on the inland side, in that case with a central doorway to each shop as part of the composition. A pair of stone bollards either side of each door stops the corners being clouted by porters' trolleys.

On the street side, a colonnade provides shelter to the row of little shops.

These long arcades fall into two sections either side of the pedestrian 'Butcher's Bridge' (so named after the meat traders: the fish market was on the lower level by the river). To forestall visual monotony, each of the two long sections is given a break-point expressed as an open classical pavilion. You can walk through these and overlook the river. In each Plečnik provided a well for the market traders to draw water from.

The joy of the composition is the way Plečnik made a relatively prosaic commission – a place for traders and shopkeepers to sell their goods – into a public promenade, part of his overall plan for the city centre. He may only have achieved

The entrance and glazing to each unit is treated as a classical composition.

various fragments of his urban ambitions, but what fragments they are: even a set of sluices he designed on the river are dignified and distinctive, while he managed to make concrete lamp-posts into strange and wonderful neoclassical totems. Today, Ljubljana is a tourist honeypot and in 2021 the city's collection of Plečnik's buildings were declared a UNESCO World Heritage Site, and rightly so. His work is a brilliant dialogue of new with old. He was a great one for breaking the supposed classical 'rules', which is why he was rediscovered by a new generation of postmodernist architects in the 1980s as something of a 'rogue architect'.[1] There is a satisfyingly playful oddness to many of his buildings, where he is inclined to mix up materials almost randomly, and place columns in curious positions. By his often exuberant standards these market buildings are relatively restrained, and in this urban context none the worse for that.

The market traders still set up their stalls in the colonnade and the squares behind. The little shops, of course, cater for the tourist trade, offering hand-made goods and food. The flower shop pavilion is an information centre. In the jargon of the retail trade it is today a tiny 'speciality shopping centre', as many former market buildings around the world have become.

It must have seemed something of an old-fashioned thing to build as the modern world was stricken by war, but it represented continuity and, for Plečnik, national pride. He essentially bowed out with this project, aged 72 when it was finished. After the war modernism was the thing and he did little more than a few renovations until his death in 1957. Now he sits high in the architectural Pantheon.

1 The term 'rogue architects' was first applied by H.S. Goodhart-Rendel to certain original and maverick Victorian neo-Gothic architects (*Rogue Architects of the Victorian Era*, 1949). Today, it is used more loosely: a 'rogue' is an architect who does not quite play by the rules of the given style, whatever it may be.

Langham Place Shopping Mall

Mong Kok, Hong Kong, 1999–2004

ARCHITECTS: THE JERDE PARTNERSHIP (JON ADAMS JERDE (1940–2015), WITH WONG & OUYANG (HK) LTD)

STYLE: COMMERCIAL HIGH TECH

Rising amid the tumult of Mong Kok, the Langham Place Mall, connected to the neighbouring curvilinear office tower, is marked by its curving roof.

Hong Kong is one of the most densely built places in the world. The buildings cling to the edge of the mountainous islands and on reclaimed land in the shallow sea of the Pearl River Delta: much of the original shoreline of the main island has been expanded in this way. A British colonial possession from 1841 to 1997, when it reverted to China under the 'one country, two systems' policy, it evolved as an ultra-capitalist, mercantile trading centre in a way that was much more Asian than British. This was especially true when the city expanded into the Kowloon Peninsula on the mainland from 1860. West Kowloon was gentler terrain. Building was easier. Streets were laid out on a grid pattern. Within Kowloon, the Mong Kok district became, and remains, the tumultuous heart of commercial Hong Kong.

It helps to have a guide when visiting Mong Kok as the whole place, packed and noisy as it is, is a sensory overload. This was the Hong Kong atmosphere drawn on and turbocharged so fruitfully by director Ridley Scott for his 1982 science-fiction movie *Blade Runner*, set in a very orientalised Los Angeles future, dated 2019. By coincidence, 2019 was the very year I visited Mong Kok. No flying cars were in evidence.

Retail centres generally tend to be relatively ground-hugging: it is hard to distribute people equally over more than four floors, say, though some department stores go a little higher. Retailers need steady footfall, passing trade. In everyday shopping streets, the shops usually confine themselves to the ground floors, sometimes the first. But in Mong Kok, thanks to land scarcity and hence high values, the shops pile up, level after level. You can clamber up within buildings jammed solid with little shops, higher and higher, generally grouped by type of products sold. Food, especially fresh food and fish, will be at or near ground level. Non-perishable goods such as clothing and electronics can go as high as they like. As has been the case throughout history and across the world, it helps for traders in one particular commodity to form an enclave with others in the same business. So it is here: Mong Kok is a place informally divided up by type of product on offer.

One could make a case for presenting the whole of Mong Kok, in all its visual and aural intensity, as one enormous retail centre built in many phases – lower, crumbly, older masonry buildings existing cheek by jowl with taller glassy-sleek modern ones. But just as the place's character came to define the look of a particular famous movie, so it came to influence an early twenty-first-century mall built there. When slum clearance (including, controversially, the demolition of the previous 'Bird Street' marketplace) in the 1980s made a site for a large commercial development, with office and hotel towers, it also included a shopping mall. This being Mong Kok, it did not sprawl in the North American, or even the more compact European, manner. It too went vertical: partly down into the ground but mostly up into the air. The Langham Place Shopping Mall has 15 levels.

This is not fine architecture such as you would expect from a cultural building, but that is not the point. Part of its appeal is the drama of the main atrium, a steel latticework structure clad in glass. The spectacle is the thing: this alone rises over nine levels. Two sets of express escalators, not stopping at intervening floors, take you up to the heights where there are many places to eat. From there you can start to wander back down again, the circulation routes designed to take you to and fro past the shops, restaurants and cinema complex.

There is something about the brazen, flaunt-it style of such malls that can be either off-putting or attractive, depending on taste, in conventional cases. Here, however, it takes on a wide-eyed glamour. Jon Jerde, founder of the Los Angeles-based practice that designed the mall, was one of the retail gurus of the late twentieth and early twenty-first centuries, and it shows. To ride those escalators (the longest is 45 metres, rising up to 76 metres) is a kind of urban exhilaration.

The interiors on each floor, full though they are of the usual competing branded shopfronts, are nonetheless calmer than the surrounding streets, so there is a sense of escape from controlled chaos. It may not quite be Milan's late nineteenth-century Galleria upended (see p. 210) – there is no fine detail or much in the way of craftsmanship to be found here – but it too feels like a public space, even though it is not. You are in 12-hours-a-day private territory here, those hours running late into the evening. Jerde knew his urbanism, and this is not a fortress as many inward-looking earlier malls were: in the circulation areas you can always see out to the city beyond. It is a good place to have lunch and watch the crowds.

From the outside it is hard to take in. This is despite the fact that its architects played the game of visually breaking down what would otherwise have been sheer cliffs of walls on both sides by angling sections of them in

The mall is all about its multi-level interior; it is far taller than is traditional for this building type.

various ways (the merest nod to the then-fashionable architectural trope of 'deconstruction'). The walls are part glass, the rest being clad in prodigious quantities of wafer-thin sheets of shiny ochre-coloured Brazilian granite – not a material usually to be found in Hong Kong. The whole edifice is topped with a curving metallic roof and is plugged in to the office tower, to the hotel via a bridge across the street, and via the basement to Hong Kong's Metro system.

In a city where etiolated, super-thin skyscrapers sprout from tiny, extremely valuable plots, the amount of land taken by Langham Place is as unusual as its slab-like form, enclosing 56,000 square metres of retail space of all kinds. It was only made possible by a wholescale government-sanctioned clearance and even then it has to jig around a small existing building at one corner that presumably declined to sell up. Nonetheless, it somehow suits the character of the district, as if all the teeming streets of shopkeepers generated an eruption, right in the centre. It is almost medieval: if too accessible to be a fortress then for once the term 'cathedral of commerce' is apt. One might lament the loss of one of the traditional Mong Kok small-trader markets and tight-packed, low-rise housing, as one might the undoubted big-money gentrification happening elsewhere; but this relentless churn and growth is also part of the nature of Hong Kong, which is nothing without the racing pulse of trade.

Magna Park Milton Keynes, UK, 1987–2020

ARCHITECT: CHETWOODS

STYLE: FUNCTIONALIST

It is a visually frictionless building, the Amazon distribution warehouse on the eastern edge of the relatively new city-scale town of Milton Keynes, right next to the UK's prime north–south motorway, the M1. However, at over half a kilometre long, even at motorway speed, you have plenty of time to take it in. It is longer than the Empire State Building in New York is tall and rather wider at 126 metres. It is also surprisingly high, as shown by the loading docks for trucks, apparently tiny relative to the facade. It rises to over 24 metres, sufficient for ten levels of storage racks inside, with catwalks running at intervals across them. Outside, it is painted in broad horizontal stripes: dark blue ascending through paler blues to light grey at the top. The idea is that it recedes against the sky. 117 trucks can dock with it at once if need be, incoming goods on one side and dispatch to customers on the other. It has three admin blocks plugged into it also.

We all shop remotely at places like this. Always close to trunk roads, the mega-warehouses are the dispatch centres for our online orders.

This is today's retail experience, not that you are likely to get any closer than the motorway view. This Amazon warehouse was built speculatively on previously green fields. It was constructed by a worldwide developer in order to attract just such a tenant to what is called 'Magna Park Milton Keynes'. The park is developed on a landscape plan, complete with lake and existing woodland. The building is designed for 100 per cent product availability (everything is always in stock), all capable of being delivered on the same or the next day, and it can handle returns and exchanges at the same time. In the trade this is known as an omni-channel warehouse, but other configurations are available in what is, when built, just a colossal empty space with a smooth, super-flat, concrete floor interrupted by a few rows of slender steel columns. Also on site here is the main national hub for the John Lewis and Waitrose chain, a legacy retailer still with physical department stores and food shops but rapidly pivoting to online.

This motorway, and motorways at strategic points everywhere, run past many such places, some hidden not by sky-blue camouflage but by being placed behind high-planted earthen banks. Worldwide, the majority do not try to hide, or make landscaped settings for themselves at all. They are just there, everywhere, proclaiming their function as much by their size as by the company logos, always placed towards the corners.

These are the dominant building typology of our age, to be found at the node points of our road, rail, seaport and airport systems. Yet our gaze slides past them. They are so big and commonplace that we hardly notice them because we prefer to look at other, more human-scale, things. Nonetheless, these are the shops we all now go to by proxy while others – the truck and train drivers and the cohorts of shelf-stackers and pickers and robots that work there – are our personal shoppers. We consumers browse and choose, place an order and then sit back. In a shed like this an impressively rapid chain of processes then ensues that you can track your order online. It cascades down to local centres and is distributed from those to our doorsteps or collection lockers nearby. Upstream of this is another chain of processes, stretching from place of manufacture anywhere in the world via ship, train and road to the big shed.

The end result everywhere is a prodigious amount of construction of very simple structures like this. Architects are involved, not least in the master-planning of developments and to make the sheds as lean, energy-efficient and as good to work in as possible. Laurie Chetwood (b.1957), founder of the firm involved here, is personally a great designer of highly complex, almost science-fantasy architecture and has exhibited in London's Royal Academy Summer Exhibition. You cannot describe these distribution centres as 'palaces of consumerism', as you can the great department stores of the past. Palatial

Designed to fade out against the skyline, these very long buildings are also surprisingly tall.

in size only, they come close to that blurred boundary between 'architecture' and just 'buildings'. They are supremely functional, with few airs and graces. Perhaps it is better that way: big-shed technology has more obviously architectural outlets such as sports buildings and transport terminals.

Writing in 1991, the architecture critic Martin Pawley (1938–2008) described his earlier generation of super-sheds as 'vast, horizontal and plain, as befits the unobstructed sites upon which (they are) built ... these big sheds are the unacknowledged international style architecture of the world consumer economy.'[1] Back then, such places were serving conventional retail centres, with no thought of delivering direct to the consumer. Since then the biggest distribution sheds have doubled in size and are now pushing 93,000 square metres.

Even such places as these have clear historical precedents: in the main introduction to this book we have already mentioned the enormous granaries of medieval tithe barns. There is a military connection, too. Just over 72 kilometres north of our Milton Keynes example is an older, but still expanding, Magna Park complex at Lutterworth in Leicestershire, masterplanned by the same architects. This consists of 32 buildings totalling 929,000 square metres on a site of more than 223 hectares. This was previously a Royal Air Force base, in operation during the Second World War and a centre for jet-plane development thereafter. It already had its big sheds in the form of hangars, in which Avro Vulcan nuclear bombers could shelter. Once demilitarised and sold, it was at first taken over by a food retailer, which saw the potential in a site with large covered storage in the centre of England. From that, everything else followed, phase after phase. Magna Park Lutterworth also has the trademark ascending blue stripes of its developer and architect. It is Europe's largest example of such a logistics complex and is planned to expand a further 557,000 square metres in area, beyond the old airfield boundaries into the surrounding farmland. Once that is done, it will employ some 15,000 people. It is, therefore, almost a small town in itself, and is the model rolled out across the world.

All this officially constitutes an industrial use but this is not manufacturing industry. It is, if you like, the back office of the retail business. Rather than ignoring such places we should be intrigued, even delighted, by them. These days we all inhabit the world of logistics.

1 Martin Pawley, 'Triumph of the Big Shed', *The Strange Death of Architectural Criticism: Martin Pawley Collected Writings*, 2007.

Gardens

Just as towns and cities are defined as much by the spaces between buildings as by the buildings themselves, so architecture can define landscape, even be landscape. Landscape in this context is never wild, but modified or completely invented by humans. It is the synthesis of buildings and nature, each as fully designed as the other to make the whole.

The designed landscape is everywhere and evolves in many hands over time. The Great Pyramids complex at Giza in Egypt is a necropolis landscape. A city is a landscape as much as a stretch of countryside. The whole of the Netherlands, created by people as a radical modification of the natural world, can be seen as a single designed object. So, landscape goes way beyond architecture: what we are concerned with here is the symbiotic relationship between the two.

Gardens can be highly symbolic places, compared to, or at any rate aspiring to, paradise in many religions. They are places of retreat, whether that be into a small town garden, such as the Romans had at the rear of their urban houses (the *hortus conclusus*) or a larger area within the public realm, such as a park. The origin of many urban parks was often simply stretches of countryside or farmland, or the estates of country houses or royal hunting grounds, beyond the edge of town which absorbed them as it expanded. The land had to be gifted or bought for this purpose because otherwise, left to market forces, it would have been rapidly built over.

Medical research has demonstrated what everyone instinctively felt anyway: access to the natural world is good for our mental health, reducing anxiety and stress. Best of all for those in the relevant climate zones is a walk in the woods, and not just for air quality or exercise reasons: we are psychologically attuned to being among trees, it seems, no doubt a product of our pre-industrial ancestry.

This awareness, that a modified version of nature is a desirable thing, goes back a long way. It is associated with contemplation and inner peace in the Far East and is seen as a foretaste of heaven (and hot climate moderator) in the Middle East and Mediterranean littoral, as well as being a place of promenade and prestige for the wealthy classes worldwide. The garden has been a continuing focus of study since the seventeenth century, when botanical gardens were created, featuring non-native plants brought back from expeditions mounted especially by the colonial powers. These in turn had a powerful influence on architecture through their ever larger and more technically advanced glasshouses.

Modern open spaces, which vary greatly in the amount of greenery ('soft landscape') to built form, including paving and walls ('hard landscape'), are informed by this heritage. Landscape-design modernism, is arguably more at ease with its preceding history than architectural modernism though it is no less susceptible to the vagaries of fashion. In all the most successful cases, as the distinguished landscape architect Sir Geoffrey Jellicoe (1900–1996) wrote

Entrance portico of Stockholm's Forest Crematorium (1935–40) by Eric Gunnar Asplund. It is set within the landscape of the Woodland Cemetery that he and Sigurd Lewerentz designed jointly from 1915 onwards.

in 1991, 'The imaginative landscape extends far beyond what the eye sees and the body enjoys.'[1] You could call this mysticism or trickery, or you could just call it art.

There is a divide between the two groups of designers involved: architects do buildings and broader planning while landscape architects (a separate if overlapping discipline) conventionally do the open space. But even that is not the whole story as, within landscape architecture itself, there is another great divide: those working on the large scale as designers and those who are 'plantspeople' first and foremost, working with the colours, textures, dimensions and seasonality of plants. So, it is normal, looking at the credits for large developments including a high proportion of open space, to find one or more landscape architects of different persuasions involved as well as conventional architects. The task in hand varies greatly, from a relatively small area of space associated with an office building, say (at ground level or on roof gardens and terraces), via the greater opportunities offered by a large housing development, then on to purpose-designed parks and garden spaces, and finally complete 'landscape-led' urban masterplans, new towns and cities. Even the tiniest well-designed open areas – for instance at hospital complexes or at urban 'pocket parks' – can have a disproportionately beneficial impact.

Public amenity and wellbeing aside, the designed open landscape also has an important functional role in urban drainage and flood mitigation, providing absorbent surfaces and regulating water features. This, along with the 'greening' of previously derelict industrial areas and corridors, encourages the regeneration of wildlife, in some instances connecting previously isolated animal habitats. Green landscape design is vital as a means to mitigate the effects of climate change at the local and regional levels.

Regarding paradise, Western cemeteries especially are frequently treated as gardens or quasi-natural places, not only by extension from the rural churchyards that preceded them in some countries but as a conscious attempt to make a place of beauty out of a place of necessity. These can be formal – as with the 140 military cemeteries across France and Belgium laid out following the First World War by English architect Sir Edwin Lutyens with his frequent plantswoman collaborator Gertrude Jekyll (1843–1932) – or informal. The vital example of the latter is the Woodland Cemetery or Skogskyrkogården (1915–1940) outside Stockholm by Erik Gunnar Asplund (1885–1940) and Sigurd Lewerentz (1885–1975), which first opened in 1920. This very beautiful place, inserted into 100 hectares of hillside coniferous forest, is dotted with chapels, a crematorium and other structures (gateways, steps, walls) and much of the architecture lies in the skilful way they navigate you through the forest and its clearings. It was, and is, a very influential design.

The broad division between formal and informal designs continues, with the plant-led informal approach perhaps prevailing at the time of writing, although national preferences apply. It is a running joke between the French and English, for instance, that the former love their very geometric formal gardens – such as the park of Versailles (1662–90) by André Le Nôtre (1613–1700) – while the English prefer their sweeping 'natural' landscapes as examined in the following pages. Both are equally manufactured, in the case of the English eighteenth-century examples, whole villages and natural features sometimes being moved to make vistas with their 'eye-catcher' temples and monuments. This is not uncommon. Urban parks (Central Park in New York among them, see p. 244) can involve displacement of people as much as any large redevelopment.

Although landscape architecture is sometimes seen as a poor relation to the architecture of buildings, the reality is that the two are, or should be, mutually dependent. In today's ultra-cost-sensitive world it helps that a good landscape design enhances the value of property developments and, in many cases, makes them possible in the first place. In this section we deal with specific examples of the architectural garden. It should go without saying that on the largest possible scale – the Earth – humankind needs to develop a global landscape strategy for our own future as a race.

1 Geoffrey Jellicoe, foreword to *Designing the New Landscape* by Sutherland Lyall, 1991.

Gardens of the Villa d'Este

Tivoli, near Rome, Italy, 1550-72

ARCHITECTS: PIRRO LIGORIO (1512–1583) AND SUCCESSORS

STYLE: RENAISSANCE BAROQUE

No matter how wealthy you may be, you can always spend yourself into debt. In the case of Cardinal Ippolito II d'Este (1509–1572) – Duke of Ferrara, advisor to the French King, aspiring Pope and Governor of Tivoli – a fair bit of his wealth went into patronage of the arts, while even more of it went into the furtherance of his perpetually thwarted ambition for supreme power. The two were, of course, connected: but at a time when aristocratic extravagance was the norm, Ippolito's prodigious displays of wealth (along with a not-unusual whiff of corruption) were thought just too much for him to take on the top job. Luckily for the rest of us, he left the extraordinary spectacle of his Villa d'Este and its gardens. This is Renaissance landscape and architecture in perfect fusion.

It is unfortunate that his governorship of Tivoli effectively made him master of the ruins of a very great palace from antiquity – Hadrian's Villa, in the valley

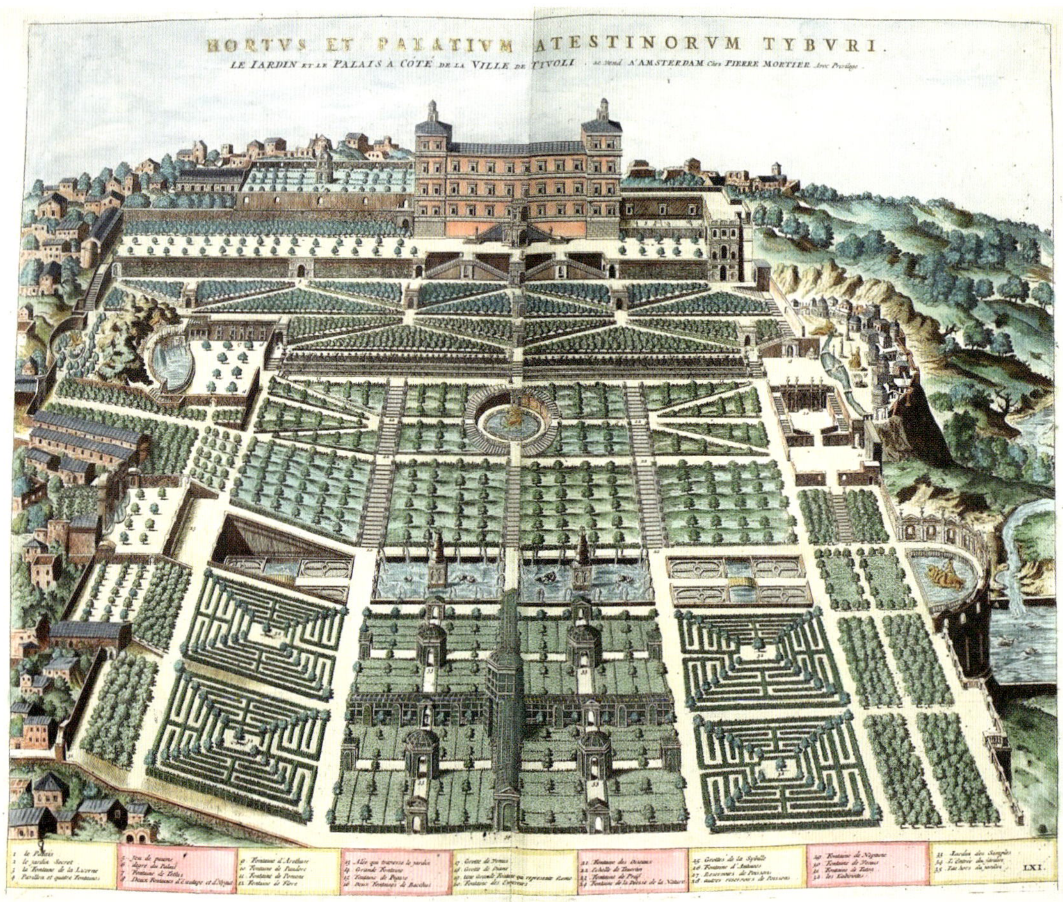

A bird's-eye plan of the gardens of the Villa d'Este by topographical artist and architect Étienne Dupérac (c.1525–1604). Drawing c.1560–75.

A sequence of pools, terraced into the slope, leads you to a vantage point overlooking the plain below with Rome in the distance.

below – because he plundered its marble and sculptures shamelessly for his own villa and gardens. He was not the first or last man of power to act in this way, so we can perhaps call this 'repurposing'. The Villa d'Este itself was later to be plundered in turn, and finally restored in the nineteenth and twentieth centuries.

Tivoli – or Tibur, to give it its Roman name – was a city-state that at times rivalled Rome. Up in the Sabine Hills 30 kilometres to the north-east, a place where an underground river burst out of the hillside, it was a delightful retreat in the hot summer months. Rich and powerful Romans had acquired the habit of building their country boltholes here long before Hadrian, let alone Ippolito. He, like Hadrian, set about making his house as much a power base as a place to escape to. To say that he designed it to impress is an understatement: it was intended to astonish, and it still does.

The slope of the site and the hillside above the town are key to the garden design, which is terraced to descend the gradient and – as was common with large Renaissance gardens – is divided into a grid of smaller square sections, each of equivalent size with a distinct character. The gradient, combined with the presence of an abundant natural water supply arriving from a height, provided the hydraulic force necessary for what seems like a thousand fountains, cascades, rills and spouts. There may be only 51 actual fountains, but there are hundreds of spouts and water jets, interspersed with 64 waterfalls and all manner of pools and channels. The ground was levelled across its centre, however, to provide a sequence of three large rectangular basins of water, based on ancient Roman examples. This terrace leads to the sharp edge of the slope and the endless view across to Rome in the far distance, as if anticipating today's 'infinity pools'.

This is anything but a 'natural' garden, not that any such thing really exists, given the need for human design and management. It is much more a work of architecture, sculpture and engineering than it is of planting, which is unremarkable if lush. It is this garden of marvels, one of the first of its kind and very influential, not the house itself, adapted and extended from a pre-existing monastery, that you remember. As you move through the palazzo with its extraordinary series of frescoes and other works of art, your eye is always drawn to the windows and what lies beyond.

As tourists today, we enter the house at the top and then move into the gardens and progress downwards level by level. This is the opposite of what was intended when the gardens were designed. Ippolito and Ligorio wanted their visitors to enter the garden from below and then ascend by degrees to the top, taking in the full ingenuity and beauty of this creation, before finally its creator would materialise on the top terrace to greet them. By that time you would be mesmerised by what Ippolito could achieve. He would want you to help him achieve more. He entertained the Pope here, with a view to succeeding him.

The original access sequence makes sense for topographical as well as personal reasons. The positioning of the palazzo, dictated by the existing buildings Ippolito took over, means that it faces away from the principal view. It is still a fine view, across the gorge of the Aniene river to the hills beyond, but it is not the view to Rome. In contrast, the garden – which entailed a lot of demolition of existing buildings and numerous lawsuits in consequence, none of which Ippolito paid much attention to – is absolutely aligned with this view. Its central axis, with the three basins, headed by the Fountain of Neptune, runs parallel with the cliff-like rear wall of the palazzo rather than leading out at right angles to it. The message to anyone ascending the gardens to the palazzo at the top was clear: Cardinal Ippolito II was quite literally overseeing Rome.

This can be a little confusing at first to today's visitor. It is not immediately obvious that you are moving across, rather than along, this roughly square garden, though it has its own internal logic and works visually in both directions. You descend, if you want, from the house by a central cross-axis, arrive at a point between two of the three great basins and at that point turn 90 degrees left and proceed out to the long view towards Rome, marked by a ruined look-out tower. More likely, however, you will be diverted to left and right or along the diagonal linking passages on the way, starting with one of many tours de force: the *viale delle cento fontane*, which is indeed a street of a hundred fountains, or rather 300 given that this is a three-level arrangement: top tier small fountains, middle tier mini-cascades, bottom tier waterspouts, each disgorging into a channel and

Transverse paths at the top of the garden are lined with waterspouts set in fern gardens.

so down to the next. Here, the spectacle is cumulative rather than singular, a beguiling place to be on a hot summer's day.

Ippolito, delayed for a decade in carrying out his plans by diplomatic postings, was still developing his gardens by the time he died in 1572, never having achieved his goal of becoming Pope. Subsequently, his successors continued to add to it: typically, a period of neglect would be followed by restoration and additions, then further neglect. For a century between 1750 and 1850 it fell into overgrown ruin, which is just how the emerging Romantic movement liked it. It inspired compositions by Franz Liszt, a frequent visitor. It was restored by its then owner, and again after the First World War, when it passed into the ownership of the Italian state. Today it, and the site of Hadrian's Villa nearby, are a UNESCO World Heritage Site.

Gardens of the Generalife Palace

Granada, Spain, Fourteenth to Twentieth Centuries

ARCHITECT: UNKNOWN

STYLE: ANDALUSIAN ISLAMIC

Across a ravine from the Alhambra, the terraces of the Generalife originally grew produce for the household.

The ancient Nasrid sites of Granada – the tightly packed old district of Albayzín, the fortress-palace of the Alhambra on its ridge and the summer palace of the Generalife, or 'garden of the architect', placed higher still – jointly form one of the most visited places in the world. Together, they mark a high point of medieval civilisation, culture and tolerance. This was the final redoubt of Al-Andalus, the Muslim-ruled area of the Iberian Peninsula from 711 to 1492. The Nasrid dynasty (1230–1492) ran the Emirate of Granada, the last to yield to Christian rule. Although affected by alterations, additions, military action, earthquake and neglect in the following centuries, today its architectural legacy still speaks clearly.

In both the Alhambra and – across a river valley to its east – the Generalife, architecture and designed green space are inseparable. The use of shaded, breeze-encouraging, interlocking courtyards with water used in ingenious and beautiful ways, a trademark of Islamic urban design, is common to both. The nearby mountain range of the Sierra Nevada provided a source of water that was 'captured' by the emirs and brought to the city in aqueducts. At the Generalife, however, the buildings are plainer and fewer, and the gardens are given greater prominence. While the palace of the Alhambra, with its gorgeous tiled interiors and vaulted ceilings, was an administrative centre, the Generalife was more of a retreat for the emirs, close but out of town, an escape from the heat and activity of urban life in what has always been a punishingly hot climate. In that respect it shares its concerns with Cardinal Ippolito's gardens outside Rome two centuries later (see p. 228). But the Generalife was also more than merely ornamental: its gardens step down the valley side to form agricultural terraces.

Consider the Water Stair (dilapidated at the time of writing), ascending south-east into the hills from the top of the site. It is intimate. It is overhung with trees, providing dappled shade. Its materials are not refined: steps in brick, circular landings paved in patterns of pebble, the balustrades finished in painted mortar. When working, water descends the stair in two ways: via little circular fountain basins set into the centre of each landing and in troughs formed in the tops of the balustrades, widening at the points the water swirls round the landings. So, as you climb or descend the stair, you can trail your hand in the running water. One hopes it will be properly restored to working order.

The Generalife was laid out around a sequence of relatively compact gardens, such as the main water court, giving it a more domestic feel than the neighbouring Alhambra.

That is merely a delightful sideline, however. At the foot of the Water Stair is the Patio of Cypresses, secret in feel as befitted what was the garden of the harem. A watercourse runs round it, a fountain rises from a pool, and the oleanders were chosen because they flower in June, the month the Emir's court arrived for the summer recess.

The main gardens begin with the Court of the Canal – again the rill running down the central axis, flanked by fountains amid lush planting. A terrace on the western side gazes out to the Alhambra and beyond, and down to the market gardens on the lower slopes. None of this is especially grand – this is part of its charm – but it is very carefully considered. From there you move through an offset sequence of other small courtyards to arrive in the more expansive modern gardens, which are good in their formal way but lack the enclosure, the relationship with buildings, that sets the originals apart. These later gardens conclude in an open-air theatre, a place of congregation and entertainment in the cool of the evening.

The architectural treatment of planting for both beauty and practical use goes back many centuries earlier. The great Mosque at Córdoba (785–987), now an architecturally unusual cathedral, is notable for the way its man-made 'treescape' of delicate internal columns and arches gives way to real orange trees in the enclosed courtyard that accounts for one-third of its rectangular site. The trees are set on a grid of gently trickling irrigation channels, continuing the grid of the columns. Originally, the two spaces were not divided. Architects today are fond of referring to 'outdoor rooms', trying to blur the boundaries between inside and outside. The success of this depends greatly on the climate, but it is revisiting an ancient idea. Equally valid to today's architects are the natural cooling attributes of such places, enough to reduce the ambient temperature by a vital degree or two and to accompany that with the gentle sound of water that we have come to associate with coolness. In modern architecture, the trickling rill in a central courtyard (see Louis Kahn's Salk Institute, p. 109, which also features an orange grove at its entrance) is influenced by such Islamic examples.

In Granada, all tourists head for the Alhambra, with its Court of the Myrtles and the Lion Court with its fountain basin. But it is well worth taking the time to visit the Generalife nearby to appreciate such gardens on a more domestic scale. This whole area is an object lesson in how the designed open spaces of the urban environment can be inseparable from the buildings.

Kyoto Temple Gardens

Kyoto, Japan, 1100–1750

ARCHITECTS: MUSŌ SOSEKI (1275–1351) AND OTHERS

STYLE: ZEN BUDDHIST

Musō Soseki was an influential man and a powerful Zen Buddhist Master. At a time of political instability, when religion and politics were closely intertwined, he advised emperors and shoguns. Inevitably, he had his enemies, but he managed to float above the various factions, adroitly switching sides when necessary. He founded a chain of great temple monasteries and was a popular teacher, artist and poet. But perhaps his best-known legacy today is this: as an intrinsic part of his design of temple complexes, he made what are now some of the most exquisite gardens on earth.

The tradition of the contemplative garden, a place of calm reflection providing an inkling of a better world – or perhaps a memory of a lost paradise – occurs across various religions and regions, as well as throughout literature. Musō's contribution in medieval Japan was to initiate Zen gardens – both lushly planted and dry – as an art form, which continued to develop for centuries afterwards. The finest examples are to be found in and around Kyoto, ancient

An unearthly paradise, a place of calm contemplation: the moss gardens at the temple of Saiho-ji.

capital of Japan from 784 to 1869. With 12 such historic gardens and associated buildings existing today, these form what is regarded as the national shrine of historic Japanese landscape architecture. A shrine of shrines, in fact.

The sense of a world beyond day-to-day experience is key to the planning of the Saiho-ji gardens.

The Rinzai denomination of Zen that Musō practised developed away from its Chinese roots (he never visited China) to become a very Japanese phenomenon. The garden was intrinsic to his practice: enlightenment could be achieved through meditation and the contemplation of landscape, which was consciously designed as a piece with its buildings: temples and shrines. With usable space for buildings and gardens always at a premium in this mountainous terrain, Japanese gardens were not as land-hungry as European examples, such as the English eighteenth-century 'natural' landscape movement (see Stowe Gardens, p. 240). On the contrary, they are relatively compact, looking in on themselves rather than to their natural or urban surroundings. They play tricks of perspective, seeming to be larger than they are. The oldest of these are the Saiho-ji temple gardens on the eastern edge of Kyoto, right next to an area of wooded rocky hills and gorges, a landscape it concentrates and perfects.

Musō did not start with a blank canvas: he redesigned an existing earlier Buddhist garden on the site. His design is nature evoked almost in paraphrase, though it makes you think of the natural world. Its plan of paths, waterways and lakes in a woodland of more than 100 species has remained intact, if frequently neglected, renewed and rearranged over the centuries. It has also acquired another unconscious layer of character purely through age: the mood of tranquillity intensifies because of the obviously venerable nature of the place.

The Japanese concept of sublimating one's spirit in natural things is the artistic concept of *yugen*, the sense of something beyond what can be said. The moss garden of Saiho-Ji, and its related gardens of pavilions, woods and water across old Kyoto attached to other temples and palaces, succeed by being aesthetically and spiritually self-sufficient – what the British landscape architect Sir Geoffrey Jellicoe described as 'a sense of boundlessness by being turned in on itself to become a complex microcosm of nature'.[1] These various gardens were designed according to common principles and subsequently evolved over time. Some became very artful with their carefully aligned sequences of views across water and bridges to buildings in the middle distance. The tea house became part of the ritual environment.

A sense of movement through life, of overcoming obstacles, began to appear in the form of dry rock gardens (another import from China, but much more sophisticated) near the watery planted ones. The oldest example is also to be found at Saiho-Ji, originally made by Musō. This line of design thought culminated in what is perhaps the modern received notion of the dry Zen garden of contemplation: precisely raked and constantly tended white quartz gravel around rocks placed in a particular geometric relationship to each other. This had a practical origin in that cleaning and raking the gravel was part of the training of Zen monks. Geometric patterning developed from this and became ritualised. A famous example of the Zen garden is at the Temple of Ryōan-ji, which is thought to be seventeenth-century. Such designs have their origins in the Shinto roots of Japanese religion, where the overall landscape – as, for instance, the distant views of volcanic peaks seen across the Seto Inland Sea and the forested mountain ranges inland – becomes an object of veneration, to be evoked and concentrated in garden form. After all, this landscape is a nurturing being, supporting the human race which lives there.

Anyone who sets out and plants a garden is responding to the natural world in one way or another, making their own paradise. But the design of places that combine buildings and landscape as part of a considered whole is

The dry Zen garden of Ryōan-ji offers an example of how the natural physical landmarks of Japan became adopted as symbolic objects of veneration.

more refined in Japan than anywhere else. Only a few natural elements are selected and idealised: nothing is cluttered. The temple gardens of old Kyoto are thus an object lesson in how to make contemplative worlds in which everything is balanced and harmonious. The effect of all this on the Western world has been considerable from the moment these exquisite places were first encountered and described. Claude Monet's famous garden at Giverny in Normandy, France, is one such, though only in part. By and large the West adopted a pick-and-mix attitude to Japanese aesthetics.

Musō's work has been changed and rearranged several times so we cannot be sure exactly how these places looked originally. The principles he established have endured, however. As the Japan-based Korean minimalist artist Lee Ufan (b.1936) wrote of these gardens in 2017: 'I am overcome by the sensation that time has stopped, that I have slipped inside another dimension.'[2]

1 Geoffrey Jellicoe and Susan Jellicoe, *The Landscape of Man*, 1975, rev. 1987.
2 Quoted in Sophie Walker, *The Japanese Garden*, 2017.

Gardens of Stowe House Stowe, Buckinghamshire, UK, 1713–51

ARCHITECTS: CHARLES BRIDGEMAN (1690–1738), SIR JOHN VANBRUGH (1664–1726), JAMES GIBBS (1682–1754), WILLIAM KENT (1685–1748), LANCELOT 'CAPABILITY' BROWN (1716–1783) AND OTHERS

STYLE: PASTORAL NEOCLASSICAL AND GOTHIC REVIVAL

The 1738 Palladian Bridge, 1741 Gothic Temple and the pillar of the 1749 Cobham Monument, all attributed to the multi-talented James Gibbs, define the Capability Brown/William Kent landscape.

Never was an apparently natural landscape more man-made, by several successive hands, than the gardens of Stowe House in Buckinghamshire, England. Here nature was tamed, cosseted and shaped in several phases of work stretching from the early eighteenth into the nineteenth century. The 101 hectares of the main gardens today include some 30 pieces of fine architecture in addition to the magnificent main house with its Robert Adam frontage. They range from large temples to small statues via bridges, grottoes, pavilions, columns and obelisks, all very carefully placed as incidents in the landscape, either as eye-catchers from afar or as curiosities to chance upon.

This grand landscape was made by a very ambitious man: Richard Temple, Lord Cobham (1675–1749) – serving colonel and veteran of several battles, diplomat, politician, leading member of the landed gentry and the (by the standards of the day) progressive Kit Kat Club, where free-trade, strongly Parliamentarian and determinedly Protestant Whigs like Cobham met to debate and let their wigs down. The fact that there are so many temples in his garden is, of course, a reference to the family name. The nobility of the time competed for attention with their Palladian buildings but Cobham and his designers took the fad to a new level of ambition, adding Gothic and Chinese as well.

Cobham started in earnest on his house and garden in 1713 during a brief lull in his military and political career. This required more money than he possessed, so two years later he married it. His bride, Anne Halsey (d.1760), was independently wealthy as sole heir to the fortune of her brewing-magnate father. The beer money she brought in was well spent. Over the next few decades they transformed an unremarkable country estate into one of the finest landscapes in Europe, and the first of its kind.

First came a relatively old-school French-style formal garden by Charles Bridgeman and Sir John Vanbrugh, of which few traces remain other than three or four pieces of Vanbrugh's garden architecture that were subsequently moved. This layout was steadily swept away from 1735 in the hands of William Kent, James Gibbs and Capability Brown. The Cobhams were wealthy and involved enough to approve the changes to the relatively recent works they had themselves commissioned.

What followed was a landscape design revolution. At first recruited in 1740, aged only 24, as head gardener, Brown quickly began to show his talent as a large-scale designer and the much older Kent – who only occasionally visited Stowe – appears to have delegated much to his disciple, with the Cobhams' approval. Kent and Brown abolished straight-line gardening. For them, and

Kent's Temple of British Worthies (1734–5) sits in the Elysian Fields section of the gardens.

The Temple of Ancient Virtue (1734–7) by Kent overlooks the Elysian Fields.

especially for Brown, what came to be known as the 'line of beauty'[1] was the carefully contrived but seemingly natural snaking line, usually defined by belts of trees, edges of lawns and lakes, the courses of streams and rivers, gently rolling hillsides and, of course, the paths that wound their way through these landscapes. However, the line of vision travels in a straight line, and here their placing of the various garden buildings is key – catching the eye like beacons, each when you reach it leading visually to one or more of the others.

The greatest concentration of garden buildings is in the valley known as the Elysian Fields, with its stream and narrow lakes. Further out, the landscape becomes more expansive: Brown's Grecian Valley is a broad ride through woodland leading to the largest and most impressive of the garden buildings: the Temple of Concord and Victory (1747–64), based on the first century Roman Maison Carrée in Nîmes. This was possibly originally designed by

Brown himself, with Cobham, and modified by others later – something that happened frequently in the restless expansion and remodelling of the garden over time. Cruelly and crudely altered in the 1920s, when the estate was taken over by a boys' school, this temple is now fully restored to its 1760s state.

Elsewhere, you find the Palladian Bridge of 1738, probably by Gibbs, artfully placed across the arm of the main lake and based on a published design by Palladio himself, which he in turn drew from his studies of the architecture of the ancient world. But then comes a great stylistic shift. Up the hill from the Palladian Bridge is the large and highly original Gothic Temple – 1741, also attributed to Gibbs – and triangular in plan. Pretty much everything in this garden is symbolic of something or other political, and in this case it is the 'Liberty of Our Ancestors', to which the temple was dedicated. In this narrative it was the Goths who freed Britain from the tyrannical yoke of the Romans. The Gothic Temple is a celebration of restored democracy. Unlike other buildings here it is built from the tough patriotic local ironstone. It is part castle, part church, part house. You can stay in it and domestically it works adequately, if eccentrically.

There is much more symbolism to be found in the general layout of the gardens. There is a Path of Vice, a Path of Virtue and a Path of Liberty. Along the way, the buildings and statuary explore these themes through classical myth. Vice is quite an easy path, Virtue involves crossing various bridges, and Liberty – as they defined it, the ultimate goal for Cobham and his political allies – is the hardest and longest, involving many obstacles. In actuality, these routes are not especially apparent because the layout of the gardens is such that you can wander at will, drawn to this point and that by the sweep of the landscape and the power of the architecture.

The approach from the town of Buckingham to the south is all about power, wealth and status. A dead-straight road leads off between two lodges, heading for the triumphal Corinthian Arch (1765, by Lord Camelford, Thomas Pitt (1737–1793), so a later addition). From there you look down into the valley across the lake and up the other side, with the long facade of the house set atop lawns in the centre of your vision. However, when you are in the gardens, walking around, the mansion very seldom impinges on your view. The different parts of the garden work at three levels of focus – close, medium and long – and at the centre of the whole design is not the house but the little valley of the Elysian Fields, a world in itself. Other worlds, other centres are to be found around the gardens. It was this expression of the gardens as self-sufficient, not needing the house, that was so original.

1 A term devised by William Hogarth (1697–1764), see *The Analysis of Beauty*, 1753.

The High Line Manhattan, New York, USA, 2004–present

ARCHITECTS: JAMES CORNER FIELD OPERATIONS, DILLER SCOFIDIO + RENFRO WITH PLANTSMAN PIET OUDOLF (B.1944)

STYLE: INDUSTRIAL SALVAGE

The line in its abandoned state in autumn 2000, photographed by Joel Sternfeld (b.1944).

Manhattan has two of the most appealing designed landscapes in the world and they are as different from each other as can be imagined. Central Park, designed by Frederick Law Olmsted (1822–1903) and Calvert Vaux (1824–1895) in 1857 and completed by 1876, is the extraordinary superimposition of a 341-hectare informal, picturesque landscape on originally inhospitable terrain, captured within the rigid boundaries of the expanding New York city grid.

It was driven through with much heavy engineering and many controversies, including the forced removal of informal settlements including Seneca Village, home to many free African Americans and Irish immigrants. Such were the methods of the time (methods also common in earlier European landscape design and prevalent today for many public works such as airports) but the end result is a lush crafted landscape-with-buildings and place of public resort made all the more impressive by its necklace of surrounding skyscrapers.

The green ribbon of the High Line threads its way down Manhattan's West Side.

The High Line set out to be something else, making use of redundant industrial infrastructure rather than rural-fringe land. The raw material was an elevated freight railway, abandoned since 1980, which ran down Manhattan's West Side, bringing meat, dairy and other foodstuffs into the Meatpacking District. The idea to make this into a public promenade was inspired by a Parisian precedent, the Coulée verte René-Dumont, a five-kilometre stretch of abandoned urban railway in south-eastern Paris, reopened as a linear park in 1993. But that is more suburban in character, sometimes elevated, sometimes sunken, sometimes at street level. It lacks the drama, the film-set quality, of Manhattan's West Side.

Espoused by campaigners and co-founders of Friends of the High Line, Joshua David and Robert Hammond, the High Line park/promenade/urban pier was supposed to arise from the communities of Manhattan's then-declining

Meatpacking District, rather than being imposed on them. It was emphatically not – certainly not at first – an official project, though it depended on official support to provide capital funding, along with private donations. It is still run by the non-profit conservancy established by David and Hammond, though now owned by the City of New York. The original concept was to capture in a linear park the atmosphere of this miraculously surviving, vegetation-sprouting railroad as it threaded its way between, and sometimes through, industrial buildings. This was a realm known mainly to urban explorers and photographers, or glimpsed from surrounding buildings.

The project had to acknowledge the obvious paradox of its creation: that by opening such a previously off-limits place up to the public, the charm of its isolation would be lost. I was lucky enough to walk the first section shortly before it opened, so experienced the final days of its being an almost-secret domain. Since it opened, the High Line has become so popular that at busy times it resembles a procession, with little opportunity for calm contemplation among the jostling crowds. It is also true that its gentrifying effect has led to cultural and commercial development along its route, which has pushed up property prices and rents, so increasingly excluding the working-class communities originally associated with the area. Unlike Central Park, then, the exodus of previous residents came after, rather than before, the construction work, through the operation of capitalism and tourism rather than court order.

In fact, the Meatpacking District – which had become an area of louche nightclubs, drug dealing and worse from the 1970s as industry moved out – had been heading upmarket since the fashion and gallery worlds began to colonise it in the 1990s. Old buildings were converted, new ones added. The High Line accelerated the process, as was inevitable with the arrival of such an intriguing visitor attraction. If the park had not been made, the steel railway viaduct would simply have been demolished, as southerly sections of it already had been.

The structure was pretty sound: this was not an especially old bit of infrastructure, dating to 1933. Prior to that, the railcars had moved along the streets, often with fatal consequences. The separation of street and railroad levels in this way allowed the urban dreamers of the 2000s to imagine a place of both activity and serenity, a walkway with hanging gardens and places to pause. Architect and landscape architect made the tough framework necessary for the footfall, incorporating sections of old railway track and making architectural spaces; plantsman Piet Oudolf provided the soft landscape that draws on the High Line's original overgrown appearance. The ambition was duly achieved with the first section opening in 2009 from Gansevoort Street in the south (where the viaduct abruptly terminates, though you can spot fragments of it further south where it used to run through buildings) to 20th Street in the north. Two further phases followed, bringing it round railway yards up to 34th Street. This took it to nearly 2.4 kilometres, with further spurs mooted at the time of writing.

At its top end it is little more than a walkway: the best parts are further south. Where it broadens and passes over busy 10th Avenue, an amphitheatre is made in the deep steel structure, with windows looking out onto the street life. Elsewhere, you can sit out on built-in sun loungers, at one point overlooking the Hudson. Everywhere, the planting bursts up through slots in the paving, or covers whole areas away from the path. One of the main appeals of the High Line is that it is anything but a straight corridor. It squirms about to a remarkable extent, a legacy of its 1930s beginning when it had to literally thread a way through a densely built-up area. All along the route it changes in character.

Dereliction is always appealing, exploring it thrilling, but for a public park everything had to be redesigned and made accessible. Stairs, lifts and lighting were needed. Key to the success of the High Line is the way it quite casually mixes old with new, highly designed with left-as-was. It became an idea that cities around the world rushed to emulate in their own leftover fragments of transport engineering but none to date can match the atmosphere created here on the West Side.

As resurrected, the High Line is a mix of architecture and planting that carries physical memories of its original function.

Further Reading

This is a short list of more general books on architecture and landscape, from entry-level to grandly academic, for those wishing to explore the subject further.

It is always worth tracking down a specialist architecture bookshop and losing yourself there. For some of these titles, second-hand sources are the better option.

Banham, Reyner, with Mary Banham, Paul Barker, Sutherland Lyall and Cedric Price (eds), 1999, *A Critic Writes: Selected Essays by Reyner Banham* (Berkeley: University of California Press)

Calder, Barnabas, 2021, *Architecture from Prehistory to Climate Emergency* (London: Pelican Books)

Curtis, William J.R., 1996, *Modern Architecture since 1900* (London: Phaidon)

Davidson Cragoe, Carol, 2018, *How to Read Buildings: A Crash Course in Architecture* (London: Herbert Press)

Fazio, Michael, Marian Moffett and Lawrence Woodhouse, 2022, *Buildings across Time: An Introduction to World Architecture* (New York: McGraw-Hill Education)

Fraser, Murray (ed.), 2019, *Sir Banister Fletcher's Global History of Architecture* (London: Bloomsbury Publishing)

Goldberger, Paul, 2009; rev. 2023, *Why Architecture Matters* (New Haven, CT: Yale University Press)

Jellicoe, Geoffrey and Susan Jellicoe, 1975; rev. 1987, *The Landscape of Man: Shaping the Environment from Prehistory to the Present Day* (London: Thames & Hudson)

Moore, Rowan, 2012, *Why We Build* (Basingstoke: Picador)

Pearman, Hugh, 1998, *Contemporary World Architecture* (London: Phaidon)

Pevsner, Nikolaus, 1979, *A History of Building Types* [1976] (London: Thames & Hudson)

Rasmussen, Steen Eiler, 1962, *Experiencing Architecture* (Cambridge, MA: MIT Press)

Stevens Curl, James and Susan Wilson, 2016, *The Oxford Dictionary of Architecture* (Oxford: Oxford University Press)

Sudjic, Deyan, 2016, *The Language of Cities* (London: Allen Lane)

Summerson, John, 1965, *The Classical Language of Architecture* (London: Thames & Hudson)

Index

A

Aalto, Aino, 25
Aalto, Alvar, 24–26
Adam, Robert, 39, 240
Adjaye, Sir David, 156–159, 199
Alberti, Leon Battista, 35, 36, 37
Aldrich, Chester Holmes, 117
Amateur Architecture Studio, 152–155
Ancient Egypt, 18, 35, 75–76, 77, 121, 187, 225
Ancient Greece, 76, 80, 161, 164–166, 170, 182, 185, 189, 203
Ancient Rome, 8, 35, 76, 80, 165, 182, 203
Andréossy, François, 120–122
Architects Co-Partnership, 58–61
architecture
  as an art, 9
  defined, 7, 10
  as a science, 7–9
Arts and Crafts, 41–43, 62
Arup, Ove, 150, 173–175
Arup Associates, 58–61, 93
Ashmole, Elias, 137
Asplund, Erik Gunnar, 224, 226
Atelier Bow-Wow, 51–53
Australia, 13, 93, 173–175
Aztec and Inca empires, 21

B

Bage, George, 100–102
Baillie Scott, Mackay Hugh, 41–43
Baker, Herbert, 124
Baroque, 30–33, 228–231
Bauhaus school of design, 47, 62
Bo Bardi, Lina, 136, 138
Boileau, Louis-Auguste, 204
Boileau, Louis-Charles, 204
Bouman, Elias, 188–190
Brandt, Carl, 170–172
Braunfels, Stephan, 33
Brazil, 13, 136–137
Bridgeman, Charles, 240–243
bridges
  Allahverdi Khan Bridge, 21–23
  engineering, 66, 105
  industrial, 117, 118
  Ironbridge, 100, 101
  Ljubljana Central Market, 215
  Millau Viaduct, 118
Brinkman, Johannes, 106–108
British Museum, 16, 18, 19
Brown, Lancelot 'Capability,' 240–243
Brückwald, Otto, 170–172
Brummerhof hall house, Germany, 34
Brutalism, 48, 109–111
Bunshaft, Gordon, 65–67
Buontalenti, Bernardo, 140–143
Burbage, Richard, 167–169
Burkina Faso, 68–70

C

Cambodia, 184–187
Canada, 198–201
canals, 97, 101, 107, 120–122, 152
cantilevers, 92–93, 126–128
caravanserai, 117
caryatid columns, 17–18, 19
Castellamonte, Amedeo di, 98
Chambers, Sir William, 78–81
Chetwoods, 220–223
China, 20, 92–95, 97, 112–115, 120, 152–155
civic buildings *see also* museums
  defined, 13
  public educational functions, 112–115
classical style
  Classical, 80, 170–172
  Georgian Domestic Classical, 38–40
  Hellenic (Ancient Greek Classical), 16–19, 164–166
  Neoclassical, 120–122, 214–216
  Pastoral Neoclassical, 240–243
  Post-Renaissance Classical, 188–190
  Renaissance Classical, 58–61
  Stripped Neoclassical, 144–147
Coalbrookdale, Shropshire, 96
Cockerell, Charles, 137
Colbert, Jean-Baptiste, 120
Cole, Henry, 139
Cooper, Don, 29
Correa, Charles, 198–201
courtyard houses, 35
courtyards
  Chilehaus, Germany, 82, 85
  cortile of the Uffizi, 140–142
  courtyard clusters, 62–64
  'empty' courtyards, 109, 110–111
  as gathering places, 25, 26
  Somerset House, 78, 80
  university quadrangles, 59, 67
Crosby, Theo, 167–169
cruciform steel columns, 44–45, 46, 100
curtain walls, 82, 85, 107
Czechia, 44–47

D

deconstructivism, 92–95, 176–179
Delano, William Adams, 117
dendriform columns, 86, 87, 88
Denmark, 62–64
design codes, 29, 38
Diller Scofidio + Renfro, 178, 244–247
Disney, Lillian and Walt, 176
Dowson, Philip, 60
Duany, Andrés, 27–29

E

Eames, Charles, 130
Eames, Ray, 130
Edinburgh, Scotland, 12, 14

educational buildings
breadth of design for, 54–55
libraries, 55, 56, 59, 61, 65–67
primary and secondary settings, 55, 62–64, 68–70
quad-based colleges, 58–61, 65–67
universities, 56–57, 71–73
University of Virginia, 54, 56–57
Egypt, 200
Eiffel, Gustave, 204
England, 13, 41–43, 58–61, 64, 78–81, 100–102, 104, 106, 124, 144–147, 162, 167–169, 181, 203, 204, 220–223, 227, 240–243
Eritrea, 126–128
Erskine, Ralph, 90, 204
Ethiopia, 128
expressionism, 82–85, 129–132, 173–175

F
Farrell, Yvonne, 71–73
Finland, 24–26
Foreign Office Architects, 133–135
Foster, Norman, 32, 118, 119
France, 93, 103–105, 106, 118, 120–122, 133, 148–151, 194–197, 202, 204, 227, 245
Franchini, Gianfranco, 148–151
Frank, Charlotte, 32
Freelon, Phil, 156–159
Freelon Adjaye Bond + Smith Group, 156–159
functionalist style, 100–102, 120–122, 220–223

G
gardens
the designed landscape, 225–226
dry gardens, 235, 237, 238–239
Forest Crematorium, Sweden, 224
informal designs, 226–227
landscape architecture, 226, 227
'natural' landscapes, 227, 236, 240–243
urban parks, 227, 244–247
water features, 229–231, 233–234, 235, 236, 237
Western cemeteries, 226
Gaudí, Antoni, 191–193
Gehry, Frank, 132, 176–179
Germany, 14, 30–33, 34, 82–85, 116, 117–118, 162, 164, 170–172, 178
Gibbs, James, 240–243
Goodhart-Rendel, Harry, 146–147
Gothic style, 58–61
Gothic Revival, 123–125, 240–243
Neo-Gothic, 193
Gottlieb Paludan Architects, 112–115
Grafton Architects, 71–73
Great Zimbabwe, 21
Greece, 16–19 *see also* Ancient Greece
Gruen, Victor, 176, 204–205
Guggenheim Museum Bilbao, 177, 178

H
Ħaġar Qim, Malta, 6
Hall, Edwin Thomas, 146–147
Hazeldine, William, 100–102
Hertzberger, Herman, 89–91
high tech style
Commercial High Tech, 217–219
Digi-Tech, 133–135
Eco-Tech, 112–115
High Tech, 105, 148–151
High-Tech Symbolist, 198–201
Techno-Historicist, 103–105
Hoger, Johann Friedrich 'Fritz,' 82–85
Hong Kong, 217
houses
emergency houses, 36–37
family homes, 36
hall-houses, 34, 35–36, 53
house-city relationships, 35
Japanese *minka*, 51, 53
Low German Houses, 34, 36
luxury houses, 36, 41–43, 44–47
multi-functional buildings, 35
Roman atrium houses, 35
terraced/row houses, 38–40
Howard, Ebenezer, 14

I
Ictinus, 16
India, 123–125, 199
industrial buildings
evolution of, 97
iron-smelting, 96
mills, 97–99, 100–102, 103–105
multi-storey factory buildings, 98
water-powered, 97–98
industrial villages, 98–99, 103–105
International Congresses of Modern Architecture (CIAM), 25–26
internationalism, 155
International Modernist, 44–47, 48, 106–108, 181
Ippolito II d'Este, Cardinal, 228, 230–231
Iran, 13, 20–23, 205
Ireland, 38–40
Islamic architecture, 20–23, 68–70, 198–201, 232–234
Italy, 54, 76, 98, 126–128, 137–138, 140–143, 160–161, 181–182, 210–212, 228–231
see also Venice

J
Jacobsen, Arne, 62–64
James Corner Field Operations, 244–247
Japan, 36, 51–53, 133–135, 235–239
Jefferson, Thomas, 55, 56–57
Jekyll, Gertrude, 226
Jellicoe, Sir Geoffrey, 225–226
Jerde, Jon Adams, 217–219

Jerde Partnership, 217–219
Jones, Inigo, 80, 81

K

Kahn, Louis, 33, 49, 109–111, 181
Kajima, Momoyo, 51–53
Kallikrates, 16
Kazakhstan, 13
Kent, William, 240–243
Kéré, Diébédo Francis, 68–70
Khan, Allahverdi, 20–23
Koolhaas, Rem, 92–95, 133
Krier, Léon, 27–29
Kuöhl, Richard, 84, 85

L

Laplanche, Jean-Alexandre, 204
Lari, Yasmeen, 36–37
Laud, William, 58, 59–60
Le Corbusier, 10, 13–14, 25, 26, 36, 110, 181, 194–197
Ledoux, Claude-Nicolas, 98
Lewerentz, Sigurd, 224, 226
Ligorio, Pirro, 228–231
Lipsius, Konstantin, 105
Loon, Ellen van, 92–95
Loos, Adolf, 41, 86
Louis XIV, 120
Lu Wenyu, 152–155
Lutyens, Sir Edwin, 41, 43, 86, 124, 226

M

MacCormac, Richard, 58–61
Machu Picchu, 21
Mackintosh, Charles Rennie, 41, 42, 86, 214
Madrid, 10
Maki, Fumihiko, 200
Malta, 6
Mandrup, Dorte, 62–64c
mannerism, 50, 140–143
materials
  of the Arts and Crafts movement, 42
  clay, 69
  concrete, 72–73
  emergency houses, 36–37
  iron- and steel-framed buildings, 77, 82, 98, 99, 100–102, 103–105, 106, 114
  marble, 66, 67
  reinforced concrete, 107
  skeuomorph, 18
  sustainable, 9, 73, 154
  timber, 18, 51
  Tudor buildings, 167
Mather, Rick, 147
Maufe, Sir Edward, 60
McNamara, Shelley, 71–73
Medici, Cosimo I de, 140–141
Mengoni, Giuseppe, 210–212
Mexico, 20, 182, 185
Millau Viaduct, France, 118
Mnesikles, 16, 17
modernism, 8, 25, 42–43, 49, 107, 128, 194, 216
  Catalonian modernisme, 191–192
  Historic Modernism, 106
  International Modernist, 44–47, 48, 106–108, 181
  Late Modern Monumentalist, 30–33
  Modern Expressionist, 129–132, 173–175
  Modern Mannerist, 48–50
  Modern Vernacular, 24–26, 51–53, 68–70
  Modernist, 58–61, 62–64, 65–67
  Streamline Moderne, 126–128
Moisant, Armand, 103–105
Moneo, Rafael, 181
Moussavi, Farshid, 133–135
multi-functional buildings, 24–26, 35, 144–146, 148–151
museums
  Aga Khan museum, 200
  Ashmolean, 137
  British Museum, 16, 18, 19
  as a building type, 138–139
  as civic buildings, 138
  Guggenheim Museum Bilbao, 177, 178
  Sao Paulo Museum of Art, 137, 138
  Tradescant's Ark, 137
MVRDV, 90

N

Nash, John, 39
Negri, Richard, 162
Netherlands, 89–91, 106–108, 188–190, 204, 225

O

Obama, Barack, 156–157
offices
  ancient *stoas* and *basilicas*, 76
  cellularised office blocks, 75, 89–91
  evolution of, 75–77
  Larkin Soap Company Headquarters, 75
  monastery scriptoria, 74, 76
  office planning, 75
  the Uffizi, 140
Olmsted, Frederick Law, 244
Olowe of Ise, 157–158
OMA, 92–95, 133
Orrell, John, 167–169
Oudolf, Piet, 244–247
Ove Arup and Partners, 150

P

Palladio, Andrea, 80, 161, 240, 243
parabolic arches, 192
Paris, France, 13–14
Pennethorne, James, 81
Pereira, William, 132
performance buildings
  amphitheatres, 165–166, 170

music/concert venues, 162, 176–179
opera houses, 162, 170–172
Teatro Olimpico, Italy, 160–161
theatres, 161–163, 167–169
Pericles, 16, 18–19
Peru, 20, 71–73
Petazzi, Giuseppe, 126–128
Phidias, 16, 18
Piano, Renzo, 105, 148–151
Plater-Zyberk, Elizabeth, 27–29
Plečnik, Jože, 86, 214–216
Polykleitos the Younger, 164–166
postmodernism, 27, 32, 48, 50
Prouvé, Jean, 197

R

Reich, Lilly, 44–47
religious buildings
Ancient Greece and Rome, 16–19, 182–183, 185, 189
Beth Sholom synagogue, 199
Blue Mosque, Istanbul, 199
Cathedral of Our Lady of the Angels, USA, 181
Coventry Cathedral, England, 181
great Mosque at Córdoba, 234
Hagia Sofia, Istanbul, 180, 182
monasteries, 55, 58, 59, 74, 76, 97, 110, 111, 186
temple complex of Ħaġar Qim, Malta, 6
through history, 182–183
Zen gardens, 235–239
Renaissance, 35, 76, 80, 137, 141, 142, 161
Neo-Renaissance, 210–212
Post-Renaissance Classical, 188–190
Renaissance Baroque, 228–231
Renaissance Classical, 58–61
retail buildings
'Bon Marché' store, Paris, 202, 204
department stores, 202, 203–204
distribution warehouses, 118, 205, 220–223
evolution of, 203
shopping malls, 203, 204–205, 209, 210, 217–219
Rice, Peter, 148–151
Riquet, Pierre-Paul, 120–122
roads
Broadacre City, 14
distribution warehouses, 118, 205, 220–223
filling stations, 126–128
grid-plan approach, 14
New Urbanism, 27–29
road networks, 13, 14–15, 118
road-to-building balance, 10, 14–15
Roe, John, 38–40
Roe, Patrick, 38–40
Rogers, Richard, 105, 148–151
Rohe, Ludwig Mies van der, 44–47, 49
rural settlements
British 'garden cities,' 14, 27
picturesque villages, 27, 29
retrospective aesthetics, 27

S

Saarinen, Eero, 49, 129–132
Saarinen, Eliel, 129
Salk, Dr Jonas, 109–110
San Salvador de Tábara, Spain, 75
Sao Paulo Museum of Art, 137, 138
Saulnier, Jules, 103–105
Scamozzi, Vincenzo, 161
Scharoun, Hans, 162, 178
Scheeren, Ole, 92–95
Schinkel, Karl-Friedrich, 33
Schmidt Hammer Lassen Architects, 112–115
Schnelle, Eberhard, 75
Schnelle, Wolfgang, 75
Schultes, Axel, 32
Schwebebahn monorail, Germany, 116, 117–118
Scotland, 12, 14, 35, 41, 214
Scott, George Gilbert, 124
Scott Brown, Denise, 48–50
Sedefkar Mehmed Agha, 199
Semper, Gottfried, 170–172
Shah Abbas I, 20–23
Shakespeare, William, 161, 162, 167, 168
Skara Brae, Orkney 35
Skidmore, Owings and Merrill (SOM), 66, 105
skyscrapers, 82, 92, 100, 101
Slater, Samuel, 102
Slovenia, 214–216
Soane, Sir John, 144–147
Soleri, Paulo, 29
Soseki, Musō, 235–239
Spain, 10, 74, 75, 178, 189, 191–193, 232–234
Spence, Basil, 181
squares *see also* courtyards
Fitzwilliam Square, 38–40
Naqsh-e Jahan Square, 20, 21, 22
Pompidou Centre, 148, 149, 151
St. Petersburg, 21
Stam, Mart, 106–108
Stein, Gertrude, 10
Stevens, Frederick William, 123–125
Street, Peter, 167–169
styles *see also* classical style; Gothic style; high tech style; modernism; Renaissance; vernacular
Afro-futurism, 70
Andalusian Islamic, 232–234
architecture and, 7, 8
Architecture Parlante, 152–155
Arts and Crafts, 41–43, 62
Bowellist, 148–151
Brutalist, 48, 109–111
Byzantine/Ottoman, 206–209
Deconstructivist, 92–95, 176–179
Expressionist, 82–85
Functionalist, 120–122, 220–223

Futurist, 126–128
Georgian Functionalist, 100–102
icon buildings (shapeism), 175, 177–178
Indo-Saracenic, 123–125
Industrial Salvage, 244–247
Internationalism, 155
Khmer Architecture, 184–187
Mannerist, 50, 140–143
Monumentalist, 148–149
Neo-Baroque, 30–33
Neo-Palladian, 78–81
New Urbanism, 27–29
Safavid Islamic, 20–23
Sculptural Primitivist, 194–197
skeuomorph, 18
Streamline Moderne, 126–128
streets in the sky, 72
Structuralist, 89–91
Sui Generis, 191–193
Symbolist, 152–155, 156–159
traditionalism, 8
Zen Buddhist, 235–239
Sweden, 204, 224, 226

T
technology
alternative power sources, 112–115
architecture and, 7–8, 9
computer-aided design, 133–135, 173–175, 176–179
High Tech style, 105, 148–151
office planning and, 75, 76–77
passive cooling techniques, 69, 70
for transport, 117
water-powered industrial buildings, 97–98, 101–102
Tenochtitlan, 21
Toyota, Yasuhisa, 178
transport buildings
airports, 117, 118–119, 129–132
engineering for, 117–118
monorails, 116, 117–118
railways, 117, 118, 123–125
Tschumi, Bernard, 19
Tsukamoto, Yoshiharu, 51–53
Turkey, 180, 182, 206–209

U
United States of America, 10, 14, 15, 27–29, 48–50, 54, 56, 65–67, 75, 109–111, 117, 156–159, 176–179, 181, 204–205, 244–247
University of Virginia, USA, 54, 56–57
urban planning
large-scale urban planning, 13–14
seats of power, 20–23
terraced/row houses, 38–40
urban settlements *see also* roads
Ancient Greek city-building, 18–19
architecture in, 9–10
house-city relationships, 35
multi-function buildings, 24–26
New Urbanism, 27–29
out-of-town malls, 204–205
parks, 227, 244–247
road-building balance, 10, 14–15
slum areas, 14
suburbia, 14, 27
urban populations, 13
Utzon, Jørn, 130, 173–175

V
Vaidya, Raosaheb, 123–125
Vanbrugh, Sir John, 240–243
Vasari, Giorgio, 140–143
Vaux, Calvert, 244
Venice, 13, 22, 40, 188, 190
Venturi, Robert, 48–50
vernacular, 41, 42, 154
Modern Vernacular, 24–26, 51–53, 68–70
Neo-Vernacular, 170–172
New Vernacular, 52
Vernacular, 167–169
Vienna, 10
Virlogeux, Michel, 118
Vitruvius, 7
Vlugt, Leendert Van der, 106–108

W
Wagner, Richard, 162, 164, 170–172
Wallot, Paul, 31
Wang Shu, 152–155
Washington DC, 10, 129, 156
Webb, John, 169
Williams-Ellis, Sir Bertram Clough, 29
Witherford Watson Mann, 81
Wong & Ouyang, 217–219
Wotton, Sir Henry, 7
Wren, Sir Christopher, 13, 137
Wright, Frank Lloyd, 14, 41, 42, 75, 86–88, 110, 176, 199, 214
Wright & Wright, 58–61
Wyatt, James, 81

Z
Zaera-Polo, Alejandro, 133–135

Acknowledgements

My thanks are due to many people, directly or indirectly, who have helped me with this book: I have learned much in writing it.

Initiating me into the workings of Wagner's Bayreuth were Hugh Canning, the Rev. Richard Coles and Alexander Schwartz. Gentle correction of my words on Japanese contemplative temple gardens was provided by Ai Hishii, Professor Masao Fukuhara of Osaka University and Jan-Carlos Kucharek.

Denise Scott Brown talked me through the background and genesis of the Vanna Venturi House. Tim Waterman, associate professor at The Bartlett School of Architecture, clarified my thoughts on the nature of the architectural garden in contrast to 'landscape'. Author David Long kindly checked my words on the Portuguese Synagogue in Amsterdam. John Tuomey helped me choose Fitzwilliam Square, Dublin as an exemplar of Georgian volume housing.

Professor Steven Semes of the University of Notre Dame helpfully critiqued my accounts of Seaside in Florida and the Acropolis in Athens. Professor William Whyte gave me an expert guided tour of St John's College Oxford, including its Cistercian wine cellar. Professor Thomas Chung of the architecture school at the Chinese University of Hong Kong guided me through the tumult of the Mong Kok district.

Stephen Witherford, via the Courtauld Gallery, explained the ingenious planning of Sir William Chambers's Somerset House. Chris Hardie, locked down by pandemic in Shanghai, laid out the rationale and technical workings of his Shenzhen Energy Ring, then under construction. Historian Tim Dunn helped me decide on the best 'golden era' railway station for the book, while the architectural community on social media, many academics among them, has been stalwart in providing informed answers to my artless questions on this and that.

My wife Kate Hobson made valuable suggestions for improving the introduction. My commissioning editor at Yale, Sophie Neve, helped enormously in refining the structure of the book, its tone and its overall balance of buildings, architects and countries represented; my thanks also to the anonymous peer reviewers who approved the book concept and critiqued the manuscript and to Simon Bradley, editor, Pevsner Architectural Guides at Yale, for correcting some of my style descriptions. With thanks also to my editor Julie Hrischeva, designers Maggi Smith and (for the cover) Steve Leard, copy-editor Lizzy Silverton, picture researcher Susannah Stone and indexer Amanda Speake.

Finally, anyone presenting architecture in this way must doff their cap to the work of the incomparable architectural historian Sir Nikolaus Pevsner (1902–1983), whose last book *A History of Building Types* (1976, based on the A.W. Mellon lectures he gave in Washington in 1970, a remarkably ambitious work by the then-ailing scholar) first piqued my interest in approaching architecture in this rewarding way.

There is no comparison between this non-academic book and that, beyond the characteristically honest remark in his Foreword when he too reflects on the agony of having to freeze the process and leave things out. 'My attempt to justify this ... is, as I am aware, only convincing up to a point. My main reason has simply been a fervent wish to see publication.'

Picture Credits

P.6 Eric de Mare / RIBA Collections
P.12 National Library of Scotland
P.16 Matte René / Agefotostock
P.17 Photo Scala, Florence
P.19 Colin Dixon / Arcaid Images
P.20-21 Lukas Bischoff / Alamy Stock Photo
P.23 Arthur Greenberg / Alamy Stock Photo
P.24 Mvlampila / Alamy Stock Photo
P.25 © Oriol Gómez
P.26 © Oriol Gómez
P.27 Reproduced from the Leon Krier Archives held by the Architecture Library of the Hesburgh Libraries, University of Notre Dame
P.28 Kristina Blokhin / Alamy Stock Photo
P.30 REUTERS / Alamy Stock Photo
P.31 Manuel Cohen Photography
P.33 Wikpedia / LoboStudio Hamburg
P.34 blickwinkel / Alamy Stock Photo
P.38 Edwin Smith / RIBA Collections
P.39 Barry Mason / Alamy Stock Photo
P.41 Allies and Morrison, photographer Nick Wood
P.42 Allies and Morrison, photographer Charlotte Wood
P.43 Allies and Morrison, photographer Nick Wood
P.44 © photo David Zidlicky
P.46 © photo David Zidlicky
P.47 © photo David Zidlicky
P.48 Library of Congress, USA / Carol M. Highsmith
P.49 Courtesy of Venturi, Scott Brown, and Associates. Photographer: Rollin R La France
P.50 Photo by Smallbones
P.51 © Shinkenchiku-sha
P.52 © Atelier Bow-Wow
P.54 Robertslisa / Stockimo / Alamy Stock Photo
P.58 Zoonar GmbH / Alamy Stock Photo
P.59 By permission of The President and Fellows of St John's College, Oxford
P.61 © Wright and Wright Architects / ©Hufton+Crow
P.62 Photo: Aage Strüwing © Jørgen Strüwing
P.63 Photo: Aage Strüwing © Jørgen Strüwing
P.65 Iwan Baan Photography
P.66 Beinecke Library, Beinecke Rare Book and Manuscript Library, Yale University © Ezra Stoller
P.67 Iwan Baan Photography
P.68 Iwan Baan Photography
P.69 Erik-Jan Owerkerk / Kéré Architecture
P.70 © Siméon Duchoud / Kéré Architecture
P.71 Iwan Baan Photography
P.73 Iwan Baan Photography
P.74 Photo The Morgan Library & Museum / Art Resource, NY / Scala, Florence
P.78 © Richard Bryant / Somerset House Trust
P.79 Look and Learn
P.81 Manuel Cohen Photography
P.82 AKG images
P.83 Peter Eberts / Bildarchiv Monheim / Arcaid Images
P.84 AKG images
P.86 Hulton Deutsch / Getty Images
P.87 Historic American Buildings Survey, Library of Congress, USA
P.89 © Foto AVIODROME Lelystad
P.90 © Herman van Doorn
P.92 OMA by Iwan Baan
P.93 Iwan Baan Photography
P.94 OMA by Philippe Ruault
P.96 © Science Museum / Science & Society Picture Library, All rights reserved
P.100 © Historic England Archive
P.101 © Historic England Archive
P.103 Cellen Wikipedia
P.104 De Agostini / Icas94 / Agefotostock
P.106 Foto AVIODROME Lelystad
P.107 Colin Walton / Alamy Stock Photo
P.108 NAI Collection Database – Het Nieuwe / Municipality of Rotterdam (City Archives) CC-BY
P.109 Iwan Baan Photography
P.110 Iwan Baan Photography
P.111. Iwan Baan Photography
P.113 © Schmidt Hammer Lassen
P.115 © Schmidt Hammer Lassen
P.116 AKG images
P.120 AKG images
P.121 Hemis / Alamy Stock Photo
P.122 Hilke Maunder / Alamy Stock Photo
P.123 Richard I'Anson / Getty Images
P.125 Snehal Pailkar / Alamy Stock Photo
P.126 View Pictures / Universal Images Group via Getty Images
P.127 ERIC LAFFORGUE / Alamy Stock Photo
P.129 Balthazar Korab / Library of Congress, USA
P.131 Balthazar Korab / Library of Congress, USA
P.132 Wikipedia
P.133 David Parker / Alamy Stock Photo
P.134 © FOA
P.135 Photo: Satoru Mishima / FOA
P.136 © MSAP
P.140 Zoonar.com / Daniel Ferreira-Leites Ciccarino / agefotostock
P.143 Catharina Lux / agefotostock
P.144 Richard Bryant / Arcaid Images
P.145 Richard Bryant / Arcaid Images
P.149 Frédéric Soltan / Getty Images
P.150 Michel Denancé
P.151 Michel Denancé
P.152 Iwan Baan Photography
P.153 Iwan Baan Photography
P.155 Iwan Baan Photography
P.156 © Nic Lehoux / David Adjaye Associates
P.157 © Alan Karchmer / David Adjaye Associates
P.159 © Alan Karchmer / David Adjaye Associates
P.160 Photo Scala, Florence / Luciano Romano
P.164 Achim Bednorz / Bildarchiv-Monheim / Arcaid
P.165 DEA / G DAGLI ORTI / Agefotostock
P.167 Wikipedia
P.168 © Peter Dazeley
P.169 © Nick Guttridge
P.171 AKG images
P.172 GmbH / Alamy Stock Photo
P.173 Dennis MacDonald / Agefotostock
P.174 MB Photo / Alamy Stock Photo
P.175 Getty Images, Goddard Photography
P.176 Los Angeles Philharmonic Association / Walt Disney Concert Hall
P.177 Los Angeles Philharmonic Association / Walt Disney Concert Hall
P.179 Los Angeles Philharmonic Association / Walt Disney Concert Hall
P.180 Photo Scala, Florence / bpk, Bildagentur fuer Kunst, Kultur und Geschichte, Berlin
P.184 Tang Chhin Sothy / Getty Images
P.185 Michael Freeman / Getty images
P.186 Jan Fritz / Robert Harding
P.188 Europa Nostra
P 189 Collection Jewish Museum, Amsterdam / Collection Arthur and Jetty Polak, purchased with the support of the Sponsor Bingo Lottery
P.191 Manuel Cohen Photography
P.192 Photo Manuel Cohen Photography / © DACS 2023
P.193 Photographer Alex Bland / Arcaid Images
P.194 Georges Engel courtesy of RPBW
P.195 Bildarchiv Monheim/Arcaid images / © ADAGP, Paris and DACS, London 2023
P.196 Photo: Cemal Emden / © ADAGP, Paris and DACS, London 2023
P.198 Photo: Shai Gil
P.201 Photo: Shai Gil
P.202 Top-Foto / Roger-Viollet
P.206 Reuters / Alamy Stock Photo
P.207 Martin Siepmann / Agefotostock
P.208 Images & Stories / Alamy Stock Photo
P.211 Gabriele Croppi / Robert Harding
P.212 Foto Andrea Scuratti / Comune di Milano
P.213 Marc Rasmus / Agefotostock
P.214 bozac / Alamy Stock Photo
P.215 © M Paternoster / MGML
P.216 © Hugh Pearman
P.217 Images courtesy of JERDE
P.219 © Hugh Pearman
P.220 Images courtesy of GLP / Sky Revolutions
P.222 Images courtesy of GLP / David Morris Photography
P.224 Photo: G. Jackson / Arcaid
P.228 Darling Archive / Alamy Stock Photo
P.229 SOPA Images / Getty Images
P.231 AA World Travel Library / Agefotostock
P.232 Archivo y Biblioteca del Patronato de la Alhambra
P.233 Archivo y Biblioteca del Patronato de la Alhambra
P.235 John S Lander / Getty Images
P.236 Damien Douxchamps / Robert Harding
P.238 Javier Larrea / Agefotostock
P.240 Glyn Fletcher / Alamy Stock Photo
P.241 © Hugh Pearman
P.242 © National Trust Images / Hugh Mothersole. All rights reserved
P.244 © Joel Sternfeld
P.245 Iwan Baan Photography
P.247 Iwan Baan Photography

First published by Yale University Press 2023
302 Temple Street, PO Box 209040, New Haven
CT 06520-9040
47 Bedford Square, London WC1B 3DP
yalebooks.com | yalebooks.co.uk

Library of Congress Control Number: 2022946433
ISBN 978-0-300-26344-2
A catalogue record for this book is available from the British Library

10 9 8 7 6 5 4 3 2 1
2027 2026 2025 2024 2023

Designed by Maggi Smith
Cover design by Steve Leard
Copy-edited by Lizzy Silverton

Printed and bound in Slovenia by DZS Grafik d.o.o.

Cover: Interior (detail) of Yokohama Port Terminal, Japan. Foreign Office Architects, 1995–2002. Photo: Satoru Mishima / FOA.

Frontispiece: Exterior (detail) of Sydney Opera House, Australia. Jørn Utzon, 1956–1973. Getty Images / Goddard Photography.

MIX
Paper from responsible sources
FSC® C106600
FSC www.fsc.org